Called to Teach

Called to Teach

EXCELLENCE, COMMITMENT,
AND COMMUNITY IN
CHRISTIAN HIGHER EDUCATION

Edited by

Christopher J. Richmann
and J. Lenore Wright

PICKWICK *Publications* · Eugene, Oregon

CALLED TO TEACH
Excellence, Commitment, and Community in Christian Higher Education

Pickwick Publications
An Imprint of Wipf and Stock Publishers
199 W. 8th Ave., Suite 3
Eugene, OR 97401

www.wipfandstock.com

PAPERBACK ISBN: 978-1-5326-8318-3
HARDCOVER ISBN: 978-1-5326-8319-0
EBOOK ISBN: 978-1-5326-8320-6

Cataloguing-in-Publication data:

Names: Richmann, Christopher J., editor. | Wright, J. Lenore, editor.

Title: Called to teach : excellence, commitment, and community in Christian higher education / edited by Christopher J. Richmann and J. Lenore Wright.

Description: Eugene, OR: Pickwick Publications, 2020. | Includes bibliographical references.

Identifiers: ISBN 978-1-5326-8318-3 (paperback). | ISBN 978-1-5326-8319-0 (hardcover). | ISBN 978-1-5326-8320-6 (ebook).

Subjects: LCSH: Learning and scholarship—United States—Religious aspects. | Universities and colleges—Teaching. | Universities and colleges—Religion. | Critical pedagogy.

Classification: BV4020 C22 2020 (print). | BX2373 (ebook).

Manufactured in the U.S.A.   August 3, 2020

The editors and publisher gratefully acknowledge permission to reprint or adapt material from the following works:

Baird, Robert. "On Becoming a Philosopher." In *Falling in Love with Wisdom,* edited by David D. Karnos and Robert G. Shoemaker, 135–37. New York: Oxford University Press, 1993.

Beaujean, A. Alexander. "Observing a Master (Teacher)." *The Score* 41.1 (2019). https://www.apadivisions.org/division-5/publications/score/2019/01/kirk-master-teacher.

Choucair, Mona M. "Lovin' the Skin I'm In: Resurrecting Stories in the Secondary English Classroom." In *Teaching Literacy in Urban Schools: Lessons from the Field*, edited by Barbara Purdum-Cassidy and Lakia M. Scott, 49–60. Lanham, MD: Rowman & Littlfield, 2018.

Glanzer, Perry L., and Nathan F. Alleman. *The Outrageous Idea of Christian Teaching*. New York: Oxford University Press, 2019.

Singletary, Jon, Helen Harris, T. Laine Scales, and Dennis Myers. "Integrating Christian Faith and Social Work Practice: Students' Views of the Journey." In *Christianity and Social Work: Readings on the Integration of Christian Faith and Social Work Practice*, edited by T. Laine Scales and Michael Kelly, 185–201. 6th ed. New York: North American Christians in Social Work, 2020.

Contents

PART 3: COMMUNITY

Contributors

Nathan F. Alleman is Associate Professor of Higher Education in the School of Education at Baylor University.

Andy E. Arterbury is Associate Professor of Christian Scriptures at George W. Truett Theological Seminary.

Robert Baird is Professor of Philosophy, *emeritus*, at Baylor University.

A. Alexander Beaujean is Associate Professor of Psychology at Baylor University.

William Bellinger is W. Marshall and Lulie Craig Chairholder in Bible, Professor of Hebrew Bible and Chair of the Religion Department at Baylor University.

Burt Burleson is University Chaplain and Dean of Spiritual Life at Baylor University.

Trey Cade is Director of Baylor Institute for Air Science and Assistant Research Professor in the Center for Astrophysics, Space Physics, and Engineering Research at Baylor University.

Candi K. Cann is Associate Professor of Religion in the Baylor Interdisciplinary Core at Baylor University.

Mona M. Choucair is Senior Lecturer in English and Curriculum and Instruction in the School of Education at Baylor University.

Perry Glanzer is Professor of Educational Foundations in the School of Education and resident scholar with the Institute for the Study of Religion at Baylor University.

D. Thomas Hanks is Professor of English, *emeritus*, at Baylor University.

Helen Wilson Harris is Associate Professor in the Diane R. Garland School of Social Work at Baylor University.

Dennis Myers is the Danny and Lenn Prince Endowed Professor of Residential Care of Older Adults in the Diane R. Garland School of Social Work at Baylor University.

Byron Newberry is Professor of Mechanical Engineering in the School of Engineering and Computer Science at Baylor University.

Elizabeth Palacios is Dean for Student Development and Special Assistant to the President on diversity at Baylor University.

Rebecca Poe Hays is Assistant Professor in Christian Scriptures at George W. Truett Seminary.

Christopher J. Richmann is Assistant Director for the Academy for Teaching and Learning and affiliate faculty in Religion at Baylor University.

T. Laine Scales is Professor in the Diana R. Garland School of Social Work at Baylor University.

Anne-Marie Schultz is Professor of Philosophy and Director of the Baylor Interdisciplinary Core at Baylor University.

Jon Singletary is Professor and Dean of the Diana R. Garland School of Social Work at Baylor University.

Elizabeth Vardaman is formerly Associate Dean for Engaged Learning in the College of Arts and Sciences at Baylor University.

J. Lenore Wright is Associate Professor of Philosophy in the Baylor Interdisciplinary Core and Director for the Academy for Teaching and Learning at Baylor University.

Laurel E. Zeiss is Associate Professor of Musicology in the School of Music at Baylor University.

Introduction

J. Lenore Wright and Christopher J. Richmann

On October 12, 2018, the Academy for Teaching and Learning (ATL) at Baylor University celebrated its tenth anniversary with a symposium titled, "Called to Teach." At this symposium, Baylor faculty representing diverse disciplines and institutional perspectives presented papers each reflecting, in their own ways, on the call to teach. These papers became the basis for the present collection.

Callings: Excellence, Commitment, and Community

When someone claims to have a "calling," what do they mean? The term, like its Latinate version, "vocation," is slippery. Does it specify devotion to a religious life? Does it refer to an occupation? Does it invoke a deep personal sense of contributing something meaningful? At different times and in various communities, it has meant all this, and more.

The Protestant Reformations of the sixteenth century were a decisive moment in the history of the concept of "callings." Martin Luther challenged the medieval Catholic hierarchical notion of "estates," or stations in life, where those occupations dealing directly in spiritual affairs claimed greatest honor and were alone considered divine callings.[1] Instead, while greatly prizing the office of preaching, Luther argued God calls people to all honest earthly tasks and equally esteems the work of these callings. This was liberating, as the mundane tasks in which most people were engaged—parenting, business, farming, government service, teaching—now enjoyed sacred status.

---

1. Luther, "Appeal to the Ruling Class," 407–12.

But as it turns out, this sacredness is not always experienced as liberation. With the twentieth-century expansion of education and opportunity, and the related cultural expectation that one's career is an intensely personal decision ("what do you want to be when you grow up?") rather than something communally determined, questions of vocation can be the source of stress and alienation. We are overburdened with options yet, in the last analysis, expected to bear the burden of decision alone, since we are told that personal fulfillment is the ultimate measure of success in one's career choice. This American individualism is expressed in popular theology, with its notion that God has a distinct "plan for your life." While many undoubtedly derive great comfort from this perspective of God's providence, others sense a daunting responsibility: because of the Reformations insight that one's calling could potentially be any productive task, this "plan" is seldom self-evident. And riding on these life choices is not only personal contentment, but alignment of one's personal decisions with God's will. In response, titles proliferate offering advice for how one should "discern" one's calling.[2]

Such a preoccupation with finding, discovering, or discerning one's calling, however, would have struck the major sixteenth century reformers as odd. Their focus—and the theological center of their doctrine of vocation—was not the *search* for one's call, but what one *finds in the midst* of the callings one has. Without fail, what one finds (or rather, *hears*) are requests from neighbors. This is the voice of God: neighbors asking for bread, advice, goods at a fair price, a listening ear, a word of encouragement.

The office, experience, and accidents of time and location all determine the requests one hears. In Luther's earthy illustration, the father with the crying baby is hearing the call to "rock the baby, wash its diapers, make its bed, smell its stench, stay up nights with it, take care of it when it cries, [and] heal its rashes and sores" in full confidence that as he does so, "God, with all his angels and creatures, is smiling."[3] The person with "Professor" before her name will get asked to teach by college students. Students may not say it in so many words, but they communicate their needs with their tuition dollars, their willingness to endure uncomfortable chairs (even for 8 am class!), and their sustained attention to material.

2. For example: Palmer, *Let Your Life Speak*; Smith, *Consider Your Calling*; Schultze, *Here I Am*. A more Reformations-grounded treatment appears in Schuurman, *Vocation*; although Schuurman also focuses on "discernment" of one's calling.

3. Cited in Tranvik, *Martin Luther and the Called Life*, 97.

Viewed this way, the excitement of vocation is not in the discovery of "what is my calling?," although many, undoubtedly, train for and pursue certain tasks out of a conviction that in such work personal interests and aptitudes intersect with human need. But the deeper and abiding excitement is in identifying how one can best respond to the requests, best serve the neighbor in the offices, relations, and stations in which one finds oneself day in and day out. This perspective framed our invitation to the contributors to this collection, who responded creatively and thoughtfully to our claim that faithful action within the call to teach (like any calling) is shaped by *excellence, commitment,* and *community.*

Of course, the essayists here are also scholars, so they are motivated also by their disciplines. As evident in many of the chapters, their work is enriched by a deep sense that what we teach is important—and therefore bringing others into the community of knowledge is important.[4] As teachers, we want to expand the circle of those who know, invite more conversation partners into the discussion of—as Robert Baird so beautifully puts it—"matters that matter."

Baylor's Vision for Teaching Excellence

God's call is never abstract. Vocation is always contextualized, precisely because it is located in the voice of the neighbor. Although we believe the insights in this collection have application in many institutional settings, we consider it equally important to name the particular setting out of which these insights emerge. The context that these essays share is Baylor University, a Christian research university in Waco, Texas, with a strong tradition of undergraduate education and more recent aspirations to achieve R1 status. This intersection of Christian mission, teaching heritage, and research impact make Baylor distinct, if not unique. None of these elements—let alone the awesome something that is greater than the sum of these parts—flourishes without rewards, support, and expectations. As we often say, Baylor "doesn't take teaching for granted." For over forty years, Baylor has been intentionally working out the practical implications of that sentiment.

In the late 1970s, William F. Cooper (Bill), Professor of Philosophy and Dean of Faculty Development, assisted by Elizabeth Vardaman (Betsy), applied for and received a grant from the Lilly Foundation to pilot a

---

4. Bruffee, *Collaborative Learning.*

faculty development program they named the Summer Teaching Institute.[5] Robert M. Baird (Bob), Professor of Philosophy, convened the first group of Institute participants in 1978.[6] Cooper, Vardaman, and Baird, inspirational and beloved teachers themselves, recognized a need for instructors to think and talk together about how to design, organize, and teach their courses. Cooper's immediate aim was for faculty participants to write syllabi for their courses, which, believe it or not, was an uncommon practice at Baylor in the sixties and seventies. Thanks to their initiative, teaching development at Baylor was born.[7] Thanks to their vision—a vision to guide That Good Old Baylor Line—teaching development has been institutionalized.

Even before teaching development was integrated formally into institutional structures, Baylor proudly proclaimed a tradition of excellence in education. A recent survey of Baylor alumni indicates that "most alumni recall the quality of the education at the university when asked about what comes to mind about Baylor."[8] Scores of our predecessors shouldered significant responsibility for creating and maintaining quality education, Cooper, Vardaman, and Baird among them. We could not be where we are without their work and example.[9] Baird, who served forty-

5. Dr. William F. Cooper has been affiliated with Baylor University for over fifty years. Cooper also became supportive of the Baylor Interdisciplinary Core in its early years and provided funding for BIC faculty development through his dean's office discretionary account. He continues to advocate for teaching development.

6. Baird served as Summer Teaching Institute leader for several years before transitioning to facilitator of the "microteaching" component of the Institute, a role he performed for approximately thirty years.

7. The STI/SFI is now a fixture of the University and ATL. Former and current leaders, based on available records, include the following: Bill Cooper, Bob Baird, Fred Curtis (deceased), Gustavo Morales, Bert Williams, Paul Rosewell, A. A. Hyden (deceased), James Nowlin, Tom Proctor (deceased), Jeter Basden, Tom Hanks, Anne-Marie Schultz, Laine Scales, Lenore Wright, Andy Arterbury, and Keith Schubert.

8. Keirns, Novak, and Smith, "Baylor University Alumni Survey," 1.

9. Cooper subsequently became Dean of Arts & Sciences and Professor of Philosophy, *Emeritus*. Vardaman recently retired as Associate Dean for Engaged Learning in A & S and Senior Lecturer in English. Baird served as Chair of the Department of Philosophy for eighteen years (1987–2005), University Ombudsperson, and Faculty Senator. Baird also directed a university self-study 1984–86 and chaired the committee that developed the Baylor Interdisciplinary Core (BIC) in the early 1990s. He earned the designation of Master Teacher and received the Piper Professor of Texas Award, the Robert L. Reid Award for Outstanding Teaching in the Humanities, the Herbert H. Reynolds Award for Exemplary Service to Students, and the Cornelia Marshall Smith Professor of the Year Award. Baird is now Professor of Philosophy and Master Teacher, *Emeritus*.

seven years on the faculty and received the highest honor for teaching, the designation of Master Teacher, reiterated his advocacy for teaching development in an April 2014 interview: "I take teaching so seriously that to be called a Master Teacher is greatly appreciated . . . though I don't think of myself as a 'master teacher.' I think of myself as a student of good teaching—I try always to improve my teaching."[10]

Herbert Reynolds, Baylor President 1981–1995, championed efforts to make teaching a priority. In the first five years of his administration, he established the Distinguished Visiting Professors Program and authorized the Robert Foster Cherry Great Teacher Award. In 1982, he created the designation of Baylor professors as Master Teachers.[11] D. Thomas Hanks (Tom), Master Teacher and Professor of English, *Emeritus*, heeded the call to excellence and dedicated himself to evidence-based, inspirational teaching throughout his forty-one-year career (Hanks won every teaching award Baylor offers). In 1982, Hanks was tapped to take over directorship of the Summer Teaching Institute, subsequently renamed the Summer Faculty Institute (SFI). He served as an SFI director and its key advocate for thirty-five years, retiring from the SFI and Baylor in 2017.[12]

The founding of the Academy for Teaching and Learning in 2008 has bolstered Baylor's tradition of educational excellence. You may be surprised to learn that at the time of the ATL's founding, Baylor was the only university of the Big XII Conference that lacked an established center for teaching and learning. University leaders recognized that increasing student enrollment, fluctuating student retention, expanding numbers of faculty, deepening investments in research, and establishing greater accountability for institutional effectiveness compelled Baylor to formalize support for faculty and ensure the continuation of transformational teaching. This resolve has ensured that our faculty and student body continue to see effective teaching as foundational to our students' significant learning, moral development, and spiritual growth. Thanks to the university's commitment, as well as extensive faculty engagement, the ATL has become a vital mechanism for the ongoing development of Baylor instructors. It is also a tangible expression—to alumni, potential students and faculty, and other stakeholders—of the institution's ongoing recognition that teaching excellence is a way of life at Baylor.

10. For the complete interview, see Baylor University, "Looking Back."

11. Baylor University, "Baylor Mourns the Death."

12. For more about Tom's career, see Baylor University, "Remembering Dr. Pennington and Dr. Hanks."

Virtually every university constituency endorsed the strategic proposal for the creation of the ATL.[13] Jon Engelhardt, former dean of the School of Education, believed so strongly in the proposed center's value that he offered funding from his own budget to help launch it. Larry Lyon, Senior Vice Provost and Dean of the Graduate School, authorized stipend funds to create the ATL's Graduate Fellows program. Former provost, Elizabeth Davis, convinced that the time had come for a center for teaching and learning, presented the proposal to the Board of Regents, who approved the ATL for operation beginning in 2008. W. Gardner Campbell, Vice Provost for Learning Innovation and Student Success and Associate Professor of English at Virginia Commonwealth University, served as the inaugural director of the ATL 2008-2011. Campbell encouraged Baylor faculty to re-imagine what great teaching might look like in a digital age. Today, members of the Office of the President, Office of the Provost, directors, deans, chairpersons, and other campus leaders champion the work of the ATL and find ways to integrate teaching development into the fabric of Baylor. Perhaps most significantly, Baylor faculty have taken ownership over the ATL, investing their expertise, time, and energy to breathe life into the ATL's mission "to support and inspire a flourishing community of learning." We are immensely grateful.

The strategic proposal identified a need for faculty members, departments, and program leaders to have a central resource to help develop meaningful and effective long-term plans for enhancing student learning. Research supports the belief that efforts made on behalf of effective teaching development need infrastructure, resources, and integration into institutional systems. A multi-year study published in 2015 concludes that faculty involvement in centers for teaching and learning depends on "whether or not the centers are integrated systematically into the expectations, support, and reward structures of the institution, and whether this emphasis on teaching excellence is reflected in the level of respect it is accorded by peers."[14]

We believe that whatever future mechanisms exist for teacher support, great teaching and significant learning will endure. Why? We believe Baylor is loyal to her core values, including teaching. But our faith in the

13. Deans, department chairs, the Faculty Senate, the Graduate Student Association, Student Congress, and individual professors and students alike declared in agreement: Baylor needs a university-wide venue that will promote a standard of excellence in teaching and foster significant learning among students.

14. Lyon, Gettman, Roberts, and Shaw, "Measuring and Improving the Climate for Teaching," 127.

future of teaching is rooted in something that is both more elusive and more palpable: That Good Old Baylor Line. Since 1845, generations of Baylor students and teachers have marched together in and out of classrooms. These students and teachers, supported by dedicated academic leaders, have forged a bold vision that unites Baylor's historic tradition of teaching excellence with a renewed commitment to teaching development, a vision realized in the Academy for Teaching and Learning and vibrantly attested in the essays of this collection. Sometimes, we need to fling our Green and Gold far *and* near. Sometimes, we teachers, like our students, need transformation as we hold that Good Old Baylor Line.

References

Baylor University, "Baylor Mourns the Death of President Emeritus Herbert H. Reynolds." May 25, 2007. https://www.baylor.edu/MEDIACOMMUNICATIONS/news.php?action=story&story=45872.

———. "Looking Back with Dr. Robert Baird." *Baylor Arts and Sciences.* April 23, 2014. http://blogs.baylor.edu/artsandsciences/2014/04/23/robert-baird/.

———. "Remembering Dr. Pennington and Dr. Hanks as They Retire." *Baylor Proud.* July 17, 2017. https://www2.baylor.edu/baylorproud/2017/07/remembering-dr-pennington-dr-hanks-as-they-retire/.

Bruffee, Kenneth A. *Collaborative Learning: Higher Education, Interdependence, and the Authority of Knowledge.* Baltimore: Johns Hopkins University Press, 1999.

Keirns, Tracy A., Chad S. Novak, and Andrew E. Smith. "Baylor University Alumni Survey 2012." The University of New Hampshire Survey Center, December 2012. https://www.baylor.edu/alumni/doc.php/193441.pdf.

Luther, Martin. "An Appeal to the Ruling Class of German Nationality as to the Amelioration of the State of Christendom." In *Martin Luther: Selections from His Writings*, edited by John Dillenberger, 403–88. New York: Anchor, 1962.

Lyon, Julie S., Hilary J. Gettman, Scott P. Roberts, and Cynthia E. Shaw. "Measuring and Improving the Climate for Teaching: A Multi-Year Study." *Journal on Excellence in College Teaching,* 26 (2015) 111–38.

Tranvik, Mark D. *Martin Luther and the Called Life.* Minneapolis: Fortress, 2016.

Palmer, Parker. *Let Your Life Speak: Listening for the Voice of Vocation.* San Francisco: Jossey-Bass, 2000.

Schultze, Quentin. *Here I Am: Now What on Earth Should I Be Doing?* Grand Rapids: Baker, 2005.

Schuurman, Douglas J. *Vocation: Discerning Our Callings in Life.* Grand Rapids: Eerdmans, 2004.

Smith, Gordon T. *Consider Your Calling: Six Questions for Discerning Your Vocation.* Downers Grove, IL: InterVarsity, 2015.

Part 1

EXCELLENCE

1

Baylor's Intellectual Heritage

Robert Baird

WHEN I GRADUATED FROM Little Rock Central High in 1955, I was headed for a small Methodist college in Arkansas and then on to law school. Religious experiences the summer before college led me in a different direction, however, and that fall I found myself in a small Baptist college in Arkansas planning to enter the ministry. But one day in the spring of that freshman year, my English professor asked me to stay after class: "You may not know it," she said, "but the questions you're raising about the literature we are reading are philosophical questions. We don't even offer philosophy here at the present time. You should transfer to Baylor University and study philosophy." I did, thus encountering the intellectual world of Baylor. My life was forever changed.

So there is much emotional satisfaction for me to begin this book by introducing the intellectual heritage of Baylor. Let me do this in two ways: first by reflecting Baylor's intellectual heritage as it was first introduced to me, and then with brief vignettes of some of Baylor's notable teacher/scholars.

My Experience as a Baylor Student

Early in my Baylor career I had among my teachers Ralph Lynn in history, Glenn Capp in debate, and Jack Kilgore in philosophy—all three well on the way to becoming Baylor legends.

In Ralph Lynn's history course early in the semester he was lecturing on Russia, the United States, and the Cold War. After class one day—everyone else had left—I said something to Lynn that seems to me now incredibly naive, even for a college sophomore. "The thing is," I recall saying, "the Russians know that we are not going to attack them. But we don't know that they will not attack us." My unstated assumption, of course: we were the "good guys," they the "bad," and furthermore, everyone knew it, *even them.*

Patiently, Lynn turned to the wall, pulled down a map of the world. "With this chalk," he said, "I am going to put an "x" everywhere the United States has missiles aimed at the heart of Russia, and an "x" everywhere Russia has missiles aimed at us." When he finished, I stared at a map that had Russia virtually surrounded by U.S. missiles and a United States scarcely threatened by Russia. What a moment! The old cliché: the scales fell from my eyes. All of a sudden it was clear to me that if I had been a sophomore at the University of Moscow that morning, I might have been petrified of the United States.

But even during that moment, I knew that the lesson I was learning had to do with much more than the Cold War. For the first time in my life, I was realizing that we see things through "colored glasses," through assumptions and presuppositions absorbed from our surroundings. But if our conclusions are colored by where we live, by what we've been taught, by whom we have become, how can we be sure that we have the truth? The door to critical thinking, Baylor style, cracked open.

I also took a course in debate from Glenn Capp, the founder of a program that had become, under his leadership, one of the premier forensic programs in the country. Capp had assigned us to read some old speeches. I came across one written by a 1936 Baylor undergraduate. It began as follows:

> On a Sabbath morning in 1914 (the great conflict, World War I, had just begun), they held a prayer service in Berlin. The Kaiser was there. The aisles were jammed. A German minister mounted the stand and, reading from the Old Testament the account of the battle between Gideon and the Midianites (and how God favored Gideon), drew across the centuries a 1914 parallel; and then they said: "Our strength is our God." Then they prayed: "God of Germany, give the victory to Germany. God of righteousness, give the victory to right."

On that Sabbath morn they held a prayer service in Paris. The war ministers were there. The aisles were packed. A French priest mounted the stand and, reading from the Old Testament the account of the battle between the Israelites and the Philistines (and how God favored the Israelites), drew across the centuries a 1914 parallel; and then they said: "Our strength is our God." Then they prayed, "God of France, give the victory to France. God of righteousness, give the victory to right."

On that Sabbath morning they held a prayer service in London. The King was there. The aisles were packed. An English bishop mounted the stand and, reading from the Old Testament the account of the battle between David and his enemies (and how God favored David), drew across the centuries a 1914 parallel. And then they said, "Our strength is our God." Then they prayed, "God of our fathers, God of England, give England the victory. God of righteousness, give the victory to right."

My sophomore's mind was reeling. The Germans see God through German eyes, the French through French eyes, the British through British eyes. And we, it seemed surely to follow, see God through our own eyes—through a glass darkly, a glass well smoked by environmental and hereditary factors. The door to critical thought, Baylor style, opened further.

Finally, I was taking my first philosophy course under Jack Kilgore. He had us read John Stuart Mill's essay *On Liberty*, a text that got inside my mind, into my blood, like no other ever had. I still remember the power of one particular passage.

> It never troubles him [the religious dogmatist] that mere accident has decided which of these numerous world [views] . . . is the object of his . . . [faith], and that the same causes which made him a . . . [Christian] in London would have made him a Buddhist or a Confucian in Beijing.[1]

Disturbing though this thought was, Jack Kilgore and John Mill persuaded me to be honest enough to acknowledge that if I had been born in a Buddhist culture, the odds are I would see God through Buddhist eyes; if I had been born in a Muslim country, the bet is I would make pilgrimage to Mecca. The question of truth and our ability to grasp it had been raised in a dramatic way. The door to critical thinking was wide open. Baylor had introduced me, a youngster from Little Rock, Arkansas, to the life of the mind.

---

1. Mill, *On Liberty*, 22–23.

Eventually, I came to see these Baylor teachers as part of a larger and longer academic tradition going all the way back to Socrates who argued that the unexamined life isn't worth living. Socrates viewed himself as a gadfly with a God-given task of stimulating individuals to think, to evaluate critically the principles guiding their lives. And that is what the Ralph Lynns, the Glenn Capps, and the Jack Kilgores were doing for me: stimulating me to think seriously about matters that matter.

But what about Baylor's religious heritage, its Christian heritage, its Baptist heritage? Is the critical spirit to which Baylor introduced me compatible with a religious culture that encourages commitment? Well, it was also at Baylor that I was led to see the mind as a gift of God and the disciplined development of the mind as a moral and religious obligation.

Quite specifically, I was led to see that devotion to the critical life of the mind is one of the ways we acknowledge the religious insight that as limited creatures of God, we are not God. And since we are not, we, indeed, always see through a glass darkly. Against this background of the acknowledgment of human finitude, uncertainty, and the need for the critical spirit, the Baylor faculty also taught me as a young sophomore that while liberal education is liberation from the limits of place and time and circumstance, it is also liberation to reflective commitment.

In one phrase, I would sum up the intellectual heritage I encountered as a young student at Baylor: the moral requirement for reasoned commitment in the face of ambiguity and uncertainty.

Influenced by the language of the British philosopher Bertrand Russell, I would say that to teach students to live the critical life of the mind without being paralyzed by doubt; to teach students to acknowledge ambiguity without being overwhelmed by uncertainty; to teach them to live with an open and tolerant spirit without sacrificing personal commitment to what one believes, after careful reflection, to be true and good and beautiful just is Baylor's intellectual heritage.[2]

Three Vignettes

And now let me turn to brief vignettes, impressionistic vignettes, of some contributors to this intellectual heritage. In these three vignettes

---

2. "To teach how to live without certainty, and yet without being paralyzed by hesitation, is perhaps the chief thing that philosophy, in our age, can still do for those who study it." Russell, *History of Western Philosophy*, xiv.

we encounter a citizen of the world, a passionate poet, and a musical conductor who undoubtedly arrived at Baylor because of the Nazi horror in Europe.

James Vardaman (1928–2018), Emeritus Professor of History and Master Teacher

Like so many Baylor students, faculty, alumni, and others, I traveled with Jim on the overnight train from London to Edinburg and the overnight boat from Wales to Ireland. Like so many, I cruised with him on the Danube River and the Baltic Sea. I explored cemeteries with him from Paris to Vienna and museums from Prague, the Czech Republic, to St. Petersburg, Russia. To travel with Jim was to be introduced to a culture and its history by one who spent his professional life immersing himself in cultures plural. There he is teaching for a year in a university in South China. There he is traversing the USSR on the Trans-Siberian railway from Beijing to Moscow. There he is lecturing at universities in Russia, in Serbia, in Egypt. There he is establishing the Baylor-European Study Program in Maastricht, the Netherlands. There he is traveling multiple times in every country in Europe, and the point: traveling almost always with students in tow—students working hard (sometimes literally) to keep up with him.

Jim was constantly teaching all along the way—teaching that included political events and the significance of geography to be sure, but teaching that also included literature, music, and the visual arts, teaching that brought laughter and, I can assure you, at times, tears. The breadth and depth of his knowledge was staggering.

If I were to try to capture Jim's contribution to Baylor in a sentence, here it is: Throughout his thirty-three years on the Baylor faculty, he was fundamentally concerned to take Baylor students to the world, to open their minds to new horizons and their hearts to new levels of compassion.

And if they could not travel with him abroad, he would bring the world to them, as he did for years chairing the most prestigious lecture series at Baylor: the Beall-Russell Lectures in the Humanities. As a result of his determination, he brought to Baylor individuals ranging from Edward Said to Carlos Fuentes, from Bill Moyers to Maya Angelou, from Czeslaw Milosz to Michael Mayne, Dean of Westminster Abbey.

And thinking of the Abbey, in 2000, Westminster Abbey honored Baylor Professor James Vardaman in recognition of his years of service to Westminster School, to Baylor University, and in recognition of his role in international education. I know of no Baylor faculty member who has had a greater influence on students than Jim. Unless it just might be that professor profiled in our second vignette.

Ann Vardaman Miller (1926–2006)
Emerita Professor of English and Master Teacher

Yes, there is a thread here. Ann and Jim: brother and sister. And yes, she too was a Master Teacher, one of the first two at Baylor to be so named. Ann loved poetry. She wrote poetry. Her life was an exuberant poem.

Ann Miller! A Baylor Icon if ever there was one. A more devoted following among Baylor alumni it would be hard to find. Here are reminiscences from three of her students:

> Professor Miller was, of course, always dazzling. But one day she actually undid me. She said she wanted to teach us something about poetic rhythm, so without any fanfare she started to recite Blake's "The Tyger" from memory. Slowly, at first, the words shaped in that gorgeous, sophisticated, Southern-tinged accent, so far from Blake, but so right. As she went on, she started to hammer out the rhythm on her desk, louder and louder with each stanza. By the third, she was standing up and pounding the desk with her fist. Declaiming the poem. No, orating it. Her fist against the hard wood with every pulse.
>
> She finished, a soft sweat lining her forehead and cheekbones. Out of breath, too. (We, stunned.) She sank into her chair, lowered her head into her hands, and dismissed the class. "Leave," she said—and then she mumbled, "Go and do what comes naturally."
>
> I did. I left, went to Pat Neff Hall, and changed my major to English. My parents thought I was nuts.
>
> (Mark Scarbrough, class of 1980, former literature professor, author of 26 books and a forthcoming memoir entitled *Bookmarked*.)

And another:

> I remember being a shy, self-conscious freshman in Ann Miller's class. The first day she went through the class roster and asked

each of us to quote a line of poetry. By the time she came to me my mouth was dry and my heart was pounding, but I was able to remember, "I have promises to keep and miles to go before I sleep, and miles to go before I sleep." Relief swept through me as I thought my job was done.

But then she asked if I knew who wrote the line and the poem. I died a thousand deaths as I replied in a squeaky voice that it was my father's standard reply to "Are we there yet?" on long trips.

Instead of the reprimand I expected, she said, "Wonderful," and launched into a discourse about how literature can enrich our lives. I don't really remember what she said after "wonderful", I just wanted to hear her say it again and again.

(Susan Sneed Alexander, Class of 1982, Master of Science in Speech Pathology)[3]

One more:

When I was a student at Baylor, and first getting to know Ann Miller, I had occasion to walk across Founders Mall with her one day. It was a gorgeous spring afternoon. The grounds crew had just planted several million daffodils, and all was right with the world.

I'm not sure where we were headed—or why—but on the way Ann spotted, at a distance of thirty or forty yards, two students she knew, sitting on a bench. They were closely entwined, very much minding their own business, which seemed to be each other. As we strode toward the romantic couple, Ann began rather loudly declaiming those immortal lines of Tennyson's "Locksley Hall."

"In the Spring a livelier iris changes on the burnished dove; / In the Spring a young man's fancy lightly turns to thoughts of love." By the time we arrived at the bench and were standing behind the pink-faced couple, Ann made a smooth segue from the 19th to the 20th century. Turning her attention to the pretty, young blonde sitting there, Ann placed a hand on the girl's shoulder, shook her head sadly and quoted Yeats['s poem "For Anne Gregory," which ends insisting that only God] "Could love you for yourself alone / and not your yellow hair."

The couples' response was a marvelous combination of embarrassment and sheer delight.

3. The reminiscences of Mark Scarbrough and Susan Sneed Alexander are from private online remembrances of Ann Miller, August 2006. They have been used by permission of Mark Scarbrough and Susan Sneed Alexander (given to me, the author).

If I hadn't understood before, I understood then that I was in the presence of a different kind of teacher—different in relation to her students, different in relation to her work—someone so in love with poetry, with what the written and spoken word can convey, that the language of books [through her] was constantly escaping the page.

(Gayla McGlamery, Professor of English Literature, Loyola University Maryland)[4]

Daniel Sternberg (1913–2000), Emeritus Dean of the School of Music

And now a most improbable tale of the intersection of a Polish Jew and a Texas Baptist University.

He was born in Poland, this magnificent Daniel Sternberg, but early in his life the family moved to Vienna where he eventually attended the Vienna State Academy of Music as a student of conducting. After graduation and seeking experience, he went to Russia to become the assistant conductor of the Leningrad Grand Opera and the prestigious Leningrad Philharmonic Orchestra.

But the political turmoil leading to World War II drove Sternberg back to Vienna where, in 1938, the Nazi SS rounded him up with other Jews. Sternberg himself has said that as the result of the SS officer who interrogated him, his life was probably spared. Instead of being taken into custody, he was told to "be out [of Vienna] in forty-eight hours or a concentration camp."[5]

Sternberg fled to Latvia with his wife, eventually to Stockholm, and finally on board a ship to the United States. In 1942 he found himself in New York among too many talented musicians competing for too few jobs. Aided by an organization seeking opportunities for émigré musicians and artists, he began a pilgrimage south, seeking work, eventually making his way to Waco and to Baylor where Roxy Grove, the chair of the Department of Music, hired herself a musical conductor—and the rest is the marvelous story of Sternberg's contribution to Baylor and to Waco.

He almost immediately became Dean of the School of Music and eventually Director of the Baylor Symphony. In 1962 Sternberg became conductor of the Waco Symphony Orchestra, a post he would hold with

4. McGlamery, "Undeniably Ann."
5. Sternberg, Interview #7, 379

distinction for the next twenty-five years. When he retired in 1980 as Dean of the Baylor School of Music, he left a legacy that makes him a pivotal figure in the history of Baylor's intellectual heritage.

Conclusion

And now, as a way of drawing together some threads and to point to a moment of courage at Baylor and to support for that courage, let me conclude this way:

Professor Bill Hillis, MD (1933–2018), was persuaded in 1981 to leave his post at Johns Hopkins University to become the chair of Baylor's Biology Department. As an undergraduate at Baylor, Bill had been encouraged to pursue medicine as a career by Professor Cornelia Smith (1895–1997), a member of the Biology Department and Director of the Strecker Museum. She graced us with her presence at Baylor until her death at the age of 101. Cornelia, by the way, was the wife of Charles G. Smith (1891–1967), Professor of English, and among the most outstanding scholars in Baylor's history. Now Cornelia, when she was an undergraduate at Baylor, had been a student of Lula Pace (1868–1925), a member of the Baylor Botany and Geology departments. Professor Pace in the 1920s began to be attacked by the Reverend J. Frank Norris (1877–1952), the notorious pastor of the First Baptist Church of Ft. Worth. She was, he said, guilty of teaching evolution. And, in fact, she was so guilty, but to her defense came Samuel Palmer Brooks (1863–1931), Baylor's president for 30 years.

After Pace died, Norris continued to attack Baylor and President Brooks for his support of the teaching of evolution. On the morning of October 29, 1926, Brooks was addressing Baylor students in a chapel service. During the service a messenger interrupted Brooks with the news that some businessmen had marched from downtown Waco to express their support of him and the university in the face of Norris' ongoing attacks. At that point the businessmen began entering the hall. The students, seeing how many of them there were, began spontaneously leaving their seats, moving to stand around the walls of the auditorium, and inviting the businessmen to be seated. And how many had marched to Baylor to support Brooks? Several hundred![6] A wonderful moment in Baylor's intellectual heritage.

6. The October 29, 1926, event recounted to the author by Kent Keeth, former

References

McGlamery, Gayla. "Undeniably Ann." *Baylor Magazine* (July/August 2002). https://www.baylor.edu/alumni/magazine/0101/news.php?action=story&story=7245.

Mill, John Stuart. *On Liberty*. New York: The Liberal Arts Press, 1956.

Russell, Bertrand. *A History of Western Philosophy*. New York: Simon and Schuster, 1945.

Sternberg, Daniel. *Oral Memoirs of Daniel Arie Sternberg*. Interview by Thomas L. Charlton and Wallace L Daniel, Waco, TX: Baylor University Program for Oral History, 1981. http://digitalcollections.baylor.edu/cdm/ref/collection/buioh/id/1190.

---

director of The Texas Collection at Baylor University.

2

An Inquiry-Based Approach to Teaching Space Weather to Non-Science Majors

TREY CADE

SCIENCE CAN BE BORING. I say that as a scientist who loves science. But sometimes it can be boring. Very often science classes (especially in my world of physics) devolve into memorizing equations and solving those equations for situations that have little resemblance to anything practical (like a block sliding down a plane). However, there is no reason why this has to be the case in our classrooms, because science can also be full of wonder, discovery, amazement, and downright really cool stuff.

The Course and Pedagogical Approach

I teach Space Weather. It's a topic I have spent most of my professional career working in, and I think it's tremendously interesting. After all, it's fun to teach about solar flares, space radiation, and all the ways the sun is trying to kill us and destroy our technology. It's also a topic that is typically only taught to physics and engineering students, because the science of space weather is grounded in space physics and it can be very complex. So when I decided I would teach a space weather course, I set a goal of broadening exposure to space weather beyond the typical physics and engineering students, which meant teaching to a larger audience that may not have a strong science or math background that would match how a course like this would typically be taught. This presented a unique challenge in teaching this topic; however, I was determined to open up this course to any student from across the university, which meant I had to assume absolutely no background knowledge or math skills beyond what a typical high school graduate would have. In presenting to these students the concepts, physical processes, and technology impacts involved in space weather phenomena, there was also a secondary goal of introducing these students to fundamental physics concepts they would need to know, as non-scientists, in understanding what we would talk about.

In determining how to teach the class, it was clear that a traditional lecture-type course would be inadequate. Studies show that "teaching by telling" is the least effective way to teach anyway, so another approach was needed.[1] I decided a storytelling approach would work well for this class. My idea was that my students would learn space weather the way humanity learned space weather. The story of space weather is a fascinating tale encompassing thousands of years of human history and includes names that many people would recognize—Aristotle, Halley, Galileo, Celsius, Herschel, Kelvin, and Marconi. From early observations and theories of the aurora, to the invention of the telescope that led to realizing the sun is a dynamic object, to the first recorded solar flare in 1859, to modern-day space weather impacts, this story has the potential to capture the students' imaginations and stir interest in a phenomenon that can significantly impact their lives. By beginning with humanity's first interactions with space science—observing the aurora and discovering magnetism—I can lay the foundation from which a more complex science can emerge. This teaching strategy then leads to scaffolding of learning that builds from foundational to higher-level understanding by the end of the course. Another benefit of using this approach is that the first third of the course unfolds like a mystery novel. This generates and maintains student interest as they follow along in key discoveries and gain some insights, which then lead to more questions that need to be answered, a cycle that repeats as you move through time and in fact very often leads to each class ending on a "cliffhanger." As one student stated, "I wish you would just skip to the end and tell us the answers. I have to come to class so I can find out what happens next!"

In further considering the method of instruction to complement this storytelling approach, and through investigating the latest pedagogical

---

1. Kober, *Reaching Students*; Freeman et al., "Active Learning," 8410–15.

research, I decided to adopt an inquiry-based technique called Process Oriented Guided Inquiry Learning (POGIL).[2] POGIL is based on research indicating that students who are part of an interactive community are more likely to be successful and that, ultimately, knowledge is personal—students develop greater ownership over the material when they are given an opportunity to construct their own understanding. The essence of POGIL is that students learn best by:

1. Following a cycle of exploration, concept formation, and application

2. Discussing and interacting with others

3. Reflecting on their progress in learning

4. Assessing their performance

To help meet these requirements, classroom activities should be developed that allow students to work in small groups on manageable problems where they can explore, analyze, and discover concepts for themselves. This turned out to be quite a natural fit with historical storytelling, as I could present the students with actual observations, data, and experiments used to create some of the initial theories and speculation about the nature of space weather. They could then explore these observations, data sets, etc., for themselves, perform their own analyses, and come to their own conclusions. This would then help fill in gaps in their knowledge and inevitably lead them to new questions that we needed to answer.

Measurements and Calculations

In one of these in-class activities, I provide the students with examples of measurements of magnetic storms at various locations around the world. These magnetic signatures are different in different parts of the world, and by examining these measurements the students gradually realize that storms at low latitudes look very different than storms in the polar regions. This dual nature of storms is discussed further but then leads to the question of "Why?" What is going on and what are the physical processes that cause these regional storm differences? This eventually leads to seeing that there are actually two types of storms, with each type measured and characterized differently.

2. https://www.pogil.org; Hanson, "Designing Process-Oriented Guided-Inquiry Activities," 281–84; Hanson, *Instructor's Guide*.

Another example is solar rotation. Shortly after the invention of the telescope, Galileo and other observers noticed that sunspots moved. After some sometimes-nasty disagreements over whether sunspots were actually on the sun (in one graphic exchange, Galileo referred to Christoph Scheiner as a "pig" and a "malignant ass") this led to the eventual realization that the sun rotated. I then give them two pictures of the sun, three days apart, and ask them to determine how fast the sun is rotating. I could just tell them that the sun rotates once an average of every 27 days, but figuring this out for themselves increases the likelihood that the information will be retained.

Hands-On Activities

Two of the more hands-on activities I use are worth mentioning, as they turned out to be much more effective than I initially anticipated. Early in the semester, we simulate the Oersted experiment, which involves connecting a wire to each end of a battery and holding it over a compass. The compass needle deflects, not only showing that electric currents create a magnetic field but also allowing students to determine the shape and orientation of the magnetic field of a line current. This experiment becomes beneficial later as we talk about possible sources for compass deflections during a magnetic storm. Another experiment later on is very simple, involving a rubber band that is pinched together in the middle, clipped with binder clips, and then cut into two sections, simulating the release of energy in magnetic fields that power solar flares.

Student comments on course evaluations have clearly shown the importance and effectiveness of these in-class activities:

> The hands-on work really helped solidify the topics in the lectures.

> The in-class group work was incredibly useful.

> The group work where we did experiments such as the rubber band and clip demonstration and the battery/compass experiment were a very cool way to learn the concepts explored in class.

> It would've been nice to do more hands on projects like the magnetic reconnection theory [rubber bands] project.

Experiments with the compass, and the rubber band with the clips caught my attention and helped me learn much more.

Student Learning Objectives

Throughout the course, students are given the opportunity to reflect on their progress and assess their performance through the use of Student Learning Objectives. Each lesson has a set of learning objectives that tell them what they need to know coming out of each lesson. They also know the exam test questions will be based on these learning objectives. Here is an example of the Student Learning Objectives for the lesson on the earth's magnetic field:

1. Explain why a compass points north.

2. Describe the difference between the earth's rotation axis and magnetic axis.

3. Know the scientific theory put forth by William Gilbert in his book *De Magnete.*

4. Explain what produces the earth's magnetic field.

5. Describe what happens to the earth's magnetic field during a field reversal.

6. Describe the three primary ways the earth's magnetic field changes over time and the characteristics of those three changes.

To achieve synthesis and application of all the material we cover throughout the semester, I implemented a capstone final exam scenario. In the scenario, the students are placed in the role of members of a Space Weather Consulting Company. They have been called to provide expert testimony before Congress regarding potential federal budget cuts to space weather services within the National Oceanic and Atmospheric Administration, and they must submit a written statement to Congress addressing their opinion on the matter. As a take-home project, the written statement gives them time to synthesize their knowledge and articulate convincing arguments based on their knowledge of space weather phenomena, technological impacts, past events, and space weather services. Depending on the size of the class, during their final exam time they must then also appear before Congress (simulated by me) to answer questions regarding this topic. Since they do not know what will be asked during the congressional hearing, they must adequately prepare for all Learning Objectives with written notes. The key here is that in the process of preparing written notes to support their questioning, they are in effect participating in synthesis and application through the process of organizing the course material into reference material.

Students' Perspectives

Since being first offered in 2012, over eighty students have taken the class, representing the following majors: business, accounting, marketing, entrepreneurship, journalism, psychology, literature, history, education, international studies, medical humanities, aviation science, astronomy, chemistry, geology, environmental science, mechanical engineering, and computer science. Overall, students have responded very well to the course, and here is what some of the students have had to say on the course evaluations:

> The class was engaging because he made it exciting, and I came into class every day anxious to know what would come next.

> How the material was presented piqued my interest. I really enjoyed how the class read like a novel, and each lesson built on the last one, with some cliff hangers.

> Structural design of the course was actually what made this class so interesting. To me it was like showing up for a TV episode because I felt like every time I was getting closer to more answers I had even more questions until the end of the course and I realized I learned stuff all along the way.

> Liked the use of groups and working on what we learned in class. Always kept you interested in the next lesson to come.
> It was taught in a very interesting way and it was so different than the rest of my classes.

Students are also given the opportunity to follow up the course with undergraduate research experiences in my Space Weather Research Lab. In this setting, they get to work with space weather data and participate in data analysis to support research outcomes. So far, ten students have worked as student researchers, with one student presenting a research poster at the 2017 Fall Meeting of the American Geophysical Union, the largest earth and space science conference in the world.

As the student comments above attest, when we strive to push ourselves beyond the norm and work from a mindset of constant learning and growth, we can connect to students and achieve true learning. Since starting this class, there have certainly been times where I have tried to do some things that haven't worked so well. I would urge educators, however, not to fear failure; if you are inspired to try something new, try it. If it doesn't work, don't do it again, or figure out how to make it better. Ultimately, that is one of the ways we grow and develop as teachers, and in the end that will benefit our students more than we realize. When we acknowledge that our own learning never ends, we are much more likely to ignite the spark of learning in our students. And we can make science not so boring.

References

Freeman, Scott, Sarah L. Eddy, Miles McDonough, Michelle K. Smith, Nnadozie Okoroafor, Hannah Jordt, and Mary Pat Wenderoth. "Active Learning Increases Student Performance in Science, Engineering, and Mathematics." *Proceedings of the National Academy of Sciences* 111.23 (2014) 8410–15.

Hanson, David M. "Designing Process-Oriented Guided-Inquiry Activities." In *Faculty Guidebook: A Comprehensive Tool for Improving Faculty Performance*, edited by Steven W. Beyerlein and Daniel K. Apple, 281–84. Hampton, NH: Pacific Crest, 2007.

———. *Instructor's Guide to Process-Oriented Guided-Inquiry Learning*. Lisle, IL: Pacific Crest, 2006.

Kober, Nancy. *Reaching Students: What Research Says About Effective Instruction in Undergraduate Science and Engineering*. Washington, DC: National Academies Press, 2015.

POGIL. pogil.org.

3

Observing a Master Teacher

A. Alexander Beaujean

PSYCHOLOGISTS AND EDUCATORS HAVE studied teaching excellence in higher education for almost a century.[1] Like many things in psychology, this research has largely consisted of common-or-garden variety concepts and has generally lacked much that is technical.[2] This does not mean that our knowledge of college teaching has been stagnant, only that assuming attributes in this domain are quantitative is not currently warranted by the state of evidence.

The current state of knowledge indicates that the phenomena constitutive of teaching excellence in higher education are qualitative.[3] This does not make them any less real than quantitative phenomena or their investigation unscientific.[4] It just means that the approach to their investigation should match the known structure of the phenomena. To that end, in this chapter I describe a qualitative investigation into how one particular master teacher approaches the process of teaching.

1. Buskist and Keeley, "Becoming an Excellent Teacher," 99–112; McKeachie, "Research on College Teaching."

2. Maraun, "Measurement as a Normative Practice," 435–61.

3. Levinson-Rose and Menges, "Improving College Teaching," 403–34. I use the term *qualitative* to refer to attributes that are not known to have additivity but may possess order. We can measure ordered attributes only in the sense that we can determine if one person has more of it than another person. See Joint Committee for Guides in Metrology, *JCGM 200:2012*.

4. Michell, "Place of Qualitative Research," 307–19.

Teaching Excellence in Higher Education

As with any other profession, there are certain attributes that professors need to have. At a minimum, they need to understand the core concepts in their field. Expertise in a given academic field does not translate automatically into having expertise in the classroom. In fact, the two skill sets are likely independent of each other.[5]

In addition to having a strong grasp of their discipline, professors who engage in teaching need to have a certain set of minimum competencies.[6] For example, they need to be able to communicate concepts in their field in an organized manner and be able to assess others' understanding of these concepts. Although they are both normative concepts (i.e., relate to some standard), competence is not the same as excellence, however. *Competence* refers to having a sufficient amount. In principle, any professor can be a competent teacher as long as they meet the minimum criteria. Such is not the case with *excellence*. Excellence requires being outstanding--of the highest quality. All professors can strive for teaching excellence, but by its nature they cannot all be excellent teachers.

If teaching excellence is not equivalent with teaching competence, then what is it? Excellence in college teaching is not a technical concept. Ask any group of college students or faculty to define or describe excellent teaching and you will get a variety of answers.[7] Not only is excellence not a technical concept, but also there is a growing consensus that there is no single set of behaviors constitutive of excellent college teaching.[8] Buskist et al. argued that *master teachers* (i.e., professors who have demonstrated a level of rare excellence in the college classroom) possess certain qualities (i.e., non-quantitative attributes), but demonstrating behaviors constitutive of any specific subset of these qualities is not sufficient to be a master teacher:

> Rather, master teachers are likely to come in all shapes and sizes, so to speak, and represent different combinations or blends of these qualities. What makes [Professor X] a master teacher is not exactly the same as what makes [Professor Y] a master

5. Hattie and Marsh, "Relationship Between Research and Teaching," 507–42; Marsh and Hattie, "Research Productivity and Teaching Effectiveness," 603–41.

6. Elton, "Dimensions of Excellence," 3–11.

7. Feldman, "Superior College Teacher," 243–88; Keeley, Ismail, and Buskist, "Excellent Teachers' Perspectives," 175–79.

8. Buskist, "Excellent Advice."

teacher, although there may be some overlap in the personal qualities and penchants relevant to teaching that each possesses . . . Master teachers are as unique as teachers as they are as human beings.[9]

When considered in the broader literature of expertise, the uniqueness of master teachers is not surprising. Experts do not only just have more of something than others in the same field but also represent a different class of individuals.[10] There is disagreement about how someone becomes an expert,[11] but there is little contention that experts both process information in their area expertise differently as well as attend to different information than other individuals.[12] This allows them to plan better and respond to situations more adroitly than non-experts.

Studying Teaching Excellence

Historically, most studies of excellent teaching have focused on *perceived* qualities of professors who exemplify excellence.[13] For example, asking stakeholders (e.g., students, faculty, alumni) what they perceive as teaching excellence[14] or investigating criteria for teaching awards.[15] Such studies can provide useful information, such as some general qualities that people believe are constitutive of being a master teacher (see Table 3.1). At the same time, these studies are limited because investigators do not examine behaviors directly. Instead, they rely solely on secondary information about excellent teaching.

An alternative to using secondary information is to observe master teachers engaged in the process of teaching.[16] Although investigators infrequently collect this type of data, this type of data is critically important

9. Buskist et al., "Elements of Master Teaching," 31–32.

10. Ackerman, "Nonsense, Common Sense, and Science," 6–17; Ericsson, "Why Expert Performance is Special," 81–103.

11. Hambrick et al., "Deliberate Practice," 34–45.

12. Dunkin, "Concepts of Teaching," 21–33; Horn and Blankson, "Foundations for Better Understanding," 73–98.

13. Buskist and Keeley, "Becoming an Excellent Teacher," 99–112.

14. Catano and Harvey, "Student Perception of Teaching Effectiveness," 701–17; Keeley, Ismail, & Buskist, "Excellent Teachers' Perspectives," 175–79.

15. Skelton, "Understanding 'Teaching Excellence,'" 451–68.

16. Hativa, Barak, and Simhi, "Exemplary University Teachers," 699–729.

for understanding teaching excellence.[17] Direct observations allow for collecting data about the specific behaviors in which professors engage that make them experts in teaching.

Direct observation of behavior is crucial to understand any type of expertise.[18] Experts often behave and extract information from their environment with automaticity. That is, they are not always conscious of what they are doing, or how what they do is any different from others. Thus, it is not surprising that master teachers approach teaching qualitatively different than their colleagues and that they are not necessarily cognizant of how or why what they do is different.[19] Consequently, direct observation of master teachers can provide a wealth of information about what it is they do that makes them experts.

In this current study, I conducted a case study of a master teacher for an entire course. Case studies are detailed examinations of a single example and have been a common part of psychological research for a long time.[20] They are occasionally used to study teaching expertise in P-12 environments[21] but are rarely used to study master teachers within university settings. This is unfortunate because case study methods are particularly useful for studying experts.[22] "[S]ometimes we simply have to keep our eyes open and look carefully at individual cases—not in the hope of proving anything, but rather in the hope of learning something!"[23]

Method

The Case: Roger E. Kirk

Since by its nature excellent teaching is rare, selecting cases randomly from the universe of professors does not guarantee being able to observe a master teacher. Instead, case studies of excellent teachers require purposefully selecting *extremes*—individuals that are much different from

---

17. Berliner, "In Pursuit of the Expert Pedagogue," 5–13.

18. Macnamara, Hambrick, and Oswald, "Deliberate Practice and Performance," 1608–18.

19. Livingston and Borko, "Expert-Novice Differences in Teaching," 36–42.

20. Bromley, *Case-Study Method*.

21. For example, Smith and Strahan, "Toward a Prototype of Expertise," 357–71.

22. Ericsson, "Why Expert Performance is Special," 81–103.

23. Eysenck, "Introduction," 9

what is typical. Extreme cases are particularly useful for exploratory studies that are "open-ended" in the investigation of a phenomenon.[24]

The case I selected was Roger E. Kirk. Kirk is an expert in the field of quantitative methods. In terms of scholarship, he has published over one hundred works in psychology and statistics, including five books. One of his books has received the rare honor of being designated a *citation classic*.[25]

Kirk's expertise not only includes the field of quantitative methods but also includes pedagogy. This is more difficult to demonstrate than expertise in a substantive area. Perhaps the best way to make the case of his pedagogical expertise is to note the numerous awards he has received. In 1992 he was named the *Outstanding Tenured Teacher in the College of Arts and Sciences* at Baylor University. In the following year, Baylor gave him the title *Master Teacher*—the university's highest teaching award. In 2005, Division 5 of the American Psychological Association (APA) gave him the *Jacob Cohen Award for Distinguished Contributions to Teaching and Mentoring*. He won the 2012–2013 *Cornelia Marschall Smith Professor of the Year* at Baylor for his "superlative teaching and outstanding research contributions." More recently, in 2015, he won the APA's *Charles L. Brewer Award for Distinguished Teaching of Psychology*. This award "celebrates Roger E. Kirk's dedication to and accomplishments in the teaching of psychology . . . His passion for teaching is legendary, his commitment to his discipline absolute, and his work ethic unmatched."[26]

The Design: Case Study

The aim of this particular study was to explore how a master teacher behaves in the college classroom—an aim that lends itself to a case study design.[27] Case study research starts from the desire to derive an in-depth understanding of a case set in a real-world context.[28] It is particularly apropos when: (a) the research questions are about "how" or "why"; (b) it is not possible to manipulate behaviors of those involved in the study; and (c) the boundaries are not clear between the phenomenon and context

24. Seawright and Gerring, "Case Selection Techniques," 294–308.

25. Beaujean and Weaver, "Roger E. Kirk"; "Bibliography of Roger E. Kirk."

26. "Charles L. Brewer Award," 384.

27. Baxter and Jack, "Qualitative Case Study Methodology," 544–59.

28. Yin, *Case Study Research*; Yin, "Case Study Methods," 141–55.

(i.e., the behaviors of a master teacher have to be considered within the context of teaching).

This particular case study was holistic, descriptive, and exploratory. It was holistic because I focused on a single case throughout the study (Kirk). It was descriptive because my goal was to describe a situation not normally accessible to investigators in its real-life context: the in-class behaviors of a master teacher. It was exploratory because I had no clear set of behaviors that I was looking to observe when I began the study.

The Context: College Classroom

I observed Kirk teaching an introductory statistics course during the spring 2018 semester. The course is designed for undergraduate students (typically sophomores) and covers topics ranging from descriptive statistics to inferential statistics. It is required for all psychology majors, but students from other majors also take the course. In the semester I observed, eighty-five students were enrolled.

The Data Collection

There are two components to the introductory statistics course: recitation and lab. I only observed the recitation component, which met three days per week for fifty minutes. I observed approximately 95 percent of the classes Kirk taught for the semester (approximately forty classes). The classes I missed were those in which an exam was administered, I had a schedule conflict, or Kirk was absent. Before beginning the data collection, I obtained Kirk's permission and the approval of my institution's IRB.

All classroom data were gathered through direct observation by a single observer. I sat in the same seat every class (front row, stage right), which allowed me to focus on Kirk instead of the students. I have taught similar courses in the past, so the content was already familiar to me. This allowed me to focus on Kirk's teaching behaviors. For each class, I brought a notepad and made notes about teaching behaviors. As this study was exploratory, I did not have *a prioiri* criteria about what behaviors I would or would not record. Instead, I made field notes about any behaviors I saw related to teaching.[29]

29. Fusch, Fusch, and Ness, "How to Conduct a Mini-Ethnographic Case Study,"

In addition to classroom observations, I also reviewed documents Kirk has authored about teaching statistics.[30]

The Data Analysis

For the data analysis, I searched my notes for themes (i.e., patterns of behavior that have meaning).[31] Specifically, I went through the data as I gathered them and noted when I saw repetitions of behaviors. I then went through these repetitions to see if they could be further combined to form meaningful themes. Eventually, I settled on five distinct classes of behavior patterns, which I then named and defined.

Results

In what follows, I provide the five themes that emerged from my observations. They are presented in no particular order. In Table 3.2, I integrated these findings with the master teacher qualities from the literature on perceived teaching excellence.

Levity

One of the most frequent behaviors I observed from Kirk was the use of humor. This made the general climate of the course positive and lighthearted. Moreover, it allowed Kirk to regain student focus when he judged that students were not being engaged.

Kirk employed many forms of humor, ranging from anecdotal (e.g., funny stories about statisticians mentioned in the textbook) to self-deprecating (e.g., making light of himself when he made an error) to situational (e.g., making funny statements about difficult content such as "boy this is hard and confusing, isn't it!"). His humor was never caustic or juvenile, and never at the expense of any particular student.

Perhaps the most unique way Kirk introduced levity was one of the ways he regained students' attention: short "dance breaks." Kirk and his

---

923–41.

30. Kirk, "Teaching Introductory Statistics"; Kirk, "Charles L. Brewer Invited Address."

31. Braun and Clarke, "Thematic Analysis," 57–71.

wife are award-winning ballroom dancers.[32] So, he spontaneously broke into a ballroom dance (e.g., foxtrot, rumba) multiple times throughout the semester. This noticeably piqued students' attention from which Kirk would segue back into teaching.

Rigor

Kirk approached the course's content rigorously and never "dumbed down" the material. For example, it was not uncommon for him to work through proofs or derivations when applicable. Moreover, he had very high expectations of his students. He frequently told them that he expected that they be able to demonstrate knowledge about not only how to calculate a given statistic but also when to apply it and how to interpret the results. His tests reflected these expectations.

Care and Respect for Students

Kirk demonstrated respect for his students and care that they did well in his course. This is not surprising given its commonality among master teachers.[33] What was surprising was how Kirk went about doing this given the inherent difficulties in this endeavor with larger class enrollments.

Kirk's demonstration of respect and care was most frequently evident in his purposeful effort to know his students. He had students complete a seating chart after the first few classes. He did not use this chart just to take attendance or call students by name during class. In addition, he came at least 10–minutes early to every class and used the seating chart to have informal conversations with students before class began. Kirk explained the origins of this practice:

> One day I got to the lecture hall ten minutes earlier than usual. Instead of standing at the front of the hall, I wandered up and down the isles [sic]. During this time, I had a number of conversations with students who never asked questions during class or called me at home. From that day on, the ten minute walk-around became a regular part of my pre-lecture routine.[34]

32. A video of Kirk and his wife dancing went "viral" in 2019: https://twitter.com/TamaraJosol/status/1099041978308796418.

33. Keeley, Ismail, and Buskist, "Excellent Teachers' Perspectives," 175–79.

34. Kirk, "Teaching Introductory Statistics," 5.

The topics of these student conversations were not random. Before each class, Kirk reviewed a notebook that contained the gist of earlier student contacts that he wanted to follow up (e.g., asking students who were ill how they were currently feeling, asking student athletes about an upcoming sports event). Thus, over the semester he made multiple personal contacts with the eighty-five students taking his course!

Another way he demonstrated respect was the way he made it safe to ask questions. He stated multiple times in class that it was typical for students to be confused or feel anxious when learning statistics. One way he tried to alleviate this confusion and anxiety was setting aside time in every class for students to ask questions about concepts they did not understand well. In other words, he *wanted* students to ask questions and planned his lessons on the assumption that part of class time would be devoted to answering questions.

Another way Kirk tried to help students not feel anxious or confused about statistics was to make himself available to students. In his syllabus, he provided both his office *and home* phone numbers so students could contact him outside of class with questions. Moreover, he encouraged them to contact him in class, and his syllabus states, "I enjoy answering questions about statistics . . . Answering your questions is an important and enjoyable part of my job; do not hesitate to contact me."[35]

It is one thing to ask for student questions, but it is another thing entirely to answer them in a way that respects the person asking the question. Kirk made a point to use body language and tone of voice and to have a level of positivity in his responses that gave students the impression that their questions were important—even those that had been asked before. It was not uncommon for students to ask the same question in consecutive classes; I counted one particular question asked four separate times. Yet, Kirk never gave the impression of appearing frustrated, nor were his answers ever condescending. Instead, he answered every question as if it were being asked for the first time.

Anecdotes and Examples

Statistics can sometimes be a dry subject. To make the content more accessible and "come alive," Kirk frequently provided anecdotes and examples throughout his classes. The anecdotes ranged from personal (e.g.,

35. Kirk, *Instructors Manual*, 12.

an experience using a given statistic, errors he made) to professional (e.g., background of individuals who developed a statistic). Sometimes he combined the two and provided anecdotes of his personal interactions with the statisticians who developed a statistic!

In addition to anecdotes, Kirk provided examples in nearly every class. Sometimes these examples involved working through data analysis from a real-world situation, in which case Kirk worked out the solution via slides (which he provided to students ahead of time). Other times, the examples were more didactic and involved Kirk working through the calculations, by hand, in class. Either way, students were afforded multiple demonstrations of how to calculate, use, and interpret every statistic that was discussed in the course.

Material Reviews

The first part of every class started the same way: ten minutes devoted to reviewing material previously covered in the course. This review could range from going over terms to working through an example. He was especially apt to repeat a previous example when it was complex and students were likely to be confused or have unasked questions (e.g., power analysis). In conducting these reviews, he often made a point to note how concepts he taught earlier in the semester fit together with more recent topics.

Discussion

In this study, I directly observed the pedagogical behaviors of a master teacher: Roger E. Kirk. Unlike many other pedagogical case studies, I observed Kirk in the same course for an entire semester. Thus, I was able to collect data from approximately forty separate classes. In those classes, I saw repeated behaviors from Kirk that fit into five themes: levity, rigor, care and respect for students, anecdotes and examples, and material reviews. Moreover, these behaviors coincide with the general themes that people perceive as being constitutive of an expert in teaching (see Table 3.2).

The first thing that stands out from this study is that the first two themes, levity and rigor, seem contradictory. How can a course with a lighthearted climate also be one that is rigorous? Honestly, I am not sure how it is done; but I know it can be done because I saw Kirk do it. Somehow, he was able to weave rigor with due levity and do so in a way that seemed seamless.

A former mentor of mine once described his own teaching philosophy as playing an accordion. Sometimes it needs to be stretched (i.e., students need to be challenged) and sometimes it needs to be relaxed (i.e., students need to have a break). Perhaps that is what Kirk is doing by weaving levity and rigor throughout a course. Knowing when to stretch and when to relax, however, is not intuitive, and likely something that differentiates master teachers.

The second thing that stands out from this study is the deliberate actions Kirk took to foster student relationships. Given Kirk's professional stature, it could be understood if he did not bother with trying to connect personally with students in courses with larger enrollments. It is not easy to connect with so many of them, nor is it easy to create an atmosphere where students feel comfortable asking questions. Yet, Kirk appeared to accept the challenge and, as a consequence, purposefully devote considerable time and effort to make this happen. I can probably count on one hand the number of professors I know who have provided their home phone number on a syllabus and asked students to call when they have questions. I can count with one finger the number of professors I know who keep a notebook about student interactions so they can follow up with students throughout the semester. This is likely another thing that differentiates Kirk as a master teacher.[36]

The third thing that stood out was that Kirk *planned* time for content review and students asking questions. These were not impromptu events that serendipitously occurred that then threw off the schedule of events. Instead, Kirk developed his curriculum with the idea that reviewing older content and answering students' questions are just as worthy of class time as providing new content.

Such behaviors may not be necessary in other courses but are vital in statistics. Students often see statistics as a disorganized collection of formulae and concepts, so they can get overwhelmed by the seemingly-unrelated details.[37] Thus, reviewing material can help tie older and newer concepts together as well as aid in student understanding.

36. Keeley, Ismail, and Buskist, "Excellent Teachers' Perspectives," 175–79.
37. Harlow, "Teaching Quantitative Psychology," 105–17.

Limitations

The major limitations of this study are the same as those of many other extreme case studies: the sample is purposeful and the approach is exploratory. Thus, the results may or may not generalize to other master teachers, and following Kirk's example will not necessarily make a professor develop into a master teacher. Moreover, since there was only one observer and the same individual also coded the data and developed the resulting themes, there could be—and likely is—some bias in the results. These factors do not necessarily invalidate the results but do indicate that others need to replicate the results before developing any notion of causality or generalizability from the results.

Implications

Personally, I learned a great deal by observing Kirk. I teach courses similar to the one in which I observed and have already started implementing changes. I try to incorporate more humor and anecdotes, plan for content reviews, and make a more purposeful effort to talk with students about non-class related material that is important to them.

For those who do not teach courses in quantitative methods, this study may not seem to have any relevance—and perhaps it does not. What could have relevance for faculty from other disciplines is observing master teachers in their own departments or universities. They may not have the particular title of *master teacher*, but they exist. I cannot recommend enough learning from them. Ask if you can observe them teach, whether for a few classes or throughout a semester. It does not really matter if you are familiar with the content or not. If you are, all the better; but, even if you are not you can still learn from observing a master teacher.

Table 3.1: Common Qualities Stakeholders Perceive in Master Teachers

Quality
Passionate about content area
Proactively improves teaching
Deep understanding of content area
Develops rapport/is approachable
Cares that students learn
Organized
Rigorous/intellectually stimulating

Note: Information taken from Buskist (in press), Buskist and Keeley (2014), and Keeley, Ismail, and Buskist (2016).

Table 3.2: How Roger E. Kirk Demonstrated the Common Qualities of Master Teachers

Quality	Example Behaviors from Kirk
Passionate about content area	Animation when discussing class topics; provided many anecdotes related to the content
Proactively improves teaching	Deliberate and purposive approach to designing his course
Deep understanding of content area	Recognized by his peers as an expert in the field of quantitative methods
Develops rapport/is approachable	Uses humor; spontaneous dance breaks; planned conversations with students before class; receptive body language
Cares that students learn	Made it safe to ask questions; made himself available to students to answer questions; patience; frequently reviewed material
Organized	Detailed syllabus and logical organized of material (for example syllabus, see Kirk, 2008)
Rigorous/intellectually stimulating	Rigorous approach to material; overtly high student expectations; provided multiple examples and content-related anecdotes

Note: Qualities taken from Table 3.1.

References

Ackerman, Phillip L. "Nonsense, Common Sense, and Science of Expert Performance: Talent and Individual Differences." *Intelligence* 45 (2014) 6–17. doi:10.1016/j.intell.2013.04.009.

Baxter, Pamela, and Susan Jack. "Qualitative Case Study Methodology: Study Design and Implementation for Novice Researchers." *The Qualitative Report* 13.4 (2008) 544–59.

Beaujean, Alexander A., and Charles Weaver. "Roger E. Kirk: A Biography." *The Score* 41.1 (2019). https://www.apadivisions.org/division-5/publications/score/2019/01/kirk-biography.

Berliner, David C. "In Pursuit of the Expert Pedagogue." *Educational Researcher* 15 (1986) 5–13. doi:10.2307/1175505.

"Bibliography of Roger E. Kirk." *The Score* 41.1 (2019). https://www.apadivisions.org/division-5/publications/score/2019/01/kirk-bibliography.

Braun, Virginia, and Victoria Clarke. "Thematic Analysis." In *APA Handbook of Research Methods In Psychology, Vol 2: Research Designs: Quantitative, Qualitative, Neuropsychological, and Biological,* edited by Harris Cooper, Paul M. Camic, Debra L. Long, A. T. Panter, David Rindskopf, and Kenneth J. Sher, 57–71. Washington, DC: American Psychological Association, 2012.

Bromley, D. B. *The Case-Study Method in Psychology and Related Disciplines.* Chichester, UK: Wiley, 1986.

Buskist, William. "Excellent Advice from Excellent Teachers." In *The Seven Keys to Excellence in Teaching.* New York: Oxford University Press, forthcoming.

Buskist, William, and J. Keeley. "Becoming an Excellent Teacher." In *The Oxford Handbook of Undergraduate Psychology Education,* edited by Dana Dunn, 99–112. New York: Oxford University Press, 2015.

Buskist, William, Jason Sikorski, Tanya Buckley, and Bryan K. Saville. "Elements of Master Teaching." In *The Teaching of Psychology: Essays in Honor of Wilbert J. McKeachie and Charles L. Brewer,* edited by Stephen F. Davis and William Buskist, 27–39. Mahwah, NJ: Erlbaum, 2002.

Catano, Victor M., and Steve Harvey. "Student Perception of Teaching Effectiveness: Development and Validation of the Evaluation of Teaching Competencies Scale (ETCS)." *Assessment & Evaluation in Higher Education* 36.6 (2011) 701–17. doi:10.1080/02602938.2010.484879.

"Charles L. Brewer Award for Distinguished Teaching of Psychology." *American Psychologist* 70.5 (2015) 384–85. doi:10.1037/a0039387.

Dunkin, Michael J. "Concepts of Teaching and Teaching Excellence in Higher Education." *Higher Education Research & Development* 14.1 (1995) 21–33. doi:10.1080/0729436950140103.

Elton, Lewis. "Dimensions of Excellence in University Teaching." *International Journal for Academic Development* 3.1 (1998) 3–11. doi:10.1080/1360144980030102.

Ericsson, K. Anders. "Why Expert Performance is Special and Cannot Be Extrapolated from Studies of Performance in the General Population: A Response to Criticisms." *Intelligence* 45 (2014) 81–103. doi:10.1016/j.intell.2013.12.001.

Eysenck, H. J. "Introduction." In *Case Studies in Behaviour Therapy,* edited by H. J. Eysenck, 1–15. London: Routledge, 1976.

Feldman, Kenneth A. "The Superior College Teacher from The Students' View." *Research in Higher Education* 5.3 (1976) 243–288. doi:10.1007/BF00991967.

Fusch, Patricia L., Gene E. Fusch, and Lawrence R. Ness. "How to Conduct a Mini-Ethnographic Case Study: A Guide for Novice Researchers." *The Qualitative Report* 22.3 (2017) 923–41.

Hambrick, David Z., Frederick L. Oswald, Erik M. Altmann, Elizabeth J. Meinz, Fernand Gobet, and Guillermo Campitelli. "Deliberate Practice: Is That All It Takes to Become an Expert?" *Intelligence* 45 (2014) 34–45. doi:10.1016/j.intell. 2013.04.001.

Harlow, Lisa L. "Teaching Quantitative Psychology." In *The Oxford Handbook of Quantitative Methods in Psychology*. Vol. 1: *Foundations*, edited by Todd D. Little, 105–17. New York: Oxford University Press, 2013.

Hativa, Nira., Rachel Barak, and Etty Simhi. "Exemplary University Teachers: Knowledge and Beliefs Regarding Effective Teaching Dimensions and Strategies." *The Journal of Higher Education* 72.6 (2001) 699–729. doi:10.1080/00221546.200 1.11777122.

Hattie, John, and H.W. Marsh. "The Relationship between Research and Teaching: A Meta-Analysis." *Review of Educational Research* 66.4 (1996) 507–42. doi: 10.3102/00346543066004507.

Horn, John L., and A. Nayena Blankson. "Foundations for Better Understanding of Cognitive Abilities." In *Contemporary Intellectual Assessment: Theories, Tests, and Issues, 3rd ed.*, edited by Dawn P. Flanagan Patti L. Harrison, 73–98. New York: Guilford, 2012.

Joint Committee for Guides in Metrology. *JCGM 200:2012. International Vocabulary of Metrology—Basic and General Concepts and Associated Terms (VIM)*. Sèvres, France: Autor, 2012. https://www.bipm.org/utils/common/documents/jcgm/JCGM_200_2012.pdf.

Keeley, Jared W., Emad Ismail, and William Buskist. "Excellent Teachers' Perspectives on Excellent Teaching." *Teaching of Psychology* 43.3 (2016) 175–79. doi: 10.1177/0098628316649307.

Kirk, Roger E. "Charles L. Brewer Invited Address: Teaching Statistics: What I Have Learned So Far." Paper presented at the annual meeting of the American Psychological Association, Toronto, Canada, August 2015.

———. *Instructors Manual with Test Bank for Statistics: An Introduction*. 5th ed. Belmont, CA: Thomson Wadsworth, 2008.

———. "Teaching Introductory Statistics: Some Things I Have Learned. In *Engaging Others in Quantitative Psychology*, chaired by Lisa L. Harlow. Symposium conducted at the annual meeting of the American Psychological Association, Chicago, IL, August, 2002.

Levinson-Rose, Judith, and Robert J. Menges. "Improving College Teaching: A Critical Review of Research." *Review of Educational Research* 51.3 (1981) 403–34. doi:10.3102/00346543051003403.

Livingston, Carol, and Hilda Borko. "Expert-Novice Differences in Teaching: A Cognitive Analysis and Implications for Teacher Education." *Journal of Teacher Education* 40.4 (1989) 36–42. doi:10.1177/002248718904000407.

Macnamara, Brooke N., David Z. Hambrick, and Frederick L. Oswald. "Deliberate Practice and Performance in Music, Games, Sports, Education, and

Professions: A Meta-Analysis." *Psychological Science* 25.8 (2014) 1608–18. doi: 10.1177/0956797614535810.

Maraun, Michael D. "Measurement as a Normative Practice: Implications of Wittgenstein's Philosophy for Measurement in Psychology." *Theory & Psychology* 8.4 (1998) 435–61. doi:10.1177/0959354398084001.

Marsh, Herbert W., and John Hattie. "The Relation between Research Productivity and Teaching Effectiveness: Complementary, Antagonistic, or Independent Constructs?" *The Journal of Higher Education* 73.5 (2002) 603–41. doi:10.1080/0 0221546.2002.11777170.

"Master Teachers at Baylor University (BU-PP 703)." 2013. https://www.baylor.edu/bupp/doc.php/211002.pdf.

McKeachie, Wilbert J. "Critical Elements in Training University Teachers." *International Journal for Academic Development* 2.1 (1997) 67–74. doi:10.1080/1360144970020108.

———. "Research on College Teaching: The Historical Background." *Journal of Educational Psychology* 82.2 (1990) 189–200. doi:10.1037/0022-0663.82.2.189.

Michell, Joel. "The Place of Qualitative Research in Psychology." *Qualitative Research in Psychology* 1.4 (2004) 307–19. doi:10.1191/1478088704qp0200a.

Seawright, Jason, and John Gerring. "Case Selection Techniques in Case Study Research: A Menu of Qualitative and Quantitative Options." *Political Research Quarterly* 61.2 (2008) 294–308. doi:10.1177/1065912907313077.

Skelton, Alan. "Understanding 'Teaching Excellence' in Higher Education: A Critical Evaluation of the National Teaching Fellowships Scheme." *Studies in Higher Education* 29.4 (2004) 451–68. doi:10.1080/0307507042000236362.

Smith, Tracy W., and David Strahan. "Toward a Prototype of Expertise in Teaching: A Descriptive Case Study." *Journal of Teacher Education* 55.4 (2004) 357–71. doi:10.1177/0022487104267587.

Yin, Robert K. *Case Study Desearch: Design and Methods*. 4th ed. Los Angeles: Sage, 2009.

———. "Case Study Methods." In *APA Handbook of Research Methods In Psychology, Vol 2: Research Designs: Quantitative, Qualitative, Neuropsychological, And Biological*, edited by Harris Cooper, Paul M. Camic, Debra L. Long, A. T. Panter, David Rindskopf, and Kenneth J. Sher, 141–155. Washington, DC: American Psychological Association, 2012.

4

Responding to Bad Questions and Poor Answers

Andrew E. Arterbury

RECENTLY, WHILE PREPARING FOR a minor surgical procedure, my doctor provided me with an information sheet. Toward the end of the information sheet, the doctor included a commonplace quote. He reminded his patients: "There is no such thing as a 'bad' or 'dumb' question." Of course, this same doctor then asked me to read three additional documents before asking him any questions. He even suggested that I write down my questions so I could ask them all at once. Finally, the doctor stressed that the nurse (rather than he) would call just once to address my questions. In essence, the doctor first claimed there are no "bad" questions, but then he took active measures to avoid bad questions and to dissuade me from bothering him or his staff with too many questions.

At times, university classrooms exhibit a similar environment. Frequently, we as professors assure our students there are no bad questions, and we often suggest that all comments are welcome. Truthfully though, we often say those things to be polite and to encourage good comments while finding subtle—or sometimes, not so subtle—ways to discourage or eliminate the bad questions and poor answers we wish to avoid. Consequently, I am suggesting that we take a more straightforward approach to this topic. I am suggesting that we acknowledge the presence of bad questions and poor answers within our classrooms. Ignoring these problems only leaves us flat-footed when the situations arise. Even worse, mishandling these situations or mistreating the offending students is beneath the calling we seek to carry out. Alternatively, professors who construct healthy strategies for responding to bad questions and poor answers before they arise are better positioned to improve the pedagogical environment in their classrooms. I am suggesting that if we respond proactively and constructively to the problems that bad questions and poor answers present in our classrooms, we may be able to create a win-win situation for us and our students.

Identifying Bad Questions and Poor Answers

In order to define better what I mean by bad questions and poor answers, I will describe three examples that arose from two students in my classes last year:

Student #1 repeatedly asked bad questions throughout the semester. His bad questions derived from two main sources. First, he never read the course syllabus. As a result, in the last month of the semester when I—for about the sixth time—reminded my students of their final writing assignment, which the syllabus clearly described, Student #1 raised his hand and asked me why he had never heard of this assignment before now. Obviously, Student #1 was the only person who could answer his own question.

Second, this same student, Student #1, sat at the back of the room and often chatted with his friend while his classmates or I were speaking. As a result, on three separate occasions Student #1 asked a question that had just been explicitly addressed within the previous thirty seconds of class discussion. I consider these types of questions to be "bad questions."

Student #2 was a contentious and hard-working student who earned a solid grade in my class. Sometimes, however—even near the end of the course—she offered poor answers to questions I raised during our classroom discussions. Akin to ancient Gnostics who sought insight that was hidden from the masses and only available to a select few who possessed the spark of divine knowledge within them, this student at times seemed disappointed by the clearly written, obvious point of a biblical book or passage. As a result, she routinely rearranged the text we were reading or essentially constructed a new text in her head that she found more interesting. She strove for a unique interpretation that no one else had ever voiced before.

At times, Student #2 would notice an exceedingly common word in two or three biblical books and suggest that they are connected thematically. In essence, she attempted to uncover a complex web of linked biblical passages that reveal a divinely encoded message for contemporary readers. For example, she suggested that the conjunction "but" in Genesis 8, Acts 2, and Romans 5 are all mysteriously connected. Without a doubt, later biblical writers frequently quoted from earlier biblical texts, but noting the appearance of a short, ubiquitous word like "but" in multiple texts without providing additional supporting evidence does not amount to a quotation of a previous source according to either ancient or modern standards. The word "but" occurs 5,012 times in the NRSV translation of the Bible. Student #2 wanted to connect only three of those 5,012 words without any justification for her decision. From my angle of vision, Student #2 provided a very poor answer. She relied upon instincts and logic in my classroom that she brought with her to Baylor's campus and that did not align with any of the course's learning objectives. In other words, she fell back on instincts and logic that she learned in a non-academic environment and imported those into my classroom.

In my opinion, Student #1 asked "bad questions," and Student #2 offered "poor answers." Of course, having argued that things such as bad questions and poor answers exist, we still need to consider how a professor—and especially a professor who senses a call to this profession—might respond to these bad questions and poor answers.

Examining Myself First

Perhaps the first thing I should do as a professor who senses a call to teach is to ask: "What can *I* do differently?" "How can *I* improve?" If my present approach fosters bad questions and poor answers, I need to ask whether I can alter my approach and eliminate some of those bad questions and poor answers—not in a way that intimidates or discourages students, but in a way that places the burden on me to prevent the problem altogether.

After reflecting on Student #1's questions, I have now decided to give a quiz over the syllabus at the beginning of each semester for all of my classes. It does no good to lament that Canvas labels a list of assignments and due dates as the "Syllabus." It also does no good for me to self-righteously conclude that a twenty-five-year old seminarian ought to be more conscientious about his education. *I* am the one who can eliminate that bad question from arising again. If I will simply hold my students accountable for reading the syllabus, I can arrive at an easy solution that benefits my entire class.

Second, after asking myself what Professor Emeritus and Master Teacher in Baylor University's Department of English, D. Thomas Hanks, would have done in response to Student #1's chatter at the back of the room during class, I concluded that once again *I* was in a position to prevent the bad questions from arising in the first place. On more than one occasion over the years, I watched as Tom graciously addressed similar classroom incivilities.[1] Tom did not merely address poor classroom behavior because it offended him; rather he addressed the incivilities for the sake of all his students. On some occasions, Tom stopped talking and smiled while waiting for the disruptive student to recognize his errant ways and correct them. On another occasion, I witnessed Tom visiting with a disruptive student after class with a gracious smile and a clear explanation of why a different course of action would be advantageous to all. In essence, Tom always acted when faced with classroom incivilities. He never let problems fester until they created more problems. When I, however, chose to ignore Student #1's back row chatter, it led to additional problems—including bad questions that disrupted the flow of our discussions. Before going any farther, I must first refine my pedagogical approach and eliminate the distractions *I* can.

Disposition toward Students

Next, if we are called to teach—that is, if we see our job as part of our God-initiated and God-directed vocation—then we must realize that our disposition and responses towards students who raise bad questions and offer poor answers will matter almost as much as the curricular content we present in class. Without a doubt, poor questions and answers can derail our curricular plans for the day or at least slow them down considerably, but our responses to offending students have the potential to make or break the entire semester. In particular, regardless of the answers we provide to bad questions and regardless of our technical responses to poor answers, as those who are called to teach we must first and foremost respond to our offending students with respect and gracious compassion, for numerous reasons.

---

1. Boice, *Advice for New Faculty Members*, 81–98.

First, practically speaking, a poor professorial response will nega-tively impact the entire class for the remainder of the semester. When students temporarily derail class by asking ill-advised questions that are clearly addressed in the syllabus or when they talk at the back of the room and then ask about the subject that was just discussed, a poor response from the professor to the offending student can have devastating effects upon the entire class. If the professor opts to treat the offending student with dismissive snobbery ("Someone didn't read his assignment last night."), condescending shame ("Surely you can do better than that."), or sarcastic mockery ("Did Joel Osteen help you with that response?"), the entire class will notice. That type of harsh, professorial response will surely *reduce bad questions* in the future, but it will also *reduce all questions and comments*. Even if the other students know their classmate asked a bad question or offered a poor answer, most students will back away from the educational endeavor if they perceive the professor to be mean, condescending, or overly impatient.

Second, a poor professorial response will negatively impact the of-fending student. Many of our international students come from honor/shame cultures where teachers and their opinions are held in especially high esteem. As professors who are called to teach, we must be hospitable hosts who recognize how our responses can either increase or decrease a student's sense of honor or shame for perhaps years to come.

In reality, regardless of our students' culture of origin, honor and shame play a significant role in every setting that involves humans. As a result, there may be no better moment for a professor to exemplify her or his sense of calling than when the professor is forced to respond to a bad question or a poor answer in front of the entire class. That moment is precisely when the professor most needs to amass all of her creativity and resourcefulness in the hope of turning a negative experience into a positive one—or at least neutralizing the threat that the situation poses to the offending student's honor.

If a student realizes that the professor sought to preserve or to en-hance her or his honor amid a potentially embarrassing situation, that student may well read more diligently and think more deeply about the subject matter of the course moving forward. Regardless, when other students in the class perceive that the professor advocated for the offend-ing student and sought to neutralize a potentially embarrassing situation, they too will take greater risks and engage in the educational endeavor more deeply because they perceive the professor to be one who has their back as well. Furthermore, it is in that moment—when a student has the potential to lose face in front of his or her peers—that the professor demonstrates to the offending student, to the class, and to herself what it means to be "called to teach." When the professor lives out the spiritual conviction that God values all persons by ardently seeking to preserve honor and save face for even her poorest students, the professor begins to understand what sets apart those who are "called to teach" from those who simply enjoy the life of the mind.

Transformative Moments

Finally, as professors, we may hope to eliminate as many of the Student #1 type of offenses as possible—failing to read the syllabus and unfocused attention that leads to repetitive questions; however, when we teach with a sense of calling, we may well embrace the poor answers of Student #2. Instead of a problem, Student #2's answer provided me with a tremendous pedagogical opportunity—one that I could not have staged on my own. Poor answers may well lead to transformational moments if we handle them properly. Student #2 applied real-world instincts and logic to the subject matter of our course. Her poor answer challenged me as a professor to define better the hermeneutic I was seeking to teach and to illustrate why an academically informed hermeneutic is more helpful than the one she brought with her to Waco.

In other words, all professors face the challenge of helping their students to inquire, reason, and write in line with the scholars from their own discipline.[2] We all face the challenge of demonstrating why our academic discipline matters. That objective can only be accomplished, however, if we show our students the benefits of migrating from the angle of vision with which they entered to the angle of vision with which we hope they will they depart.

Years ago, I recall Professor Mikeal C. Parsons from Baylor University's Department of Religion explaining to his graduate students that professors in the Humanities are not simply called to answer the questions that our students ask. Rather, we are first and foremost called to teach our students to ask better, higher, and more important questions. When I think back on the professors who most impacted me, each of them taught me to ask better questions.

2. Clines, "Learning, Teaching, and Researching Biblical Studies," 15.

Student #2 started out well, but she ended up offering a poor answer that grew out of her misguided, semi-Gnostic questions. Her responses rightly assumed that God has a word for God's people, but she failed to consider the word of the Lord that was first addressed to the original recipients of Genesis, Acts, and Romans. In addition, she believed that the sixty-six books of the Bible are interconnected—notably, both Paul and Luke saw a similar type of connectedness between the events of the Old Testament and their day—but the student focused her attention on commonplace, English words rather than major, biblical themes like the redemptive work of God during the times of Moses, the Babylonian exile, and Jesus—redemptive works that transcend modern translations of ancient events and texts. In essence, she opted to focus on English conjunctions rather than God's saving activity throughout the Scriptures.

Regardless, poor answers like the one that Student #2 voiced can set the stage for a teachable moment. If a caring professor can invite her to ask better questions and to try out better interpretive approaches, the door to transformational education may be opened. Professors who foster transformational moments, however, will first need to start at a similar beginning point as their students, and they will likely need to mine for the gold that lays amid the dross of the student's initial answer.

Perhaps the professor who responds to Student #2 will explain how a quasi-Gnostic reading of the text actually defies the very standardizing purpose of the Scriptures, which the student herself passionately affirms. Perhaps the professor will describe the types of criteria Biblical Studies scholars frequently employ when identifying a quotation or an allusion to an earlier work. Perhaps the professor will demonstrate the exegetical payoff that accompanies informed interpretation of a singular biblical text instead of attempting to weave together all sixty-six books of the Bible at a single moment. Yet regardless of the tack professors may take, professors who are called to teach must recognize the grand opportunity that poor answers can sometimes provide when we aim for transformational education.

In other words, professors who are called to teach should realize that at times bad questions and poor answers can provide professors with a kernel of genius with which to work. If we can find and highlight that kernel of genius amid the student's comments while allowing the chaff to fall away, we may be able to teach students to ask better questions and articulate better answers. Furthermore, professors who are called to teach should realize that one student's misstep can benefit every student in the room while simultaneously making the professor a better teacher. In essence, one of the most important challenges facing professors who are called to teach surfaces when she seeks to identify the insightful but miniscule kernel of insight that is present in a poor question or answer and to demonstrate how someone in her own academic field might cultivate that same insightful kernel into a full-grown plant.

Conclusion

In conclusion, I am arguing that our sense of calling as teachers and professors is revealed (perhaps, most clearly) in the way we respond to the repetitive, unnecessary, or ill-conceived questions that our students raise as well as the inadequate answers that they offer to our questions. Bad questions and poor answers may indeed impede our lesson plans. As a result, at times we need to think creatively about eliminating those dynamics in future classes. At other times, however, bad questions and poor answers provide us with golden opportunities to establish a hospitable classroom environment and to open the door for transformational moments. Shaming students has no place in the classroom of a professor who has been called to teach. Alternatively, if we think through our strategies for responding to bad questions ahead of time and if we listen for the kernel of genius that is often embedded in poor answers, we may help the offending students become better students while encouraging the entire class to test the waters of our academic field.

REFERENCES

Boice, Robert. *Advice for New Faculty Members*. Boston: Allyn & Bacon, 2000.
Clines, David J. A. "Learning, Teaching, and Researching Biblical Studies, Today and Tomorrow." *Journal of Biblical Literature* 129.1 (2010) 5–29.

5

The Outrageous Idea
of the Christian Teacher

PERRY L. GLANZER AND NATHAN F. ALLEMAN

IN THIS CHAPTER THE core point that we address relates to the basic truth that teachers are not solely teachers. They may also be spouses, parents, Democrats or Republicans, Jews or Muslims, environmentalists, feminists, members of particular ethnic or racial groups, a country, a particular sexual identity and more. All of these identities orient us metaphysically and morally. As Charles Taylor observes, "to know who you are is to be oriented in moral space, a space in which questions arise about what is good or bad, what is worth doing and what is not, what has meaning and importance for you and what is trivial and secondary."[1] When a person becomes a mother or father, for example, he or she immediately inherits the moral tradition within our culture about what it means to be a good mother or father. The person may reject this tradition, but it still exists.

Furthermore, when we try to be excellent in any of our identities, such as being a good teacher, a good mother, a good citizen, a good environmentalist, or a good Christian, these identities and the moral traditions associated with them may come in conflict. In this respect, although our identities orient us morally within particular traditions of practice, they also can cause moral problems. After all, we each have multiple identities. Many of these identities connect the individual to moral traditions housed within historical narratives, and sometimes metaphysical

1. Taylor, *Sources of the Self*, 28.

metanarratives from which the teacher may derive particular moral ends, virtues, rules, and practices.[2] Thus, teachers interested in pursuing the good life in every dimension of their lives must not only try to figure out what it means to be a good teacher. They must also contemplate what it means to be excellent in each of these identities as well (e.g., a good parent, woman, Muslim, Democrat, etc.), and then prioritize their identities when moral conflicts occur.

We do not necessarily think teachers are unique in this regard. Individuals in any other employment or social role may seek congruence and consistency among their various roles. Still, there is something unique about being a teacher that conjoins and creates an unusual confluence of these elements. Young people will look to them as models (or examples of what to follow or not to follow) regarding how to be excellent not only in a particular field of study (e.g., biology, the visual arts, English literature) but also in other areas of life (e.g., marriage, citizenship, and/or friendship). They likely do not look at their dentists, doctors, or bankers the same way.

One of the most important life questions concerns how we prioritize, mesh, and draw boundaries between our different identities. The answer to this question pertains to how we prioritize and mix the normative ideals associated with these identities and their associated moral traditions. There may be plenty of overlap between being a good teacher, a good feminist, and a good Muslim, but these identities may also produce conflicts. Consider how the female teacher with these three identities decides what to wear to class. Each of the three identities may provide her with particular ways of thinking about or expressing answers to this question ("dress professionally," [teacher identity]; "dress modestly," [Muslim identity]; and "dress to express yourself and your voice" [feminist identity]). Indeed, one of the areas where there is a wide degree of disagreement concerns the answers to the following key question: *how can or should one's other identities outside of being a teacher, along with their associated narratives, virtues, practices, etc., inform one's teaching?*

We will not attempt to address all of the difficult matters that arise from the dilemma of how our various identities interact with the identity of being a teacher. Instead, we will focus primarily on the relationship between two particular identities—being a Christian and being a teacher. We hope to answer the questions: (1) *How does being a Christian change one's teaching?* (2) *How should it?* A great deal of sloppy thinking exists

2. Glanzer, "Building the Good Life," 177–84.

around this topic that often reduces the options to simplistic dichotomies such as indoctrination vs. true teaching. Consider this Catholic literature professor, Chris Anderson, who teaches in a pluralistic university setting. He observes, "The university either ignores my faith or sees it as a potential problem."[3] He then notes:

> When I first read [Parker] Palmer urging teachers and students to live "divided no more," to act with "integrity," no longer disguising their real identity and commitments, I said, "yes, of course," in a general way. But for a number of reasons "congruence" like this didn't seem to apply to me as a Catholic Christian in a contemporary university. In my case, congruence seemed more dangerous and problematic than for a feminist, or an environmentalist or a person of color.[4]

Many educators believe that particularly when it comes to religion, we need to make sure these teachers simply draw boundaries between their identities.

In contrast, we suggest that the basis for this approach involves recognizing that our identities consciously and unconsciously influence our teaching. As professors develop, they should become conscious of how their identities influence their teaching. After all, part of being a critical thinker is learning how to order the priority we place upon our specific identities in particular situations. We will use empirical examples from Christian faculty members at institutions associated with the Council for Christian Colleges and Universities (CCCU) to help us understand the multiple and complex ways this applies in a Christian context.

What Difference Does Christianity Make for Teaching?

What difference does a professor's faith tradition make for teaching? We think the best way to answer this question is simply to ask experts who would know: Christian professors at Christian colleges and universities that give attention to how faith animates learning. What George Marsden said about Christian academic communities and scholarship can apply to Christian teaching, "In such communities there is a constant alertness to Christian perspectives and what difference they may or may not make."[5] We would also add that such an environment creates constant attention

---

3. Anderson, *Teaching as Believing*, 9.

4. Palmer, *Courage to Teach*, 16.

5. Marsden, *Outrageous Idea of Christian Scholarship*, 61.

to the practice of Christian teaching in all its dimensions as well. Scholars find that alertness and attention to deliberate forms of practice are what is necessary for excellence.[6] Moreover, as anyone familiar with obtaining excellence in a practice knows, experts tend to understand things differently than a novice. Just as a seasoned golf pro can analyze a developing golfer's swing and see all the problems or marks of excellence or a great musician can hear the subtle flaws or beauty of an emerging musician, an experienced teacher can analyze data and see significant weaknesses and nuances. In contrast, the novice will fail to see subtle or important nuances.

To date, few scholars have addressed the general topic of how a Christian teacher's *identity* influences their *teaching* in higher education.[7] Indeed, broad, empirical surveys examining the extent to which faculty serving in faith-based institutions embrace and express their Christian or specific denominational identity in their teaching (as opposed to simply in their scholarship) are completely absent from the scholarly conversation about the value of a religious identity within American higher education.[8] While there are some rich individual statements,[9] scholars have not undertaken a national study of this matter until now.

Surveying Christian Teachers

To address this gap in the scholarship, we conducted a survey in which we asked over 2,300 professors at 48 CCCU institutions in North America about the relationship of their Christian tradition to their teaching. Surveying Christian professors at these Christian colleges and universities helps us understand the myriad ways Christian professors incorporate their identity in a supportive context.[10] In our survey, we asked

6. Ericsson, Krampe, and Tesch-Romer, "Role of Deliberate Practice," 363–406.

7. There are a few more works that address Christian teaching at the K-12 level. See for example, Van Dyk, *Craft of Christian Teaching.*

8. One review of literature by two scholars found "only a tiny percentage of the scholarly writing that emerges from Christian higher education is devoted to the development of . . . nuanced accounts of how teaching and learning are supposed to work in a Christian setting." Smith and Smith, *Teaching and Christian Practices,* 3.

9. Anderson, *Teaching as Believing*; Elshtain, "Does, or Should, Teaching Reflect the Religious Perspective of the Teacher?," 193–201; Hughes, *How Christian Faith Can Sustain the Life of the Mind,* 97–133; Haynes, *Professing in the Postmodern Academy*; Van Dyk, *Craft of Christian Teaching.*

10. The CCCU states: "We are committed to supporting, protecting, and promoting

participants to identify the broad theological tradition with which they identify. Survey respondents selected from a menu of faith tradition options that included Anabaptist, Anglican, Baptist, Catholic, Eastern Orthodox, Evangelical, Pentecostal/Charismatic, Reformed, Wesleyan, or Other (see Table 5.1 for the results).[11] Since our sample came from Protestant institutions (a limit of our study), the sample largely included professors who identified with a Protestant tradition.

Table 5.1: Broad Theological Traditions
of Faculty Respondents (n = 2,309)[12]

Broad Theological Tradition	
Baptist	20%
Evangelical	19%
Wesleyan	18%
Reformed	12%
Pentecostal/Charismatic	8%
Anabaptist	7%
Other	5%
Anglican	5%
Catholic	4%
Lutheran	3%
Eastern Orthodox	1%

the value of integrating the Bible—divinely inspired, true, and authoritative—throughout all curricular and co-curricular aspects of the educational experience on our campuses, including teaching and research." Christian Colleges and Universities, "Our Work and Mission."

11. This list of faith traditions reflects those used in other national religion surveys, such as the Baylor Religion Survey. We do not suppose that we know all that each respondent assumes about their selected tradition. Nevertheless, most traditions do include important points of convergence, each requiring more explanation than is possible here. We recommend readers interested in better understanding the implications of these faith traditions consult the following resources: Hughes, *How Christian Faith Can Sustain the Life of the Mind*; Hughes and Adrian, *Models for Christian Higher Education*; Foster, *Streams of Living Water*; Jacobsen and Jacobsen, *Scholarship and Christian Faith*.

12. This table originally appeared in Alleman et al., "The Integration of Christian Theological Traditions."

We then asked the respondents whether this theological tradition influenced the following areas of their teaching: 1. Course Objectives; 2. Foundations, Worldview, or Narrative Guiding the Course; 3. Motivations for or Attitude toward the Class; 4. Ethical Approach to the Course; and 5. Teaching Methods. As can be seen from our questions, we understood "teaching" in our survey as involving all of the background thinking and practical work related to conducting a class. The resulting faculty responses to this question, by percentage, are in Table 5.2:

Table 5.2: Does your theological tradition influence the following areas of your teaching?[13]

Question (responses by percentage)	Yes	Don't know	No
Course objectives	48	9	43
Foundations, worldview or narrative guiding the course	79	5	16
Motivations for or attitude toward the class	78	6	16
Ethical approach to the class	84	4	12
Teaching Methods	40	20	40

Over three-fourths of teachers understood their particular Christian identity to be an influencing factor in their motivations, guiding foundations, worldview or narrative, and their ethical approach to the class (Table 2). In contrast, less than half of survey respondents believed their faith tradition was relevant to the formation of course objectives and/or their teaching methods. In fact, the professors we surveyed demonstrated the most division as to whether their particular Christian identity influenced their specific teaching methods. This is reflected by the largest number of "I don't know" answers in this category when compared to other ways that faculty members may integrate their particular Christian identity into their pedagogical practice.[14] Still, forty percent of faculty respondents to our survey thought their particular Christian identity informed their teaching methods.

13. This table originally appeared in Alleman et al., "The Integration of Christian Theological Traditions."

14. Smith and Smith, *Teaching and Christian Practices.*

As this process reveals, we initially set out to find the difference particular Christian traditions (e.g., Baptist, Wesleyan, Reformed, Catholic, etc.) made to the participants' teaching. Therefore, the teachers who indicated "no" in Table 5.2 may still think Christianity in general did make a difference in their teaching, since we asked them to think in terms of their specific intellectual and theological tradition within the broader identity of Christianity.

So why then do we think our research can answer both questions of what difference Christianity makes *and* what difference a particular Christian tradition makes? In our survey, we also gave respondents an opportunity to provide qualitative examples from their experience.[15] In the qualitative answers, we found that sixty percent of professors included answers to our question that exemplified what difference Christianity makes in their teaching. Of course, the other forty percent of answers related to the difference their particular tradition made. In other words, it is clear from the qualitative answers we received that many professors either simply understood the phrase "theological tradition" to mean their general Christian identity and the broad Christian theological tradition or they wrote down answers they considered differences their tradition made, but they are really differences Christianity in general makes. A few professors even recognized the possibility of the dual types of answers in their responses. For example, the following respondent distinguished both the general influence of Christianity and particular influence of a theological tradition on his teaching. The professor noted,

> My broader Christian tradition leads me to view my students as "divine image bearers" who are worthy of my best efforts, patience, and faith in their ability to grasp and employ effectively what I am teaching them "for Christ and his kingdom." My evangelical piety causes me to not only teach but also seek to mentor, pray for, and spiritually nurture my students.

In this chapter we focus specifically upon the responses we classified as generally Christian. We placed responses in this group if respondents did not mention a particular Christian tradition in their answers and if virtually all Christian traditions would find agreement with the types of emphasis the professors mentioned.

15. Although one might be critical of the fact that professors often only mentioned one part of a learning taxonomy instead of the full range of objectives that would entail understanding and applying a theological tradition in a critical manner, we should note that professors were only asked to give one example.

Generally, we found Christianity animated these professors' teaching in six different ways (see Table 5.3), all of which are also aspects mentioned in the literature that discusses distinctive Christian scholarship.[16] We classified three of these activities as undertaken solely by the teacher: one focused solely upon students, one focused solely on the subject taught, while another three involved the teacher, the student and the subject. Teachers from all faith traditions mentioned in our survey engaged in these activities, but did so to varying degrees.

Table 5.3: Ways Christian Identity Animates Teaching

THE TEACHER	THE STUDENT	THE DISCIPLINE
The Overall Metanarrative or Worldview		
Motivation		
Identity beyond Teacher, Student and Subject		
	Ends of Teaching	
Class Content		Class Content
Pedagogy		

One's Metanarrative or Worldview

Thinking about teaching requires that one orient oneself in a narrative context. In fact, we contend there is no such thing as critical thinking apart from a particular standpoint, identity, and narrative. You need an identity and standpoint from which to reason. As Charles Taylor observes, "Our identity is what allows us to define what is important to us and what is not."[17] In fact, identifying as a Christian often serves as a kind of shorthand for a whole tradition of theological and moral thinking formed by a unique understanding of the characters and setting in the universe as well as the larger story in which we find ourselves. It should be no surprise, then, that someone who claims God exists, acts in human history, and reveals these realities to us considers these beliefs important in how one approaches the practice of teaching. This is true no matter what the subject.

16. For a summary, see Ream and Glanzer, *Christian Faith and Scholarship*, 47–57.
17. Taylor, *Sources of the Self*, 30.

For most teachers we surveyed, identifying as Christian linked them to a metanarrative that they derived primarily from the Bible, but that Christians also developed over time within their communities. They used this metanarrative to engage in *Christian critical thinking*. Some talk about it as a worldview or paradigm.[18] Some suggest a narrative provides an understanding of the key characters as well as the overall story we use to make sense of our world and the ends of education.[19]

In the survey responses we received, the nature of the relationship between Christian identity and course-shaping perspectives that teachers expressed often followed a particular pattern. Teachers first articulated a primary theological belief rooted in their Christian identity and its associated story and then drew an implicit or explicit connection to their teaching. For example, this education professor shared,

> God has gifted each of us to join in His work in the world. Because I am a prof in teacher education that translates into the understanding that I am equipping teacher candidates who will effectively represent Christ in what, where, whom and how they teach.

As this example demonstrates, a respondent's theological perspective was often a statement about God or God's actions in the world. In other words, the professor made God and God's story the starting place of their views about teaching (e.g., "My learning outcomes derive from my view of God and who He is in my life."). Of course, teachers did not always express this outlook in a uniform fashion. Three particular ways of articulating these foundations emerged as a result of our coding process.

First, some professors focused upon a multi-faceted understanding of God's story with humanity using broad, theological themes (e.g., "The framework of historic Christianity is the ultimate story: God, Creation, Fall, Redemption, Judgement, and Restoration, Final Estate"). Often professors would mention they begin with this type of narrative framework and then apply it to their discipline: "Believing in the narrative of creation, fall, and redemption shapes our approach to literature." Although this particular way of summarizing the Christian drama is quite common among the Reformed Christian tradition,[20] we found it employed by scholars from almost all traditions.

18. Kuhn, *Structure of Scientific Revolutions*; Naugle, *Worldview*.

19. Postman, *End of Education*.

20. Ream and Glanzer, *Christian Faith and Scholarship*.

Second, other teachers took a similar theological approach, but they would mention only one specific aspect of God's character or one part of God's story with humanity that influenced or shaped their thinking about teaching. For instance, with regard to God's character, professors referred to a variety of characteristics such as God's sovereignty (e.g., "The sovereignty of God guides all that I do, including my understanding of how faith and politics interface. I can't teach political philosophy or legal theory apart from that view."); God's creative power (e.g., "All of our work and thoughts are done before the face of God. All things should be done unto Him who is the Creator of all we study and the gifts we have to study this creation."); or God's grace and love (e.g., "I approach the class with an attitude that we all deserve grace. As free receivers of God's grace and love, I offer the same to my students.").

With reference to God's story with humanity, teachers linked their injunctions to the specific content of their disciplines. A number of professors, particularly those in the sciences, emphasized some aspect of what theologians call the "doctrine of creation." One professor in the sciences shared, "Understanding God created everything means that nature is real, good, orderly, and contingent, all of which affects how we think about science." Others, however, emphasized a different part of the Christian story. For instance, a modern language teacher provided a theological exposition of how to think about languages in light of God's view of languages as revealed at the end of the Christian narrative:

> The narrative into which I fit my work is this: My work is predicated on at least two assumptions: (1) languages are important to God, so important that in the apocalyptic vision of people gathered around the throne praising God and celebrating God's salvation (Rev 7:9–10), languages (plural) remain: the acclamations of the throng are multi-lingual; (2) diverse creatures, and by implication a diverse humanity, can abide in peace and harmony within the holy realm of God (Isa 11:6–9). Because, in the ultimate scheme of the universe, languages are important and peaceful diversity is the direction in which God is moving the world, I engage in the work of teaching and learning languages and using language education for promoting intercultural understanding and peacebuilding.

In this case, the end of the Christian story proved especially important for shaping how the professor understood the ultimate importance of diverse languages.

Finally, other professors wrote less about broad or particular theological themes and focused more upon the source of knowing from which these particular theological beliefs derive: the Bible itself (e.g., "My goal is to teach biblically"). For these professors, the Christian scriptures provided the foundation or starting point for their worldview and therefore directly shaped how they thought about teaching. Of course, professors might combine two or three of these approaches (what we termed: theological narrative, theological themes, and Biblical emphasis). For instance, the following literature professor indicated how she brought particular theological themes from the Bible into her class discussions: "Because I believe the Bible is truth, my writing courses include discussions of what the Bible says about language and creativity. We are image-bearers, and our creative work can/should glorify God." Overall, our survey answers revealed that Christian teachers reason about teaching in light of God and God's story with humanity.

Motivation

God motivates Christian teachers. This finding should not be surprising.[21] What proves to be illuminating, however, are the variety of ways teachers expressed the nature of this motivational relationship. The professors we surveyed focused on three aspects of their relationship with God that inspired them: (1) the need to glorify or worship God; (2) their response to God's presence or call; and (3) their response to God's character.

Throughout the Christian Scriptures, the first response to recognizing God's presence involves worship. Not surprisingly, numerous Christian educators in our survey articulated this end as well. One science professor simply explained, "Christians can do science to the glory of God and the benefit of our neighbor." Although somewhat similar to those who talked about bringing glory to God, other teachers contended that their work comprised a form of worship of God.

Some professors also wanted to make clear that this attitude of worship in class meant one could not split education into two spheres, with one addressing the sacred and the other the secular. These teachers explained that everything is sacred and therefore everything, including teaching, involves worship. For these professors, the concept of glorifying or worshiping God involved more than what occurs in a church or

21. Nord, *Does God Make a Difference?*

university chapel service. Participants believed engaging in the professorial vocation with a certain kind of God-directed-motive is itself a form of worship. Worship occurs in front of a class and at one's desk: not merely in a sanctuary.

Second, Christian teachers also talked about ways that a relationship with God transformed how they thought about the teaching profession in light of God's presence or actions. This transformation happened a variety of ways. One group of professors simply understood themselves as, first and foremost, working for God and not merely an earthly boss. Consequently, they perceived this kind of working relationship as increasing their efforts at striving for excellence (e.g., "Do your work as unto the Lord and not as unto men [Col 3:23]. I worked harder than any of them, but it was not I but the grace of God working in me").

Moreover, a number of teachers suggested that God must then be the one to initiate this sacred responsibility. Indeed, a common way God's actions transformed the teaching profession for professors from a variety of disciplines had to do with the concept of God's calling. In most cases, the calling was stated rather straightforwardly: "Teaching is a calling I have from God, which is precious. I am eager to be a godly influence on my students." (Arts professor). In this understanding, respondents do not teach simply because it feels good when they see students learn or they have some particular passion for a certain subject (although we do not doubt that these two elements may inform their experience). Teaching is something God invited and equipped them to do.

A third group of teachers focused less upon the ways God's presence or actions changed their view of the teaching profession and concentrated more explicitly upon the way particular aspects of God's character as revealed through the Biblical narratives motivated them. Three particular themes stood out among those mentioned by professors: grace, love, and truth. This extended quote from a nursing professor provides the most extensive reflection upon this theme of grace:

> God has done amazing and gracious acts and transformation in my life. His gracious acceptance of and validation of me and His design in me makes me a faculty of graciousness. I have high expectations b/c I believe that if God calls students to a line of study (nursing in my case) that He will also provide all that is needed to meet the inevitable and character-building qualities encountered in the journey/process. So, I can expect a lot [because] I know He delivers and provides a lot. But, the process,

> the journey is long, winding, different for each person and grace
> for that process/journey needs to be part of the support and un-
> dergirding and coming-along-side that is a part of the provision
> God lends for the process/journey to progress and be endured
> (at times).

Although grace served as a motivation for professors' work, they also saw it extended to the whole of their life.

A similar type of motivation stemmed from a teacher's understanding of God's love. A philosophy professor shared, "Because the love of Christ constrains me, I work day and night to teach my classes and disciple individuals." Similar to the concept of grace, this understanding of agape love served as a motivational factor.

Finally, a number of professors used the phrases "God's truth" or "All truth is God's truth" to connect God to their professional endeavors. Similar to expanding the concept of worship, this outlook allowed them to move beyond narrow conceptions of Christianity's role in the educational enterprise. Again, these kinds of emphases upon God's character are not at all mutually exclusive: occasionally teachers combined them with grace and love.

If one combines the previous ideas together, a broad theological narrative about God's role in motivating professors emerges. God calls individuals to teach and therefore endows them with a particular identity. God has called them to serve their students and the academic community. Indeed, God is a teacher's ultimate supervisor and one remains responsible to God in the stewardship of this responsibility. In addition, God provides teachers with gifts, including love, grace, and mercy, that compel them to act. God's grace and love also motivate them towards empathy, understanding, perspective taking, truth-speaking, equipping, and other ends. The larger purpose of the proper exercise of this calling is God's glory, and the nature of this work is itself worship.

More Than Teachers, Students, and Subjects

Being a Christian teacher transforms how one views students, other teachers, one's subject and one's own self. Christian teachers do not simply view their students according to one identity (student) or according to other identities that might receive exalted attention in the academy today, such as gender, race, sexual identity, or socio-economic status.

They draw upon other identities (e.g., "Makes me place more emphases on what it means to be a Christian student rather than just a student"). This additional emphasis takes four different forms.

First and foremost, Christian teachers talk about viewing students as being made in God's image and then unpack the implications of that identity. For example, one art teacher commented, "Made in the very image of God, I teach that we cannot help but reenact creation, as we do that of God which has been implanted in us by the Great Creator, as we embody God's image and being." This idea provides an ideal for ultimate human development: to be fully developed as a human being is to demonstrate the moral character qualities revealed by God (e.g., love, wisdom, forgiveness, creativity, etc.). Second, Christian teachers also talk about their students in familial ways that could be foreign to nontheistic teachers. One psychology professor in our survey shared, "Each one is a beloved child of God, even when they don't meet course requirements." In other words, they see both their students and themselves as part of God's family. Third, Christian teachers also view their students, as well as their subject, in another way that transforms the teacher-student-subject relationship. They often mentioned, as this professor did, "My students are gifts from God." This perception about students as gifts with gifts extends the identity of the teacher and their responsibility with students. Because God entrusts teachers with the gift of students with gifts, they perceive themselves as stewards entrusted with their students' care and development.

Fourth, this view also extended to the teacher's disciplines. Christian professors also viewed their subject or specialty as a gift that needed stewardship. A literature professor shared with us, "Because I believe that all people are made in the image of God and that language is a gift from God we are to treat other people and language with the respect and admiration we would give a gift." This outlook reflects the view that just as God takes care of his whole creation, humans are to be God's embodied representatives on earth and stewards of all of God's creation, including the creations that humans make.[22] For the Christian professors we

22. This aspect of being placed as stewards of creation is aptly captured in Psalm 8, where David asks a poignant question. "What is man that you are mindful of him, the son of man that you care for him? You have made him a little lower than the heavenly beings and crowned him with glory and honor. You made him ruler over the works of your hands; you put everything under his feet: all the flocks and herds, and the beasts of the field, the birds of the air, and the fish of the sea, all that swim the paths of the seas (Ps 8:4–8).

interviewed, academic disciplines are an extended human dimension of God's creation. Humans continue to build up storehouses of knowledge that need to be stewarded.[23] If we are to summarize these two themes, it is that teachers receive multiple gifts from God—their students and their gifts as well as the gift of their discipline, and if we want to go farther, the whole world. All of these gifts are to be stewarded, and teachers recognize that they will need to teach their students how to steward all these gifts. This theme, of course, reflects the themes of stewardship found in Jesus' parables and other New Testament teachings.[24]

Overall, we find these statements about how to best understand the core identity of teachers and students to be striking, especially when compared to the AAUP's *Statement on Professional Ethics*. This professional statement talks about the responsibilities of professors in light of five identities: as scholars of a discipline, teachers, colleagues, members of an academic institution, and as citizens. In the teacher relationship, professors serve in their "proper roles as intellectual guides and counselors."[25] Although the statement insists professors should respect students, the AAUP statement does not link this basis for this respect to any particular view of our common humanity.

In contrast, Christianity adds further dimensions by which one can think about the teacher-student relationship that supply a supporting set of reasons for demonstrating respect and even love for students. Students are made in the image of God and are children of God; therefore, they deserve respect and love. Furthermore, although Steven Cahn makes the ethical claim that a faculty member should not be a students' friend,[26] these Christian teachers who participated in our survey claim they want to see their Christian students as brothers and sisters in Christ and as gifts from God who need to be stewarded wisely. This kind of identity transformation can make a radical difference in how one lives out one's calling to teach. When it comes to their students, it certainly means that Christian faculty operate with different anthropological assumptions.

---

23. For similar writing on this theme see Golde, "Preparing Stewards of the Discipline," 10–12.

24. Matt 25:14–30; Luke 16:1–15; 1 Pet 4:10.

25. American Association of University Professors, "Statement on Professional Ethics."

26. Cahn, *Saints and Scamps*, 34.

The Classroom

When it comes to the areas linked more closely to the classroom, teachers in our survey articulated and differentiated between two major perspectives on how Christianity changed the ends, content, and methods of their courses. We call them the Spiritual Addition and Christian Transformation approaches. *Spiritual Addition* professors simply understood their Christian identity as inspiring the addition of certain objectives, content, and methods to their classroom. *Christian Transformation* professors drew upon the Christian tradition to re-conceptualize or re-enact major parts of their objectives, content, and methods in ways that are more radical. In the following sections, we illustrate these differences and classify the specific ends, curricular views, and teaching methods that the professors in our study claimed were influenced by their Christian identity.

The Ends of Classroom Teaching

The majority of Christian professors in our survey claimed their particular Christian identity led them to conceptualize the outcomes of their teaching differently. Teachers variously communicated these ends as objectives, goals, expectations, hopes, or aspirations. In other words, they did not simply discuss course objectives listed on a syllabus and instead took a more expansive view. One professor articulated this outlook: "It's not an objective I would state in the syllabus, since it's not one that can be assessed, but I tell students in courses that my primary objective is that they encounter Jesus Christ and grow as his disciples in love of God and neighbor."

Spiritual Addition professors' Christian faith tradition led them to identify ways they expanded their objectives. In addition, they often used the language of "spirituality" to refer to a dimension different from "secular" learning.[27] For instance, one teacher shared, "I aspire to see my students growing spiritually as well as intellectually." These professors understood the Christian faith to *relate* to one objective while the rest of the objectives were not considered to be related to it.

27. One also finds this characteristic in the scholarly conversation as well. See for example Tisdell, "Spirituality, Diversity, and Learner Centered Teaching," 151–65.

Curricular Sense-Making, Construction, and Content

One might expect Christian teachers simply to add Christian material to classroom content or curriculum to make their classes more "Christian" in nature. While this assumption is accurate for Spiritual Addition professors, it fails to capture the complex picture of the various ways Christian Transformation professors perceive their Christian identity to influence their curricular sense-making, construction, and content. Since Christian Transformation professors understand all of life to relate to sacred and spiritual matters, they did not separate out some parts of a curriculum as being more spiritual or religious than others (e.g., "There is no distinction between 'sacred' and 'secular' knowledge."). Since everything God created relates to how Christians understand God and God's world, they viewed what others might call "secular" content, theories, and approaches as religious in nature, (e.g., "All disciplines are valid; God is working in redeeming the whole world . . ."). Moreover, they saw certain totalizing secular theories as actually functioning as a religion, similar to how Marxism functioned in the former Soviet Union and current communist countries.[28]

Christian Transformation professors did not write about adding extra Christian content, instead, they discussed how they added theological perspectives to their whole discipline, course or particular subject under discussion. The Christian Transformationists also took particular parts of a course and then discussed them using a wider Christian perspective. In the following example, a chemistry professor talks about this approach:

> A major topic in general chemistry is energy relationships in chemical reactions. Burning of fossil fuels for energy is a chemical process. These ideas lead to a discussion of our God-given roles as stewards of creation and a conversation about God-glorifying ways to use energy resources, both fossil and renewable.

In this case, the professor emphasizes that in the Christian story, we are stewards of God's creation.

Spiritual Addition professors discussed three types of additions to their curriculum due to their Christian identity.[29] The first type of addition

28. Indeed, a wide variety of scholars have observed religious nature of certain totalizing secular theories. Crisp, D'Costa, Davies, and Hampson, *Christianity and the Disciplines*; Ream and Glanzer, *Christian Faith and Scholarship*.

29. We should note that we are not necessarily arguing that this spiritual addition approach is ideal or represents faith and learning. Indeed, Rick Ostrander argues,

pertained to the inclusion of specific Christian scripture passages to illustrate or support points (e.g., "I may utilize passages of Scripture to illustrate points."; "I incorporate Biblical scripture into writing prompts and lessons . . ."; "Always include Biblical examples to support content."). The second form of addition involved simply adding Christian material to the content of the course such as the following professor mentioned:

> I sometimes draw examples from the music literature of specifically Christian works and discuss what I know of the circumstances of the composition, the composer's faith, work and situation. I discuss musical techniques/tools/tendencies that have known theological references.

Finally, the most predominant addition involved ethical material, usually summarized by saying, "I choose texts that emphasize ethical issues." In some cases, professors combined the inclusion of ethical material with the teaching found in the Bible ("In nursing it is logical to bring in the teachings of Christ regarding the value of human life"; "When discussing ethical business practices I bring in the biblical teachings of Christ."). In general, these additions influenced the focus of the course as a whole, instead of simply functioning as supplementary course material.

Pedagogical Practices

One of the complaints about pedagogy at Christian colleges and universities from David Smith and James K. A. Smith is that "the typical pedagogical practices of the modern university often remain largely unrevised as the default medium within which attempts to think, speak, and educate Christianly are conducted."[30] Our quantitative survey would appear to affirm that claim for a majority of the faculty surveyed. However, the faculty who affirmed this connection provided us with a variety of ways they believe their faith tradition influences their pedagogy.

Once again, we noticed a difference between Spiritual Addition professors and Christian Transformation professors. The Spiritual Addition professors mentioned how they added a particular spiritual practice such as devotional Bible reading, prayer, or shared personal examples of Christian conversion to their classes. The following example is representative

---

"professors who insert religious material into their classes are not necessarily integrating faith and learning." Ostrander, *Why College Matters to God*, 109.

30. Smith and Smith, *Teaching and Christian Practices*, 5.

of this outlook: "I begin each class with a meditation. The meditation is begun by a Bible connection. There is always a time of joys and concerns for students to share needs in their personal lives." We should also note that professors did not solely mention these practices as in-class additions. For instance, professors also shared about how they engaged in these practices outside of class (e.g., "I pray privately for the class and intercede for my campus and my students."). Still, it is important to note that educators understood these activities as additions to the regular pedagogy of the class.

In contrast, Christian Transformationist educators focused upon three different types of pedagogical approaches. First, Christian Transformation professors would look at the area of pedagogy differently. As one teacher noted, "Teaching methods are influenced by belief in teaching as a gift from God, to support students in their role of gaining knowledge to develop their gifts from God." Similar to the whole idea of viewing students or subject matter as a gift, this teacher understood pedagogy as a gift to be stewarded for others.

Second, while these educators used the Bible or prayer while teaching, they were not practices simply added to the start of class. Christian Transformationists mentioned trying to integrate these practices into class content in ways that connected with the content in class. For example, instead of placing prayer at the beginning of class, they incorporated prayer into the class when it related to the particular topic (e.g., "For example, in current events based classes, we might stop in the middle of a news story or current issue, identify some of the affected parties, and have three or four students pray for what we are learning about."). They took a similar approach with the use of the Bible ("I may utilize passages of scripture to illustrate a point"). They might also include a certain kind of content or assignment for Biblical reasons, even if it actually involves learning how not to rely on the Bible. This professor shared the following example:

> In Business Ethics, the reason I insist that students need to be able to make a case for asking a non-Christian colleague in a secular business setting to do the right thing by using a secular argument rather than "Bible-thumping" is that, based upon Rom 1:18ff; 2:14, all persons have a moral awareness. Hence, secular ethics, at best, focuses on some aspect of this God-given moral awareness all persons have or had until they repressed it (Rom 1).

In these cases, faculty did not necessarily see the addition of these practices as something disconnected from course objectives.

Third, professors articulated their perspectives on *why* a particular teaching practice should be incorporated into their teaching in light of their Christian outlook or narrative. Since a teacher must justify a particular method in some way, teachers drew upon their Christian identity and its associated narrative to justify the importance of particular pedagogical practices.

Ethics

When providing examples of how their Christian identity influences pedagogy, teachers often used virtue language to describe how they applied a particular practice or justified their choice for using certain practices. In other words, the teachers discussed not merely teaching students about these virtues (as was discussed in the content section) but emphasized the need to demonstrate them in their classroom practice ("An attitude of service and hospitality towards all students.").

While in some cases, teachers simply identified virtues and their use (e.g., "Justice should be tempered with grace"), in many cases, teachers tied them to some of the identities and/or larger theological narratives we described previously. In many cases professors specifically identified how the application of virtue changes their classroom pedagogy. The particular academic or professional practices varied widely (e.g., course discussion, test-taking, writing, discipline, etc.) as this professor exemplifies:

> Ethics is one of many important ways that one brings faith to bear on the educational enterprise. An ethical classroom experience goes beyond fair treatment and honesty. In an ethical classroom students are not pitted against each other as winners and losers; the class is set up to build bonds of trust and support. Forgiveness, one more chance, and respect describe the teacher's response to students who struggle to learn.

Much like this teacher, other respondents mentioned several particular virtues or groupings of virtues. For instance, respondents regularly linked fairness and justice to the importance of virtues such as grace, mercy, and forgiveness.

Similar to grace, mercy, and forgiveness, some faculty respondents employed a general ethos of Christ's love and compassion generally as expressions of professional empathy, understood as a grounding orientation to life and teaching. The following example demonstrates teachers' expression of care for the individual students' well-being: "I love my students as individuals, am committed to exploring the reality of truth with them, and demonstrating patience toward them by encouraging them to ask 'big' questions about life and faith." Again, teachers often linked this virtue to some particular aspect of educational or professional practice and saw this as part of their pedagogy.

Modeling

By far, the most frequently mentioned pedagogical method Christian teachers noted was modeling. These teachers shared Parker Palmer's perspective, "I teach more than a body of knowledge or a set of skills. I teach a mode of relationship between the knower and the known, a way of being in the world."[31] For example, this teacher provided an extensive explanation of this common practice:

> I think that students learn by example and repetition. I think that they are influenced by mentors and therefore, I try to [be] a good role model. Lead by example, if you will. I think it is a tremendous responsibility to be a role model to these students, more so than just providing them with coursework or factual information.

While one might expect this obvious pedagogical approach from any teacher, the Christian teachers expressed it uniquely (e.g., "I model the expectation of working unto the Lord."). This uniqueness took three different forms. First, a few professors mentioned the importance of modeling particular practices related to their spiritual life, such as prayer or being a witness for Christ. To this end, the faculty tries, "to model for students this type of life in all my interactions, including within the classroom." In most cases though, the modeling related to two other matters. Some emphasized the need to model the virtues they expected of students:

> One of my course objectives and attitudes that I hope to model in the classroom is developing the intellectual virtues of humility, courage, wonder, understanding and wisdom. The humility to recognize my fallibilism and hence the need to carefully listen

31. Palmer, *To Know as We Are Known*, 30.

to those whose assertions differ from my own. The courage to subject my own beliefs and those of others to critical scrutiny in my pursuit of godly wisdom and truth. A wondrous receptivity to new truths and strange persons that come my way. The requisite understanding to grasp how various things hang together and the wisdom to conduct myself in accordance with what I trust that God has entrusted me with.

The most common way teachers expressed this outlook involved imitating or modeling Christ, which usually meant exhibiting particular virtues Christ demonstrated (e.g., "servant leadership"; "treating my students with love in my heart"; seeing it as the teacher's personal responsibility "to model God's love to my student[s] while encouraging and helping them to master the content of my courses.").

The second form of modeling teachers mentioned involved demonstrating what it means to be *good* or *excellent* in a specific professional context (e.g., "I set the model for them to follow with the patients in how they are treated."). Of course, what it means to be a good professional also involved demonstrating particular virtues. The teachers in our study, however, emphasized the application of the virtues in this professional context—usually focusing upon what it means to be a good Christian scholar or teacher. The following example illuminates this approach:

> I aim to bring both elements of the descriptor "Christian scholar" to bear in my classroom work by modelling and expecting Christ-centered, intellectually rigorous engagement with literature. As well, I try to model and encourage the practice of humble, patient reading–not to mention humble, patient interpersonal relations–described earlier in this self-study.

Furthermore, in a number of these cases, teachers emphasized how Christ served as a model, not only regarding teaching methods, but also regarding other professional practices. The following example provides the application of this perspective to the broader professional vocation of teaching, removing it from the isolated perspective on pedagogical practices:

> I teach journalism and public relations courses . . . The most powerful example I know of is reminding students that God had/has a message for humanity that we, the audience, need to receive, hear and act upon. How did God craft that message to meet the audience's needs and prove the credibility of the message? By sending Jesus, who is the Word, is God and is

human—Jesus is the content, the person and the medium—totally integrated for powerful, effective outcomes when we act.

Overall, we suggest that modeling is the ultimate incarnational expression of Christian teaching in that one imitates Christ by incarnating the highest life ideals revealed by God.

Combining All the Elements

While our brief qualitative responses provide only short, clear examples of a particular strand of emphasis, we want to be clear that we doubt most Christian professors employ just one of these approaches. In fact, the lengthier and more sophisticated responses involved mentioning a combination of some of the strands that we just described. Often, these combinations involved setting forth a particular Christian identity, unpacking its narrative implications and then moving to its importance for teaching objectives, content, and/or methods. For example, one professor described how the Christian narrative influenced her classroom teaching:

> I believe that all students (people) are created in the image of God and need a Savior. I approach my students and subject matter through a biblical worldview, respect each person as a creation of God, provide an example for my students to emulate, and show them that we all fall short of perfection.

The combination of different types of emphasis took many different forms. The following professor provides a helpful extended example of how a Christian Transformation educator sets forth a brief understanding of important theological views regarding identity, ethics, and Christian practices and then applies those elements to the particular practice of dealing with a student who plagiarized an assignment:

> My understanding of the importance of truth, human sinfulness, the need for confession, and forgiveness shapes how I have responded to a student who has cheated. For example, when I have discovered a student who has copied a classmate's paper, I will ask both students for a private meeting. In the context of that meeting, I will show the student the evidence for the act, and ask for his/her explanation. Typically, a student will confess right away. Occasionally, a student may make excuses, and I gently but firmly encourage them to acknowledge their error. When they have done so, I explain the consequences for their

act, but also offer forgiveness and a plan for the future to avoid
such acts.

We contend combining several strands in this way creates a stronger
Christian understanding and presence in the classroom. Ideally, a Christian teacher would draw upon the Christian narrative to shape their view
of students, objectives, curriculum, pedagogy, and grading, and they
would seek to apply a variety of the different themes we discovered.

Conclusion

So how does Christianity change a professor's teaching? As the responses
above indicate, the answer for these Christian teachers is multi-faceted
and complex. First, it involves elevating God and God's story. Teachers
perform for God on God's stage, and they perform for reasons that link
to the larger story God creates and weaves together. To this end, they
view their task as more than helping advance a profession, providing
students with capacities, or creating citizens (ends that are common to
non-Christian teachers and more pluralistic settings). They understand
themselves and their students as God's image-bearers, needing to show
particular types of virtue both within and outside the classroom.

In the classroom, professors tend to take either a Spiritual Addition or Christian Transformation approach to their teaching purposes,
content, and methods. As the name implies, for the former group, this
involves adding some biblical, theological, or scriptural objectives, content, or methods to what might be understood as the "usual fare." For the
latter group, this approach changes everything about the class, especially
the lens and story by which one examines course purposes, content, and
methods.

Overall, both groups add objectives that involve the holistic recovery of God's intention for human persons, the development of a deeper
relationship with God, the integration of a Christian worldview, and the
formation of ethical thinking and behavior. They also apply broad interpretive views or particular curricular choices to the curriculum that
reflect the broad Christian tradition. Finally, they add Christian practices
to their courses and justify their methods, ethical teaching, and modeling
using the Christian narrative.

To tie all the strands we found in our qualitative coding process together, we summarized them in the chart below.[32] The activities of the teacher lie on one side of the chart and the objectives for the students lie on the other side.

Table 5.4: Ways of Integrating One's Faith Tradition in the Course Objectives[33]

ACTIVITIES OF THE TEACHER	OBJECTIVES FOR STUDENTS
1. Apply Broad Interpretive Views to Teaching, the Discipline and Students from the Christian Story	1. Holistic Recovery of God's Story and Intention for Human Persons and the Discipline
2. Make Distinctive Curricular Choices (e.g., introduce Scripture, add Christian material)	2. Develop a Deeper Relationship with God/Spiritual Growth
3. Add Christian practices (e.g., prayer)	3. Learn to Integrate a Christian World-view
4. Justify Methodological Approaches within the Christian Narrative	4. Develop Ethical Thinking and Behavior
5. Be a Spiritual, Ethical, and Pedagogical Model to Students, i.e., Imitate Jesus	

While we based this typology on descriptive data, we think it has some normative implications for the Christian colleges and universities we surveyed and perhaps other types of Christian colleges and universities we did not (the large number of Catholic institutions). Faculty development courses at Christian colleges could help faculty become increasingly conscious of these types and consider how to apply them all to their teaching. We find that sometimes faculty think they are failing in this endeavor when in reality they simply are not conscious of the different ways their teaching is shaped by their Christian faith.

32. We should note that we do not believe this chart summarizes every type of integration that occurs.

33. This table originally appeared in Alleman et al., "The Integration of Christian Theological Traditions."

Christian educators, we suggest, should include and synthesize many of the different strands that emerged from our descriptive study into their teaching. By adopting this practice, the Christian nature of their teaching would not rest on one or two strands that may easily become weak and tattered when left to themselves. Instead, Christian professors ought to weave together a thick cord of several strands to provide a strong and robust line of help to students seeking the wisdom of faith-shaped course objectives in the classroom.

References

Alleman, Nathan F., et al. "The Integration of Christian Theological Traditions into the Classroom: A Survey of CCCU Faculty." *Christian Scholar's Review* 45.2 (2016) 103–25.

American Association of University Professors. "Statement on Professional Ethics." Last updated and approved by Association's Council in 2009. https://www.aaup.org/report/statement-professional-ethics.

Anderson, Chris. *Teaching as Believing: Faith in the University.* Waco, TX: Baylor University Press, 2004.

Cahn, Steven. *Saints and Scamps: Ethics in Academia.* Lanham, MD: Rowman & Littlefield, 2011.

Council of Christian Colleges and Universities. "Our Work and Mission." https://www.cccu.org/about.

Crisp, Oliver D., Gavin D'Costa, Mervyn Davies, and Peter Hampson, ed. *Christianity and the Disciplines: The Transformation of the University.* New York: T. & T. Clark, 2012.

Elshtain, Jean B. "Does, or Should, Teaching Reflect the Religious Perspective of the Teacher?" In *Religion, Scholarship, and Higher Education: Perspectives, Models, and Future Prospects*, edited by Andrea Sterk, 193–201. Notre Dame: University of Notre Dame Press, 2002.

Ericsson, K. Anders, Ralf Th. Krampe, and Clemens Tesch-Romer. "The Role of Deliberate Practice in the Acquisition of Expert Performance." *Psychological Review* 100.3 (1993) 363–406.

Foster, Richard J. *Streams of Living Water: Celebrating the Great Traditions of Christian Faith* San Francisco: HarperCollins, 2001.

Glanzer, Perry L. "Building the Good Life: Using Identities to Frame Moral Education in Higher Education." *Journal of College and Character* 14.2 (2013) 177–84. doi: 10.1515/jcc-2013-0023.

Golde, Chris M. "Preparing Stewards of the Discipline." In *Envisioning the Future of Doctoral Education: Preparing Stewards of the Discipline Carnegie Essays on the Doctorate*, edited by Chris M. Golde, George E. Walker, and Associates, 10–12. San Francisco: Jossey-Bass, 2006.

Haynes, Stephen R. ed. *Professing in the Postmodern Academy: Faculty and the Future of Church-Related Colleges.* Waco, TX: Baylor University Press, 2002.

Hughes Richard T., and William B. Adrian. *Models for Christian Higher Education: Strategies for Success in the Twenty-First Century*. Grand Rapids: Eerdmans, 1997.

Hughes, Richard T. *How Christian Faith Can Sustain the Life of the Mind*. Grand Rapids: Eerdmans, 2001.

Jacobsen, Douglas, and Rhonda Hustedt Jacobsen. *Scholarship and Christian Faith: Enlarging the Conversation*. New York: Oxford, 2004.

Kuhn, Thomas. *The Structure of Scientific Revolutions*. Chicago: University of Chicago Press, 1962.

Marsden, George. *The Outrageous Idea of Christian Scholarship*. New York: Oxford University Press, 1997.

Naugle, David K. *Worldview: The History of a Concept*. Grand Rapids: Eerdmans, 2002.

Nord, Warren. *Does God Make a Difference? Taking Religion Seriously in Our Schools and Universities*. New York: Oxford University Press, 2010.

Ostrander, Rick. *Why College Matters to God: An Introduction to the Christian College*. Rev. ed. Abilene, TX: Abilene Christian University Press, 2012.

Palmer, Parker J. *To Know as We Are Known: A Spirituality of Education*. San Francisco: Harper & Row, 1983.

———. *The Courage to Teach: Exploring the Inner Landscape of a Teacher's Life*. San Francisco: Jossey-Bass, 2007.

Postman, Neal. *The End of Education*. New York: Vintage, 1995.

Ream Todd C., and Perry L. Glanzer. *Christian Faith and Scholarship: An Exploration of Contemporary Developments*. ASHE-ERIC Higher Education Report. San Francisco: Jossey-Bass, 2007.

Smith David I., and James K. A. Smith, eds. *Teaching and Christian Practices: Reshaping Faith & Learning*. Grand Rapids: Eerdmans, 2011.

Taylor, Charles. *The Sources of the Self: The Making of Modern Identity*. Cambridge: Harvard University Press, 1989.

Tisdell, Elizabeth J. "Spirituality, Diversity, and Learner Centered Teaching: A Generative Paradox." In *The American University in a Postsecular Age*, edited by Douglas Jacobsen and Rhonda Hurstedt Jacobsen, 151–65. New York: Oxford University Press, 2008.

Van Dyk, John. *The Craft of Christian Teaching*. Sioux City, IA: Dordt, 2000.

6

. . . Lovin' the Skin I'm In

The Need for "Stories" via Young Adult Literature in the Secondary English Classroom

MONA M. CHOUCAIR

RECENTLY I HAD A conversation with one of my former pre-service candidates, who was elated because "she actually got to teach young adult literature" in her new high school teaching position. She said that her students loved Sharon Flake's *The Skin I'm In* so much that they *actually* read the book cover to cover, passed the unit test, and even started a school-wide book club just because they got so excited about reading. And what got them excited?, you might ask: the need for stories that are relevant in teenagers' lives—stories that involve characters that look like them and themes that address issues that they actually face today.

I am becoming more aware of the necessity of resurrecting stories in secondary English courses as each year goes by. I am convinced that the more teens read and know, the better readers and writers they will become. It's a paradigm shift of sorts. Kelly Bull affirmed this idea: "[F] acilitating rich literacy opportunities for young adults is essential in order to provide a student-centered approach to reading that teaches young adults how to read, think, make connections, and take action."[1]

By emphasizing the importance of resurrecting "story" through traditional young adult (YA) novels, graphic novels, and digital media,

1. Bull, "Connecting with Texts," 229.

English teachers can increase young people's love for reading, improve their reading comprehension skills, and better facilitate their writing as well.

The Fault in Our Stars author John Green discusses the need for story in our middle and secondary English classrooms. He remembers what children's literature meant to him as a kid; it was good "because I saw myself in it."[2] Green contends that authors are always resurrecting storylines, making them their own, and that we must allow students to read young adult fiction so that they too can start to understand and write their own "stories."

The main character, Melekee, in *The Skin I'm In*, learns to love herself again despite being bullied because of a skin condition. Her "story" resonates with teenagers who face bullying in schools and online. By giving teens a chance to read stories of young people that look like them, have the same issues as them, and so forth, teachers will hopefully help them to love the "skin they are in."

Young Adult Novels (in Traditional Print Form)

Initially, English teachers must embrace young adult literature not as a replacement for the canon but as companion pieces to the canon. YA titles such as *The Skin I'm In* offer a sophisticated reading alternative to students, provide relevant plot lines to adolescents, offer multicultural awareness, and even help reluctant readers enjoy English class more.

Kelly Bull explains that YA literature is "rich and complex," offering students "authentic language and addressing issues that are relevant to contemporary adolescent readers." She affirms other research that emphasizes the "importance of choice in student reading."[3]

Relevance, Relevance, Relevance

Leah Emig advocates that students are more apt to read and understand literature to which they can relate: "Young adult literature shows students that there are other people who are struggling with the same thoughts and feelings [that] they are."[4] YA literature is a great way to approach

2. Green, "Does YA Mean Anything Anymore?," 2.

3. Bull, "Connecting with Texts," 228.

4. Emig, "Combining Young Adult and Classic Literature," 6.

complex issues that adolescents often face.[5] So English teachers must select literature that is appropriate and relevant.

Contemporary realistic fiction, the broad category under which most YA titles reside, proves relevant because the narrator's voice is one that teens easily recognize: "Teens respond to young adult literature in part because they can relate to the voice conveyed. Successful young adult literature usually sounds like real teens talking . . . [and] it is the authenticity of these voices that makes for rich complex narratives."[6]

Giving students a choice in what to read scares most teachers. Yet what teachers don't realize is that they do not have to read all of these books! They just have to make them available to the students either by having them in the room or suggesting titles. In order to "foster a love for reading," students must have some choice in what they read in a secondary English classroom.[7] Doing so will help them become more engaged and increase their reading comprehension as well. Megan Truax notes that "it is a well-known fact that people enjoy reading texts that interest them,"[8] so it should be no different for adolescents. The more these [adolescents] are allowed to choose what they want to read, the more motivated they will be to read.

Asking *students* to make connections between young adult literature and the canon involves them in the learning process, allows them to transfer prior knowledge onto a new text, and inspires them to read more:

> Perhaps the greatest positive benefit of books is that young people can relate to [them]. When these struggles are realistic, they present the concept to teen readers that although growing up is never easy, other teens around the world share similar problems and generally manage to struggle through adversity.[9]

Bucher and Manning suggest:

> One of the best ways to teach young adults to appreciate novels and other literature is to provide an interesting, diverse, and well-written selection of literature . . . Teaching young adults to enjoy literature and the reading process should be a major priority in any literature program.[10]

5. Gibbons, Dail, and Stallworth, "Young Adult Literature," 53–61.

6. Bond, *Literature and the Young Adult Reader,* 253.

7. Emig, "Combining Young Adult and Classic Literature," 6.

8. Truax, "Reaching Reluctant Readers," 7.

9. Bond, *Literature and the Young Adult Reader,* 246.

10. Bucher and Manning, *Young Adult Literature,* 57.

By integrating contemporary YA novels *into* their lesson plans and novel units, teachers simultaneously offer adolescents a rich experience well beyond that of the traditional classroom. Much of the popularity of young adult literature lies in its great diversity as seen below in a pairing list that has proven very successful in English classrooms:

Young Adult Novels	Traditional Canon
The Fault in Our Stars, John Green	Emily Dickinson's poetry
Sunrise over Fallujah, Walter D. Myers	*The Red Badge of Courage*, Stephen Crane
The Outsiders, S.E. Hinton	*Flowers for Algernon*, Daniel Keyes
Postcards from No Man's Land, Aiden Chambers	*The Diary of a Young Girl*, Anne Frank
The Hunger Games (series), Suzanne Collins	"The Most Dangerous Game," Richard Connell and "The Lottery," Shirley Jackson, short stories
The Book Thief, Markus Zuzsak	*Number the Stars*, Lois Lowry
Speak, Laurie Halse Anderson	*A Thousand Sisters: My Journey into the Worst Place on Earth to Be a Woman*, Lisa Shannon
The Giver, Lois Lowry	"Harrison Bergeron," Kurt Vonnegut, Jr. short story
The Secret Life of Bees, Sue Monk Kidd	*Uncle Tom's Cabin*, Harriet Beecher Stowe
Silent to the Bone, E.L. Konigsberg	*The Diving Bell and the Butterfly*, Jean-Dominique Bauby
Buried Onions, Gary Soto	*The House on Mango Street*, Sandra Cisneros
Night, Elie Wiesel	*The Boy in the Striped Pajamas*, John Boyne
The Battle of Jericho, Sharon Draper	*The Perks of Being a Wallflower*, Stephen Chbosky
Looking for Alaska, John Green	*A Separate Peace*, John Knowles
The Lightning Thief: The Graphic Novel, Rick Riordan and Robert Venditti	The myth of Persephone
Sold, Patricia McCormick	*The Scarlet Letter*, Nathaniel Hawthorne
Monster, Walter D. Myers	*The Count of Monte Cristo*, Alexander Dumas
13 Reasons Why, Jay Asher	Slam Poetry
Coraline: The Graphic Novel, Neil Gaiman and P. Craig Russell	Edgar Allan Poe's short stories
The Skin I'm In, Sharon Flake	*Their Eyes Were Watching God*, Zora Neal Hurston

One of the results of pairing YA novels with the traditional canon is that reading comprehension improves. Brock, Goately, and Raphael note that English teachers must be aware of the ever-changing technological world in which our students live—constantly on their iPhones and iPads. Therefore, students must re-learn to interpret text—the actual written word—very carefully. And "as teachers we must make sure that students see their own cultures represented in literature or current issues and topics . . ." (again, this is a nod to said title, *The Skin I'm In*.). And English Language Arts and Reading teachers must ensure that adolescents have access to "age-appropriate materials and complex texts."[11] By focusing on the power of story—stories like their own—they can hook students into a love of reading and foster in them a sense of confidence to approach both reading and writing in the classroom.

Offering students appropriate stories also ensures better discussion of literature afterwards. If adolescents can articulate their thoughts about literature and feelings toward literature, then they can better understand the *power* of stories, increase their reading confidence and speed, and improve their ability to write about literature. "[R]egardless of the form it takes, effective discussion [of story] is goal directed, structured, and paced to allow students time to share their thoughts."[12] And if we let students write in various free-write forms such as blogs, diary entries, journals, Facebook posts, tweets, and so forth, they will not even recognize that they are doing academic writing. Excellent strategies for sharing about literature are book talks, literary circles, or pair-and-share workshops. If teens like something they will talk about it.

Digital Media

Secondly, teachers must embrace digital media to hook teen readers, especially reluctant ones. "The reluctant reader dilemma reaches its peak in middle school. At this time, academics become less important than the many other factors happening in these students' lives."[13] And as Rebecca Hill confirms, "Nowadays, young readers are tech savvy . . . This generation of readers has more distractions than any previous group, thus creating a tectonic shift in how educators must assess and motivate struggling

11. Brock, Goatley, and Raphael, *Engaging Students*, 4,5,11.

12. Brock, Goatley, and Raphael, *Teaching Students*, 15.

13. Truax, "Reaching Reluctant Readers," 4.

readers. This is where technology and books collide."[14] Multiplatform books fuse traditional print books with fun computer applications, making books fun and easily accessible. Furthermore, multiplatform books cross subject lines as in *The Mackenzie Blue* series, which "includes money tips" and could be used as a "jumping off point for mini lessons in economics and ecology."[15] Another popular multiplatform tool is fan fiction, "where readers get involved as a reviewer or author," giving students a chance to "develop a sense of story elements online."[16]

Obviously, the key to getting teens to actually read and enjoy the reading process is a good platform and a good story. Digital media has proven successful in getting reluctant readers to read because it is "a convergence of story and the arts . . . for the purpose of aiding human connection and expression."[17] In their article, "Digital Booktalk: Digital Media for Reluctant Readers," Gunter and Kenny note that teachers must use cutting edge technology to help remove the stigma for poor readers. Many adolescent students cannot or will not read simply "because they do not interact well with text based materials."[18] Therefore, "the effective use of digital media as a part of an integrated instructional strategy [teaches] reading and writing to otherwise reluctant readers."[19] The authors affirm that for today's teens "the preferred first language of the media culture may help . . . [in] overcoming literacy deficiencies."[20] They also recommend movie trailers as part of the pre-reading visualization that "has been shown to increase reading proficiency by providing an organizing structure" for poor readers.[21] After all, teens love images as evidenced by their love for Instagram, Facebook, and Snapchat; this love for image translates easily to digital media.

14. Hill, "When Technology and Books Collide," 9.

15. Hill, "When Technology and Books Collide," 11.

16. Hill, "When Technology and Books Collide," 10–11.

17. Gunter and Kenny, "Digital Booktalk," 85.

18. Gunter and Kenny, "Digital Booktalk," 86.

19. Gunter and Kenny, "Digital Booktalk," 86.

20. Gunter and Kenny, "Digital Booktalk," 87.

21. Gunter and Kenny, "Digital Booktalk," 88.

Diversity and Multicultural Literature

Third, the power of story must be presented through a diverse, multicultural lens. Multicultural literature presents a "powerful medium for understanding the world in which we live . . . [and offers students methods for] develop[ing] new meanings and conceptualizations of what diversity means."[22] "People rarely belong to just one culture; we have varying levels of competency in several cultures and especially when we are teens, there is a fluidity of identity as we seek to discover who we are."[23] Diverse stories that appeal to young people present a mirror through which students can see glimpses of themselves. Christopher Palmi presents a case study whereby teacher candidates were asked to read certain YA novels in order to raise their awareness of multiculturalism. The results were convincing: YA literature proves successful as an "effective approach to addressing the culture gap . . . and for encouraging cultural receptiveness."[24] Teacher candidates walked away from the study more equipped to face their future students of various cultural backgrounds. Some of the successful YA novels included in the study were Budhos's *Ask Me No Questions*, Alexie's *Absolutely True Diary of a Part-time Indian*, Draper's *Romiette and Julio*, and Flake's *The Skin I'm In*.

Palmi coined "multicultural insight," a noteworthy result of the above case study, stressing the importance of YA novels in the secondary classroom. He argues that teachers must,

> think about, value, and develop their understanding of multiculturalism in the classroom . . . [the] most important weapon a teacher has is information; a teacher [must have] some degree of cultural education in the classroom . . . and an understanding of how their pedagogy might be shaped through the design of lessons and management of resources in order to meet the potential needs of their students.[25]

The following are a sampling of YA novels that I have taught to promote multicultural awareness:

Flake, Sharon G. *The Skin I'm In*. 2000. An African-American author.

---

22. Bond, *Literature and the Young Adult Reader*, 30.
23. Bond, *Literature and the Young Adult Reader*, 34.
24. Palmi, "Transforming Preservice Teachers' Awareness," 13.
25. Palmi, "Transforming Preservice Teachers' Awareness," 17–18.

Maleeka, the thirteen-year-old main character, is an African American girl with a rare skin condition that makes her a prime target for teen harassment and bullying. She struggles with low self-confidence and loneliness. The novel won the coveted Coretta Scott King award.

Ryan, Pam Munoz. *Esperenza Rising*. 2000. A Latin American author.

Esperenza, the young main character in this epic novel, is trying to learn her place in life as her family unit is turned upside down. The novel takes place in Mexico and addresses family tragedy and reconciliation.

Satrapi, Marjane. *Persepolis*. 2003. A Persian author.

Marjane Satrapi, the main character in this popular graphic novel, lives in Tehran during the war between Iran and Iraq. As a child in 1980, Marji lives in a war-torn land, and as an adult, she becomes a rebel with a cause. The novel is complex and deals with many important topics related to identity, crisis, and family.

Draper, Sharon. *Tears of a Tiger*. 1994. An African-American author.

Andy, the main character of this novel, must struggle with the guilt of killing his friends in a drunk-driving accident. The content of the novel is all too familiar to its teen audience. The attraction of this novel lies in its multimodal format, relying on newspaper accounts, personal stories, and journal entries.

Alexie, Sherman. *The Absolutely True Diary of a Part-time Indian*. 2007. A Spokane Coeur d'Alene American author.

Arnold Spirit, Jr., the main character of this controversial novel, moves from the Spokane Indian Reservation to an all-white public school in Washington. Junior's life is presented in diary form and addresses teen crushes, sexuality, alcoholism, and so forth. The novel is very popular with young male readers.

Soto, Gary. *Buried Onions*. 1999. A Latin American author.

Eddie, the main character in this often depressing novel, tries unsuccessfully to escape poverty and makes many mistakes along the way. Set in the crime-ridden barrio of Fresno, California, the novel addresses very real effects of poverty on teens such as stealing, drinking, and depression.

Myers, Walter Dean. *Monster*. 1999. An African-American author.

Steve Harmon, the main character in this multilayered novel, proves fascinating to young readers. Steve tells his story from prison through the vehicle of his own screenplay and journal entries. The novel is very personal and has won numerous awards including the prestigious Michael J. Printz award as well as the Coretta Scott King award for young adult fiction.

Nye, Naomi Shihab. *Habibi.* 1997. A Palestinian American author.

Liyana Abboud, the protagonist of this beautiful story, is a young woman who must move from St. Louis to Palestine, the native land of her Arab father. This bildungsroman captures the raw emotions of a young girl transplanted in a strange place as she navigates the normal emotions of a teenager and learns about living in two worlds with two identities. The novel has won the American Library Association best young novel award and numerous others.

The Graphic Novel

Perhaps the most popular way to hook teen readers is through the medium of graphic novels. English teachers may ask, why the graphic novel?

Visuals generally capture attention . . . Kids love movies and graphic novels have a close relationship with movies . . . It is helpful to remember that graphic novels use the language of young people—filmic, visual, immediate—capable of handling multiple characters and storylines in a flexible, original way.[26]

Therefore, teachers must accept graphic novels as valid literature. Joy Lawn suggests that "graphic novels are worth investigating . . . because they are enjoyed by students and have many features that are both motivating and able to underpin explicit and worthwhile teaching opportunities."[27] Graphic novels help students learn strategic reading patterns and promote close, careful readings of text. Being adept at visual literacy helps students learn to "decipher and de-code" texts, which are defined as "graphic," meaning "graphics, pictures, illustrations, and comics."[28] Graphic novels serve as "natural progression[s] of the picture book, the novel, the art book, [and so forth]."[29]

26. Lawn, "Frame by Frame," 30.
27. Lawn, "Frame by Frame," 26.
28. Lawn, "Frame by Frame," 27.
29. Lawn, "Frame by Frame," 27.

Along with promoting visual literacy through "reading" and navigating the white/black spaces of the various plates, the graphic novel presents a unique form of storytelling. Alverson advocates that graphic novels "reinforce left-to-right sequence like nothing else. The images scaffold . . . [sentences] and [offer] a deeper interpretation of the words and story. The relative speed and immediate enjoyment build great confidence in readers."[30] Recent research by Karen Gavigan suggests that graphic novels increased reading motivation for boys, English Language Learner students, and special needs students and can help teach multiple literacies.[31] Leading reading researchers agree that the very appearance of plates and bubbles focus students' attention on the page. And so "[f]or weak learners and readers, graphic novels' concise text paired with detailed images helps them decode and comprehend the text."[32] Moreover, one tenth grade English teacher asserts that graphic novels help adolescents write better; after students learn to "read" panels, they should be encouraged to "write out the action of a page or two using descriptive prose . . . which usually demonstrate[s] two things: One, their ideas about what actions connected the images we see in each panel. Two, how effective comics can be at communicating information."[33]

Another excellent writing assignment stemming from studying graphic novels is to ask students to create original plates of a graphic novel complete with dialogue bubbles, narration, and illustration. Therefore, they are actually creating their own stories and learning to appreciate another art form.

Bond offered a list of popular, successful graphic novels:

- *Batman: The Dark Night Returns,* by Frank Miller and Klaus Janson
- *Deogratias: A Tale of Rwanda,* by J.P. Stassen
- *Fagin the Jew,* by Will Eisner
- *Hikaru No Go,* by Yumi Hotta and Takeshi Obata
- *Persepolis,* by Marjane Satrapi[34]

30. Alverson, "Graphic Advantage," 3.

31. Gavigan, "Caring Through Comics," 20.

32. Meryl Jaffe, as quoted in Alverson, "Graphic Advantage," 42.

33. Ronell Whitaker, as quoted in Alverson, "Graphic Advantage," 42.

34. Bond, *Literature and the Young Adult Reader,* 82.

Additionally, Rick Riordan's *Percy Jackson & The Lightning Thief* remains a favorite among young male students.

Digital Storytelling

Finally, students must create their own stories. That's where digital storytelling comes in to play in the English classroom. Fortunately, "the tools needed for digital storytelling—computers, scanners, digital cameras, and high quality digital audio devices—have become increasingly more affordable and accessible."[35] Costello and Reigstad advocated that digital storytelling allows teens to use their computers to "become creative storytellers . . . This material is [then] combined with various types of multimedia, including computer based graphics, recorded audio, and [so forth]."[36] Often called "multiliteracy," this approach to writing/storytelling provides students with "opportunities to design multimodal narratives that represent and reflect on their sociocultural identities and their lives."[37]

Several case studies have proven that when students craft their own narratives, their overall understanding of writing improves. One recent Canadian study focused on immigrant students, noting that each student was encouraged to write and research in his/her own native language. After choosing a topic, each student wrote a narrative, learned how to download software such as Photostory 3, created a virtual space, and finally displayed and viewed his/her "story" in digital form.[38] The outcome was a resounding success as students were fascinated with the inherent differences between print and digital texts. The most interesting aspect of the study was the sharing of their projects with one another: "Overall, students showed great interest and enthusiasm in their peers' productions, especially those on topics with which they were not familiar . . . [Afterwards], we taught them how to upload projects to YouTube to reach a wider audience."[39] Teens obviously take great pride in creating their own stories and images in their real lives, so it is quite natural for them to post things in the digital sphere. And so the best aspect of digital

---

35. Robin, "Digital Storytelling," 222.

36. Costello and Reigstad, "Approaching YAL," 4.

37. Angay-Crowder, Choi, and Yi, "Putting Multiliteracies into Practice," 38.

38. Angay-Crowder, Choi, and Yi, "Putting Multiliteracies into Practice," 41–42.

39. Angay-Crowder, Choi, and Yi, "Putting Multiliteracies into Practice," 43.

storytelling is that students actually want to share what they read and what they learned. And the benefits of digital storytelling for educators are numerous: teachers may use these stories to "enhance current lessons within a larger unit, as a way to facilitate further discussion," teach "digital literacy, global literacy, technology literacy, and visual literacy" simultaneously, and teach students to "critique their own work, as well as the work of others, facilitating social learning and emotional intelligence."[40]

In summation, John Green has made his mark on the literary world through his best-selling young adult novels like *The Fault in Our Stars* and *Looking for Alaska*; he knows his audience: "For contemporary kids, who can find sufficient distractions in gaming and video, I think books must do something more," he says.[41] He is right, and educators must do more as well. By adopting young adult literature, digital media, graphic novels, and digital storytelling, English teachers can do more. And while he enjoys the many accolades of his literary success, Green remains positive that "we can grow the breadth and diversity of YA literature. We need to get more books to kids . . . And *then* the stories will endure."[42]

REFERENCES

Alverson, Brigid. "The Graphic Advantage." *School Library Journal; New York* 60.9 (2014) 24.

Angay-Crowder, Tuba, Jayoung Choi, and Youngjoo Yi. "Putting Multiliteracies into Practice: Digital Storytelling for Multilingual Adolescents in a Summer Program." *TESL Canada Journal* 30.2 (2013) 36. https://doi.org/10.18806/tesl.v30i2.1140.

Bond, Ernie. *Literature and the Young Adult Reader*. Boston: Pearson, 2011.

Brock, Cynthia H. *Engaging Students in Disciplinary Literacy, K-6: Reading, Writing, and Teaching Tools for the Classroom*. The Common Core State Standards for Literacy Series. New York: Teachers College Press, 2014.

Bucher, Katherine Toth. *Young Adult Literature: Exploration, Evaluation, and Appreciation / Manning, M. Lee*. Upper Saddle River, NJ: Pearson Education, 2006.

Byrne Bull, Kelly. "Connecting With Texts: Teacher Candidates Reading Young Adult Literature." *Theory into Practice* 50.3 (2011) 223–30. https://doi.org/10.1080/004 05841.2011.584033.

Costello, Adrienne M., and Thomas J. Reigstad. "Approaching Young Adult Literature through Multiple Literacies." *The English Journal* 103.4 (2014) 83–89.

Emig, Leah. "Combining Young Adult and Classic Literature in a Secondary English Classroom." *A Rising Tide* 7 (Summer 2015) 1–27.

40. Robin, "Digital Storytelling," 224. For further information and examples, see University of Houston, College of Education, "Educational Uses of Digital Storytelling."

41. Green, "Does YA Mean Anything Anymore?," 4.

42. Green, "Does YA Mean Anything Anymore?," 5–6.

Gavigan, Karen. "Caring through Comics—Graphic Novels and Bibliotherapy for Grades 6–12." *Knowledge Quest* 40.5 (2012) 78–80.

Green, John. "Does YA Mean Anything Anymore?: Genre in a Digitized World." *Horn Book Magazine* 90.6 (2014) 15–25.

Gibbons, Louel C., Jennfer S. Dali, and B. Joyce Stallworth. "Young Adult Literature in the English Curriculum Today: Classroom Teachers Speak Out." *ALAN Review* (Summer 2006) 53–61.

Gunter, Glenda, and Robert Kenny. "Digital Booktalk: Digital Media for Reluctant Readers." *Contemporary Issues in Technology & Teacher Education* 8.1 (2008) 84–99.

Hill, Rebecca A. "When Technology and Books Collide." *Book Links* 19.3 (2010) 9–11.

Lawn, Joy. "Frame By Frame: Understanding the Appeal of the Graphic Novel for the Middle Years." *Literacy Learning: The Middle Years* 20.1 (2012) 26–36.

Palmi, Christopher, Deborah Augsburger, and Dorene Huvaere. "Transforming Preservice Teachers' Awareness and Understanding of Multiculturalism Through the Use of Young Adult Literature." *Illinois Reading Council Journal* 44.4 (2016) 12–22.

Robin, Bernard R. "Digital Storytelling: A Powerful Technology Tool for the 21st Century Classroom." *Theory Into Practice* 47.3 (2008) 220–28. https://doi.org/10.1080/00405840802153916.

Truax, Megan. "Reaching Reluctant Readers in Middle School." *Illinois Reading Council Journal* 39.1 (2010/2011) 3–11.

University of Houston, College of Education. "Educational Uses of Digital Storytelling." 2019. https://digitalstorytelling.coe.uh.edu/page.cfm?id=27&cid=27&sublinkid=30.

Part 2

COMMITMENT

7

Training Future Philosophy Teachers

Using A Plato Graduate Seminar as Professional Development

ANNE-MARIE SCHULTZ

I thought I had found in Anaxagoras a teacher about the cause
of things after my own heart.

—Plato, *Phaedo*[1]

All this she taught me, on those occasions
when she spoke on the art of love.

—Plato, *Symposium*

PLATO'S DIALOGUES ARE FILLED with numerous examples of teacher-
student relationships. Yet, graduate seminars on Plato typically focus
on traditional philosophical concerns, like metaphysics, epistemology,
and ethics. As a result, the opportunity to use the Platonic dialogues as
resources for pedagogical training is lost. In this chapter I report on an
innovative approach to teaching a graduate Plato seminar that focuses
both on the content of the Platonic dialogues and on preparing graduate students to become better classroom teachers. First, I provide some
institutional and autobiographical context that explains why I decided to

1. All references to Plato are from Cooper, *Plato: Collected Works.*

reorient my graduate seminar in this way. Second, I engage with some scholarship of teaching and learning that discusses effective pedagogy at the graduate level. Third, I describe the primary changes I made to my graduate seminar so that it could provide both philosophical content and pedagogical training. Finally, I provide some initial indications of the success of this model of teaching.

Autobiographical and Institutional Background

Several years ago, I was selected to be a Baylor Fellow. This is a program started by a former provost, Elizabeth Davis, in 2009. Each year, eight to ten faculty are selected from across colleges and schools of the university. These fellows are tasked with two major goals. First, to rethink a course from the ground up. Second, to report on how the new version of the course progresses in monthly meetings. I decided to restructure my graduate Plato seminar. I did so because the undergraduate philosophy teacher in me was deeply dissatisfied with the fact that I was not helping the graduate students become better teachers of philosophy.

Baylor's philosophy graduate program specializes in the philosophy of religion and ethics. Most of the faculty work within the dominant analytic style of philosophy. The program covers the history of philosophy through various course offerings, such as the Plato seminar, and through our comprehensive exams. As is true in the discipline of philosophy more broadly, the primary research interests of the faculty cluster around metaphysical, epistemological, and ethical concerns. Not surprisingly, student interest reflects the philosophical interests of the faculty. As a result, students often approach texts quite differently than I do as a historian of ancient philosophy. Our graduate students typically approach Platonic dialogues with an eye toward analyzing the arguments in the texts and trying to ascertain Plato's views about a variety of contemporary philosophical issues. I, on the other hand, was trained to look at the dialogues as literary creations in which the form of the dialogue is inexorably tied to the content. The social, political, and historical context of ancient Athens shapes how we read Plato's dialogues. Students, at least initially, have difficulty recognizing the merits of the philosophical approach I take because it differs so dramatically from the overall focus of their training.

For many years, I tried to bridge this gap in my philosophical interests and theirs by encouraging students to write papers on aspects of the dialogues that bear directly on the contemporary subfield of philosophy they were focused on in their other seminars. For example, students would write on topics such as "The Euthyphro Problem and its Relationship to Contemporary Divine Command Theory" or "Precursors to the Gettier Problem in Plato's *Theaetetus*." We read the dialogues like I wanted to read them, and they wrote papers that they wanted to write. I was reasonably happy with this approach and with the papers that the students crafted. Beyond that, my students had enormous success getting their papers accepted to conferences. In fact, most of my seminar participants over the past five years have had their papers accepted at venues such as the Ancient Philosophy Society, Society for Ancient Greek Philosophy (SAGP), Southwest Philosophical Society, or Society of Christian Philosophers. It was clear that the Plato seminar was resonating with their broader work in analytic philosophy and enhancing their overall professionalism. In fact, one student, Chris Tweedt, attended the SAGP for several years. He now has a job at Christopher Newport University and has hosted the SAGP at this institution for the past three years.[2]

Despite this clear indication of preparing students to be professional philosophers, a part of me remained dissatisfied. I felt like students did not develop an appreciation for the Platonic dialogues in a way that broadened their overall approach to the practice of philosophy. I wanted to give them multiple tools of analysis (and teaching approaches) for the texts, regardless of the methods they might use in their scholarship. I worried that when these graduate students had their own undergraduates to teach, they might not teach Plato in a way that was accessible to undergraduate students from a variety of majors and cultural backgrounds. In my mind, Plato is the sort of philosopher that should cause one to think differently about why we think the way that we do, why we believe what we do, and what we hope to accomplish in the world. Plato is the philosopher who gives us a vivid portrait of his teacher Socrates, at work in the messy reality of the world. Differently and more Platonically stated, I worried that the way I was teaching Plato was not reaching the souls of my graduate students, and as a result they would not reach the souls of their students when they taught Plato.

---

2. See the conference announcement for 2019, http://christweedt.com/sagp.html.

Effective Graduate Teaching

Unfortunately, there is very little research on effective graduate level teaching and learning in the philosophy classroom. The journal *Teaching Philosophy* is almost exclusively geared toward the undergraduate teaching experience. There are only four articles that touch on these issues at all since 2002.[3] Outside the field of philosophy, there are some scholars who explore best practices by which we might train the next generation of faculty. For example, Burton Clark argues, "We need to move conceptually beyond the dichotomy of research and teaching. Drawing a fault line between these two principal faculty activities, the incompatibility thesis portrays teaching and research as distinctively different operations that are basically opposed to each other."[4] I began to see that the way I was teaching my seminar actually reinforced the fault line between teaching and research. I was attempting to reach my graduate students by appealing to their research interests rather than their teaching interests.

Carolyn Kreber's work further motivated me to think about how to restructure the Plato seminar as a different sort of professional development opportunity: teaching. Kreber seeks to integrate the scholarship of teaching and learning into graduate education. She rightly notes that, "Most programs allow for little synthesis between discipline knowledge and pedagogy."[5] This is particularly unfortunate because "programs pay little attention to the reality that the one form of knowledge dissemination their graduates will practice most frequently upon securing a faculty position is teaching the subject to other students."[6] Kreber explains that "We learn about teaching in at least two ways. One way is to learn from our own teaching practice; we reflect on our experience-based knowledge of teaching. The second way is to learn from existing education theory and findings from education research."[7] Kreber's concern about whether "educating students exclusively in the discipline, that is, in the structure, critique, and advancement of discipline-specific knowledge—as crucial and necessary as such an education is—is sufficient to adequately address the broader education goal of fostering lifelong learning" resonated with

---

3. Jacquart and Wright, "Teaching Philosophy Graduate Students," 123–60; Concepción, Messineo, Wieten, and Homan, "State of Teacher Training," 1–24.

4. Clark, "Modern Integration," 241–55.

5. Kreber, "Scholarship of Teaching," 80.

6. Kreber, "Scholarship of Teaching," 80.

7. Kreber, "Scholarship of Teaching," 85.

me.[8] I already was using the Plato seminar as a means to get students to write papers to enhance their scholarly credentials. However, after reading Kreber's work, I realized that most philosophers, regardless of research specialization, teach Plato in a variety of undergraduate contexts. Almost every Introduction to Philosophy class includes Plato in some way. Plato also figures prominently in Introduction to Ethics courses and even Philosophy of Religion and Critical Thinking courses. Beyond that, in small liberal arts colleges and community colleges, where most of our graduate students end up teaching, faculty will be called upon to teach survey courses in Ancient Philosophy. I decided to capitalize on this dimension of the profession of philosophy. I would train my graduate students to be excellent teachers of Plato. I decided to make developing a competency in teaching Plato specifically, and ancient philosophy more generally, a sub-goal of the course.

We have a teaching preparation course in our department, "Workshop in Teaching Philosophy," that all graduate students are required to take either before they become instructors of record or during the first semester they teach.[9] Also, all graduate students serve as teaching assistants for three different undergraduate courses before teaching, and they are evaluated every semester by faculty members in the department, so there is already some culture of teaching preparation present in the department. However, integrating teaching into a "content" course had no precedent. Nonetheless, I decided to forge ahead. I restructured the course to include a pedagogical focus.

How I Restructured the Course

The first time I taught the course, I came up with four concrete things to try. First, I consistently drew our attention to pedagogical content of the dialogues. Second, I emphasized how the dialogues are structured to draw the reader into the practice of philosophy. Third, I modeled how I taught various aspects of the dialogues to undergraduates. I also asked students to reflect on how effective my pedagogical strategies were for them. Fourth, I shared how the Socratic model of teaching influences my

8. Kreber, "Scholarship of Teaching," 86.

9. For perspective on pedagogical training in graduate philosophy programs, see Concepción, Messineo, Wieten, and Homan, "State of Teacher Training," 1–24.

own teaching persona and my classroom strategies for promoting discussion. In what follows, I provide examples of each of these activities.

Pedagogical Content of the Dialogues

Early in the *Apology*, Socrates defends himself against the charge of corrupting the youth by claiming not to be a teacher like the sophists. He asserts, "If you have heard from anyone that I undertake to teach people and charge a fee for it, that is not true" (19e). However, Plato's dialogues portray him in constant conversation with his peers and young men of Athens about ethical questions concerning the nature of justice, piety, temperance and friendship. What Socrates is probably disavowing in the *Apology* is the fact that he received money in exchange for his pedagogical endeavors and not that he engaged in pedagogical activity.[10] While philosophers often approach the dialogues with an eye toward the philosophical arguments they contain, the pedagogical content of the dialogue is always present. Consider the *Protagoras*, for example. The bulk of Platonic scholarship on the dialogues concerns the questions about the unity of the virtues which arises midway through the dialogue when Socrates is having a long conversation with the famous sophist Protagoras. While I do ask students to think about whether we can have one virtue without having all the other virtues, what I focus more on are the pedagogical dimensions of the dialogue.

To explain, Plato's *Protagoras* begins with an exchange between Socrates and a friend (309a–310a). The friend is eager to hear about Socrates' burgeoning relationship with the youthful Alcibiades.[11] Socrates complies but mentions that he has just left a long meeting with the sophist Protagoras. The friend forgets all about Alcibiades and asks Socrates to tell him about his encounter with Protagoras. Even in this opening exchange, a question of how to teach arises. First, we see Socrates sharing his philosophical activities with others. Second, we get a glimpse of two different pedagogical models, the one of Protagoras, traveling teacher of political virtue, and the one of Socrates, citizen of Athens who tried to

10. On why Socrates makes this claim, see Mintz, "Why did Socrates Deny that he was a Teacher?," 735–47. On Socrates as a teacher, see Nehamas, "What Did Socrates Teach?," 279–306; and Scott, *Plato's Socrates as Educator.*

11. Plato writes two dialogues, *Alcibiades* I and *Alcibiades* II, about Socrates' attempts to teach Alcibiades the value of philosophy. The *Symposium* also attests to Socrates' long pedagogical relationship with Alcibiades (212d–222b).

teach Alcibiades philosophy. Socrates assents to the friends' request and tells the story of an early morning encounter he has with the youthful and exuberant, Hippocrates (310b-314c). Hippocrates has just heard Protagoras is in town but has no way to introduce himself to Protagoras, so he solicits Socrates' help.

As in the opening dialogue between Socrates and his friend, teaching and learning are a central issue. Hippocrates is eager to learn, even though he does not know exactly what Protagoras will teach him. In the course of their conversation, Socrates cautions Hippocrates to be careful because all learning will affect his soul and he should be discerning in his selection of a teacher. I often teach this passage to undergraduates because Hippocrates shares many qualities with them. He is young, eager to do well and make his mark on the world. He is excitable and not particularly focused in his life direction other than wanting to be successful in the world. Socrates warns Hippocrates that he needs to guard his soul against pernicious pedagogical influences: "You cannot carry teachings away in a separate container. You put down your money and take the teaching away in your soul by having learned it and off you go, either helped or injured" (314b). I ask students if they consider their souls in the course of their education. In the graduate seminar, I ask the students how they plan to be beneficial pedagogical examples.

I also point out that Socrates also appears as a student in the dialogues. He is a student of Diotima in the *Symposium*. He says she "was wise about many things" (201d). He adds further that "She is the one who taught me the art of love" (201d). In the *Phaedo*, Socrates reflects on his delight in finding the books of Anaxagoras. He reports, "I eagerly acquired his books and read them as quickly as I could in order to know the best and the worst as soon as possible" (8b).[12]

The Pedagogical Structure of the Dialogues

Plato wrote his dialogues in such a way that they draw the reader into the practice of philosophy. Some scholars describe the overall shape as a "pyramid" or "pediment."[13] I prefer to use the image of the mountain

---

12. For more on Socrates as a student, see Schultz, "Socrates on Socrates," 123–41.

13. See Thesleff, "Looking for Clues," 17–45; and Thesleff, "Pedimental Structure of the Dialogues," 150–54. See also Tejera, *Plato's Dialogues One by One*. For an excellent account of how similar modes of reading Plato have gained a great deal of traction over the past two decades, see Press, "State of the Question," 9–35.

because mountain imagery suggests that the practice of philosophy, like mountain climbing, is a natural human activity, whereas a pyramid or a pediment suggests that philosophy is constructed by humans. The mountain imagery accords well with the philosophical journey as Plato describes it in the Allegory of the Cave, where the former prisoner is "dragged along the rough steep upward way (*Republic*, 515e). The dialogues typically begin at the bottom of the mountain, in a not particularly philosophical context. For example, the *Republic* begins as Socrates and Glaucon are walking back to Athens from Piraeus. They have just seen a festival in honor of the goddess, Bendis. Polemarchus stops them and insists that they return for an evening of conversation at his father's house (327a-328b). The *Euthyphro* begins with Socrates meeting Euthyphro on the porch of the King Archon as he is about to receive the formal charges against him for impiety and corrupting the youth (2a).

After a short conversation, Socrates typically turns their attention to some philosophical question. The *Republic* considers the question of justice. The *Euthyphro* explores the nature of piety. Socrates' interlocutors offer a series of answers to the philosophical question and Socrates refutes them. The interlocutor typically admits that he does not really have the answer to the philosophical question. Differently put, the interlocutor admits that he is in a state of perplexity (*aporia*). At this point, Socrates leads the interlocutor to the top of the philosophical mountain, offering his interlocutors a new way of looking at the subject under discussion.[14] After this philosophical provocation, Socrates, either explicitly or implicitly, offers his interlocutors what Mitchell Miller calls "a test for philosophical kinship."[15] The reader, then, has the opportunity to see how the interlocutors respond to Socrates' philosophical provocation. Usually, the interlocutors fail the test, and the reader has a new opportunity to see what the interlocutors did not recognize.

Regardless of the level of the class I am teaching, I typically spend the first class period of any discussion of the dialogues with a discussion of this structure and use it to guide the discussion of the dialogues. I

---

14. I am currently developing an article that explores mountain and cave imagery in Plato's dialogues. See also Kingsley, *Ancient Philosophy, Mystery, and Magic*; and Corcoran, *Topography and Deep Structure in Plato*.

15. See the introduction to Miller, *Philosopher in Plato's Statesman*; and the introduction to Plato's "Parmenides," in Cooper, *Plato: Collected Works*. When talking about this moment in the dialogues with my students, I often refer to it as a "philosophical pop quiz."

often remind the students of where we are in the overall journey up and down the mountain. The Plato seminar is no exception. I start the first class by drawing a picture of a mountain on the board and diagramming the various parts of the dialogue. I ask the graduate students to consider why this is a helpful pedagogical image and what the mountain structure tells us about Plato's conception of philosophy. In this way, students come to recognize that the dialogues have both pedagogical content and pedagogical form. Their appreciation for Plato's commitment to philosophical education increases dramatically.

Modeling How I Teach

As I alluded to in the previous section, I teach the graduate students in ways that are similar to how I teach undergraduates. The only difference is that I am explicit with them about what I am doing in any given lecture or discussion. For instance, after I draw the image of the mountain on the board, I ask them to reflect on why this mode of presentation is useful pedagogically. Similarly, when I present Plato's theory of forms, I again draw an image of the forms on the board and then lead them through a discussion. I stop at numerous points and ask them to describe the specific methods and procedures I am using to draw students into conversation. Again, when I teach the Allegory of the Cave, I use the same method with them that I do with undergraduates. I have them draw the various stages of the prisoner's journey out of the darkness of the cave and into the light of the good forms, showing how I teach the Allegory of the Cave.[16] Some days, I might show a short movie clip that illustrates some Platonic concept and ask them why movies are an effective mode of philosophical provocation.[17]

Having students engage in this ongoing reflective process about what they are experiencing as students in the seminar helps them begin to think about how they would teach Plato to undergraduates most effectively. About halfway through the semester, I asked the students to prepare a mini-lecture on a small part of a dialogue. Some examples include Socrates' testing of the oracle's pronouncement that no one is as wise as he is in the *Apology*, the Euthyphro problem, the first definition of knowledge in the *Theaetetus*, the Divided Line, and the different stages

16. Bowery, "Drawing Shadows on the Wall," 121–32.
17. See Bowery and Wright, "Socrates Goes to the Cinema," 21–41.

of Diotima's ladder of love in the *Symposium*. We then offer each other feedback on these mini-lectures, and students have the opportunity to explain why they decided to teach the various sections of the dialogues in the ways that they did.

The second time I taught the course, I added articles from the scholarship of teaching and learning on teaching Plato to our reading assignments. I also crafted pedagogically oriented assignments that asked students to describe how they would teach two Platonic dialogues, the *Symposium* and the *Euthyphro*, to their own undergraduates at various levels of the curriculum. They had to explain what aspects of the text they would focus on in introductory level classes like Introduction to Philosophy or Introductory Ethics and then how they would teach the dialogue differently in an upper-level class like an ancient philosophy survey. I found the papers very enjoyable to read. In addition, the level of reflection that students brought to the text particularly when I asked them to reflect on how they would teach the dialogues in different contexts brought out more sustained engagement with the text than the typical assignment I use in graduate seminars, namely a 3000–word conference paper.

Socrates as a Pedagogical Model

As I began my teaching career, I imitated a rather standard conception of Socratic pedagogy. Much like Aristodemus imitated Socrates by going around barefoot, I embraced "the Socratic method." The rigorous process of elenchus, of refutative questioning and answering, aims at drawing out the correct answers from the souls of the willing and unwilling participants in the process.[18] However, the elenchus often left me feeling detached from my students. I wondered what my role as educator was beyond facilitating their understanding of ideas. I wondered where to situate myself in the story of philosophy that I was inviting the student to love. Reading bell hooks' *Teaching to Transgress* when it was first published in 1994 started my revolution of thinking about the kind of teacher I aspired to be. I was in the second year of my teaching career. I knew I wanted to be a teacher who educated for "the practice of freedom."[19] I began to examine my own practice. Why was I always positioning myself

---

18. For an excellent reassessment of the Socratic Method, see Scott, *Does Socrates Have a Method?*

19. hooks, *Teaching to Transgress*, 4.

as the questioner? Why did I imitate Socrates rather than speaking from my own experience and love of philosophy?

I went back to the source: the Platonic dialogues. I started to look more carefully at everything Plato's Socrates did when he attempted to engage his interlocutors. In addition to engaging in argumentative refutation, he cites Homer regularly. He makes countless jokes. He tells myths of the ascent of the soul to the place beyond being and the journey of the soul in the afterlife. I reflected again and again on his query in the *Phaedrus* where he wonders what kind of creature he is. He explains his interest in self-inquiry to Phaedrus asking "Am I a beast more complicated and savage than Typhon, or am I a tamer, simpler animal with a share in a divine and gentle nature?" (*Phaedrus*, 230a). After a while, I noticed that he told a lot of stories about himself, his philosophical practices, and what he learns from his teachers. His pedagogical methods involve autobiography and strategic self-disclosure as much as they depend upon the elenchus, perhaps more. As I explored these Socratic stories, I also started to share some of my own stories with my students.

After a few semesters, the classroom dynamic shifted. My teaching became more dynamic, conversational, and egalitarian. Like Socrates, I try to meet students where they are. Like Socrates, I tell stories about myself to engage students in the practice of philosophy. Like Socrates, I try not to give students the answers but lead students to a different way of looking at the world around them. I find that the strategic use of self-disclosure is an effective means of getting students to reflect more deeply about their lives, and I encourage the graduate students to be willing to share stories of their own lives with their students.[20]

Conclusion

I will end by pointing to three initial indications of the success of this method of graduate instruction. First, as I mentioned above, faculty observe graduate students teach once they become instructors of record. I have had the opportunity to observe three students who took the Plato seminar in this new format. All of them included Plato in their course syllabi. I chose to attend on a day they were teaching Plato. They all did a commendable job with the text itself and were able to generate a high level of student engagement, particularly at the introductory level. Second,

---

20. For more on Socratic self-disclosure, see Schultz, *Plato's Socrates on Socrates*.

some students have started publishing in the scholarship of teaching and learning in addition to publishing in traditional content areas of philosophy. For instance, Derek McAllister, a member of the second restructured Plato seminar, became fascinated with the concept of aporia and its role in the learning process. He wrote a paper, "Aporia as a Pedagogical Technique," which appears in a special volume of the journal of the American Association of Philosophy Teachers.[21] Finally, one colleague of mine at Baylor, Dr. Paul Carron, is a graduate of our PhD program. He frequently shares with me how he has adopted these pedagogical practices in his own classroom to good effect. He also developed a sophomore-level class in the Baylor Interdisciplinary Core, an alternative core curriculum at Baylor, that places Plato into conversation with a variety issues in contemporary social psychology.

Based on these initial indications of the success of this method, I feel confident in recommending that teachers take up similar pedagogically oriented strategies in their own content driven graduate seminars.

References

Bowery, Anne-Marie. "Drawing Shadows on the Wall: Teaching Plato's the Allegory of the Cave." *Teaching Philosophy* 24 (2001) 121–32.

Bowery, Anne-Marie, and J. Lenore Wright. "Socrates Goes to the Cinema: Using Film in the Philosophy Classroom." *Teaching Philosophy* 26 (2003) 21–41.

Clark, Burton R. "The Modern Integration of Research Activities with Teaching and Learning." *Journal of Higher Education* 68 (1997) 241–55.

Concepción, David W., Melinda Messineo, Sarah Wieten, and Catherine Homan. "The State of Teacher Training in Philosophy." *Teaching Philosophy* 39.1 (2016) 1–24.

Cooper. John M., ed. *Plato: Collected Works*. Translated by Mary Louise Gill and Paul Ryan. Indianapolis: Hackett, 1997.

Corcoran, Clinton DeBevoise. *Topography and Deep Structure in Plato: The Construction of Place in the Dialogues*. Albany: SUNY Press, 2016.

hooks, bell. *Teaching to Transgress*. New York: Routledge, 1994.

21. McAllister, "Aporia as a Pedagogical Technique," 5–34. Here is an abstract of the paper, "In this essay, I muse upon *aporia*'s value as a pedagogical technique in the philosophy classroom using as a guide examples of *aporia* that are found in Plato's Socratic dialogues. The word *aporia*, translated as 'without passage' or 'without a way,' is used metaphorically to describe the unsettling state of confusion many find themselves in after engaging in philosophical discourse. Following a brief introduction in which I situate *aporia* as a pedagogy amicable to experiential learning, I examine various ways in which *aporia* appears in certain Platonic dialogues, which enables us to draw out some paradigmatic features of *aporia*. I then discuss how I apply *aporia* as a pedagogical technique in the contemporary philosophy classroom, taking up three specific concerns in detail: aporetic discomfort, right use, and potential misuse" (5).

Jacquart, Melissa, and Jessey Wright. "Teaching Philosophy Graduate Students about Effective Teaching." *Teaching Philosophy* 40.2 (2017) 123–60.

Kingsley, Peter. *Ancient Philosophy, Mystery, and Magic: Empedocles and Pythagorean Tradition.* Oxford: Oxford University Press, 1995.

Kreber, Carolin. "The Scholarship of Teaching and Its Implementation in Faculty Development and Graduate Education." *New Directions for Teaching and Learning* 86 (2001) 79–88.

McAllister, Derek. "Aporia as a Pedagogical Technique." *AAPT, Studies in Pedagogy* 4 (2018) 5–34.

Miller, Mitchell. *The Philosopher in Plato's Statesman.* Las Vegas: Parmenides, 2004.

Mintz, Avi. "Why did Socrates Deny that he was a Teacher? Locating Socrates among the new educators and the traditional education in Plato's Apology of Socrates." *Educational Philosophy and Theory* 46 (2014) 735–47.

Nehamas, Alexander. "What Did Socrates Teach and to Whom Did He Teach It?" *The Review of Metaphysics* 46.2 (1992) 279–306.

Press, Gerald. "The State of the Question in the Study of Plato: Twenty Year Update." *The Southern Journal of Philosophy* 56 (2018) 9–35.

Schultz, Anne-Marie. "Socrates on Socrates: Looking Backward to Bring Philosophy Forward." *Proceedings of the Boston Area Colloquium in Ancient Philosophy* 30 (2015) 123–41.

————. *Plato's Socrates on Socrates: Socratic Self-Disclosure and the Public Practice of Philosophy.* Lanham: Lexington Press, forthcoming (2020).

Scott, Gary Alan, ed. *Does Socrates Have a Method? Rethinking the Elenchus in Plato's Dialogues and Beyond.* University Park: Penn State Press, 2004.

————. *Plato's Socrates as Educator.* Albany: State University of New York Press, 2000.

Tejera, Victor. *Plato's Dialogues One by One.* Lanham: University of America Press, 1999.

Thesleff, Holger. "Looking for Clues. An Interpretation of Some Literary Aspects of Plato's Two-level Model." In *Plato's Dialogues: New Studies and Interpretations,* edited by Gerald A. Press, 17–45. Lanham: Rowman & Littlefield, 1993.

————. "The Pedimental Structure of the Dialogues." In *The Bloomsbury Companion to Plato,* edited by Gerald Press, 150–54. London: Bloomsbury, 2015.

8

Our Future Faculty as Stewards
of the Academy

T. Laine Scales

THE OCCASION OF THE tenth anniversary of Baylor University's Academy for Teaching and Learning (ATL) provides a fine opportunity to reflect upon one of the ATL's most important commitments: preparing doctoral students for university teaching and the academic life. This chapter draws upon a body of research that profoundly influenced my own mentoring of doctoral student instructors. I supplement the research with applications from fifteen years of experiences in my role as Associate Dean in Baylor's Graduate School—a position that involved working regularly with the next generation of university professors.

When I first began working in the Baylor Graduate School in 2004, our nation was sounding the alarms loudly, calling attention to many disastrous features of doctoral education. Researchers cited a sobering statistic: nearly half of all doctoral students dropped out before finishing. This high rate of attrition, especially when considering the steep costs of doctoral education, sparked a flurry of proposals for reform in the first decade of the twenty-first century. Scholars like Chris Golde provided helpful case study analysis of students leaving doctoral education, data that would lead to solutions if we listened carefully to their experiences.[1] Barbara Lovitts's *Leaving the Ivory Tower* argued that retention was

1. Golde's scholarly work broke new ground as she listened carefully to student experiences in interviews and pointed out that outdated practices were "at cross purposes" with students' needs. Golde later became a key part of the Carnegie Initiative

bound to improve if we offered clear and straightforward explanations about the purposes and expectations of time-honored practices like dissertation committees, comprehensive exams, and oral defenses.[2]

In the midst of these alarms, Baylor University was undergoing a struggle of its own: our institution explored how to increase its research productivity and grow its graduate programs while retaining its commitment to teaching well and remaining "unapologetically Christian."[3] Since an overwhelming majority of Christian colleges and universities served undergraduates, models for Christian research universities with robust graduate programs were few. Thus, we would have to create our own pathway for maintaining this triple commitment: to research, to teaching, and to Christ.

I was encouraged to find a hopeful proposal and some realistic solutions from the Carnegie Initiative on the Doctorate (CID), which conducted a comprehensive research and action project from 2002 to 2006; I became aware of the CID about a year after I took up my work in the Graduate School. This was a multidisciplinary and forward-thinking group of experts asking a courageous question: How do we rethink doctoral education to meet the needs of the twenty-first century? The CID carried the imprimatur of Carnegie Foundation for the Advancement of Teaching, an organization well known for educational innovation, and it challenged academics to "preserve the best of the past for those who will follow," and to consider how to "prepare and initiate the next generation . . ."[4] The CID's progressive and creative recommendations were appealing, as it called upon academics to take up our moral responsibility for making the academy relevant and tackling twenty-first century problems. It suggested realistic reforms grounded in research with eighty-four departments across forty-four universities. Implementing these solutions would take all of us working collaboratively: administrators, faculty, and graduate students, with each group taking an active role in the reforms.

The CID's book-length report, *Formation of Scholars,* was inspiring and practical, and it sparked our energy for implementing many of its practical suggestions at Baylor. It was exciting to involve students and

on the Doctorate's research team; See her early work, Golde, "Should I Stay?," 199–227.

2. Lovitts, *Leaving the Ivory Tower.*

3. For a scholarly analysis of Baylor's changing vision over the past thirty years see Hankins and Schmeltekopf, *Baylor Project.* For a compelling personal perspective see Schmeltekopf, *Baylor at the Crossroads.*

4. Walker, et al., *Formation,* 10.

even a few administrators in building intellectual communities, creating models for multiple mentors, and organizing reading and writing groups. We even managed to establish new graduate housing communities and a parental leave policy, honoring the CID's findings on the importance of wholistic living for graduate students. As an administrator in a Christian university, what I found most inspiring about the CID's work were two "church words" the researchers appropriated in surprising ways: formation and stewardship.

When the Carnegie researchers outlined their compelling vision of a formation process for doctoral students, higher education was sorely in need of a fresh way of looking at the steps one takes toward a PhD. A growing literature in doctoral education commonly described the process of becoming a faculty member as *socialization,* a term borrowed from sociology and particularly workforce development. Although helpful in some ways, the paradigm of socialization to describe the doctoral process had limitations. First, it assumed there was one right way to do academic work and that the person being socialized simply had to be shown one model (the faculty mentor) and imitate it. Through feedback—correction when she got it wrong or praise when she got it right—the well-socialized graduate student could be molded and shaped into a junior version of the doctoral advisor and other approved faculty mentors. Diversity was not considered in a socialization framework. Everyone, no matter what gender, ethnicity, personality, or giftedness, was supposed to imitate the faculty assigned to socialize her.

A second problem was that the socialization process focused too narrowly on one's occupation. In today's academic marketplace, we can no longer assume that doctoral students will become professors; their degrees may be used in a variety of ways, as the CID reminded us. Furthermore, socialization failed to acknowledge that the focus of graduate students' lives should be much wider than just their careers. Today's doctoral students are keenly aware that they are whole people with many competing responsibilities, identities, and choices. In my role as associate dean, I had multiple opportunities to watch women and men grow and mature as whole people: they built their families, invested in our city as volunteers, and committed to their local churches. Doctoral students have made a healthy change in recent years toward caring for their families, their communities, their friendships, and themselves while they are studying.

Socialization toward a career may be part of what they are engaged in, but the term *formation*, given to us by the CID, became a much better aspiration for the doctoral journey, and the word fit us well at Baylor. When we invite our students into questions about their formation, we can help them to move from the immediate and anxiety-ridden question of "How will I teach this class?" to ask instead "What kind of person am I becoming within this academic context and beyond it?" I knew that as we invited these larger questions, we were compelled to create connections and communities where this conversation could take place. The outline of my work in the Baylor Graduate School came into view, and I was fortunate to have good colleagues and energetic graduate students to begin creating the environment for this kind of formation.

If formation is the process, then what is the aim of doctoral education? The Carnegie researchers surprise us again by using another church word: stewardship. The goal of doctoral education, says the CID, is forming stewards of their disciplines. Academic stewards see a much larger purpose for their work—a purpose that far exceeds managing their own careers. Instead, they imagine themselves sustaining and growing the discipline for those who will come after. Jesus's parable of the entrusted money, found in the gospels of Luke and Matthew, describes the practice of stewardship. A nobleman goes on a trip and before leaving gives his servants money to take care of while he is away. Two servants make wise investments, and when the man returns, they present him with their profits. The nobleman expresses his approval in those familiar words, "Well done, my good and faithful servant!" However the third servant, afraid of losing the money, buried the treasure, and although he was able to return the same amount to the nobleman upon his return, he was chastised and punished for his failures. The Carnegie authors remind us of the point: "Here the emphasis is on investing, risk taking, and putting talents (whether coins or abilities) to work, not on hoarding and saving.[5]

Seeing our academic work as a process of stewardship caused us to look beyond career management and toward something much more inspiring: the faithful investment of our God-given gifts.[6] As graduate students sometimes became disillusioned with what they found in the academy, they became animated conversation partners, seeking new meaning for academic life, beyond what some of their models had made

---

5. Walker et al., *Formation*, 11.
6. Scales and Howell, "Stewardship Reconsidered," 1–15.

of it. Admittedly, our conversations at Baylor mostly focused on steward-ship as it relates to research and scholarship. We have not given as much attention as we might to how the practice of stewardship can follow from our calling to teach.

To engage this question, we return to the Carnegie Initiative on the Doctorate and its description of the academic steward. The CID describes a triad of commitments for the steward: generation, conservation, and transformation. *Generation* is easily associated with a scholar: conduct-ing original and important research to move the field forward. Related to generation is *conservation*, when scholars make expert judgements about which ideas are worth keeping and which should be discarded while, at the same time, articulating how her research contributes to the larger in-tellectual landscape. The third task, *transformation*, speaks to the focus of this chapter and the scholar's teaching role. The CID leads us to consider a much broader context than formal education only but asks how schol-ars share ideas in a variety of ways and disseminate research to transform our world. By passing on ideas that one has generated or conserved, a steward engages in "a dynamic process of transforming knowledge so that new learners can meaningfully engage with it."[7] Since learners are found everywhere (not just in classrooms), the academic steward lives out a commitment to moral responsibility and "embraces a larger sense of purpose."[8]

In the midst of the celebration for the ATL's first decade, as we con-sider our callings to teach, let's turn our attention to this question: What would it mean to reimagine our teaching as a practice of stewardship? I suggest six tasks for the teaching steward, which may include all of us who teach, but here we consider especially our future faculty. I will pro-vide concrete examples, many from among our Baylor doctoral students, and invite you to imagine examples from your own teaching context.

First, a steward cultivates a growing commitment to the teaching subject that is sustained over a lifetime. Bringing a scholarly lens to the teaching moment, the steward's continuing exploration brings a conta-gious love of new learning to the classroom. The teaching steward pre-serves the useful ideas and practices of the past that should be conserved, but at the same time, looks with critical eyes upon the disciplinary canon, discarding what is no longer appropriate. She never settles for the tired

---

7. Walker et al., *Formation*, 12.

8. Walker et al., *Formation*, 11.

old curriculum, but takes risks in the teaching context. A doctoral student in our Department of Religion, Stephanie Peek, is a great example of risk-taking in the classroom. In order to deepen her students' learning around the Gospel stories, she brings alive the ancient world by assigning the students roles to inhabit: a wealthy Roman man, a prostitute, a Jewish merchant, or a poor artisan. From those perspectives, students analyze the scriptures and learn something about how to make applications of Gospel principles. While they are learning about social justice, there is also an opportunity, if they take it, to grow in their understanding of the Gospel message and in their faith.

Second, a teaching steward is generous with time, resources, and knowledge. The culture of the academy increasingly has become one of ownership. Lacking humility, academics often claim ownership over ideas without remembering that all knowledge is a gift from God. Jenny Howell, a Baylor alum and bright young faculty member spent several years in conversation with me and others about the pervasive ownership culture in the academy, inspired by our reading of Paul Griffiths' compelling book *Intellectual Appetite*.[9] For-profit journal companies, research sponsored by corporations, intellectual property rights: the ownership culture within academic circles has been normalized in ways that do not acknowledge God as the source of our gifts. I have been disheartened more recently to see examples of this ownership culture creeping into college teaching, as instructors begin to copyright their syllabi and other teaching materials. Generosity should be the very motivation for teaching others, and the steward embodies that generosity by sharing ideas and materials with other graduate students and colleagues. Several years ago a few of us established the Baylor Teaching Commons, a pre-ATL faculty development program that served as a space simply for sharing teaching ideas. Graduate students and faculty met together in groups, and the spirit of generosity among these Baylor teachers, young and old, presented a memorable picture of stewardship. Today, the ATL serves this function, creating multiple opportunities for sharing teaching ideas.

Related to generosity is the third quality that the stewardship framework can inspire: collaboration. Good stewards want to move the whole field forward and understand that this is done by working cooperatively

9. Here we learned a great deal from Paul Griffiths, who came to dialogue with us at Baylor on two occasions during our exploration. While he brought his own personal stories and examples to our meetings together, many of these ideas are presented in Griffiths, *Intellectual Appetite*.

with others. One of the points of pride we take in our Baylor doctoral programs is the cooperative culture among our students. Many students remark how unusual this is when they talk to doctoral students at other universities. Recognizing that the highly competitive environments found in some universities can be soul-crushing, they appreciate the mutual support they find at Baylor. This is exactly the kind of environment one would hope to find in a Christian university. As we create our teaching environments, we can pass on this practice of meaningful collaboration by setting up learning situations that require cooperation. Our graduate students can practice by coaching their undergraduates and debriefing with them, providing explicit instruction on the skills of cooperation, which are essential for our teaching stewards to cultivate and share.

Fourth, a steward who teaches does not remain closed off in a silo, but builds intellectual communities that are broad and inclusive. I have had the pleasure in the Graduate School over the past eight years of meeting monthly with an interdisciplinary group of doctoral students known as Conyers Scholars. We pray and break bread together as we talk about faith and vocation and other formative topics. What I have observed in these very lively conversations is that talking across disciplines comes much more readily to the current generation of graduate students, who think quite naturally in integrative ways. If we facilitate their meeting one another, they seem to be more inclined toward interdisciplinary work than my own generation.[10] However, the outdated structures still maintained in our universities often discourage a genuine interdisciplinary dialogue. If you doubt this is true, try proposing an interdisciplinary dissertation. The sciences have broken out a bit in that regard, but I hope that our future faculty will lead the way in bringing down the silos of the academy and strive for intellectual communities that draw scholars together in a spirit of stewardship.

Fifth, a teaching steward values a rich diversity in the academy and teaches students about the importance of dialogue across differences. A faculty member on our campus, Dr. Michael-John DePalma, challenges me by his faithful commitment to exploring differences. An associate professor in English, DePalma led in the organizing of the Rhetoric and Religion in the 21st Century conference, where faculty, graduate students, and professionals from many different religious traditions came together across disciplines to talk about their area of religion and rhetoric. We can

10. For a full description of the origins and purposes of Baylor's Conyers Scholars program see Scales and Howell, "Stewardship Reconsidered," 1–15.

imagine the power of a rabbi, a Christian English professor, and a Muslim scholar, all dialoguing respectfully about their common interests. DePalma explains, "we are not all trying to get on the same page; we are exploring all of our different points of view and learning in the process."[11] A steward like DePalma understands that listening to more than just the predominant point of view enriches our academic resources. DePalma practices his stewardship not only in his guild, but in his own classroom, providing multiple opportunities for students to engage in interfaith rhetorical activism as he guides them in the process.

Finally, a steward embraces a larger sense of purpose and reimagines the teaching task as preparing the next generation to take their place as stewards, not just of the academy, but of our world. While teaching a doctoral seminar of new teachers, I had the privilege weekly of listening to them dialogue about the classes they were teaching, often for the first time. They told stories that celebrated the small victories of teaching: a class discussion that really took off, an enthusiastic undergraduate hanging around after class to talk about a reading, or the pride of a student who, on the third try, was able to successfully complete the day's lab experiment. These new teachers celebrate the delights of their teaching and learning moments, and there is a palpable feeling of relief (and sometimes surprise) that they really can do this thing called teaching that initially made them anxious. After a few semesters of teaching experience, they begin to talk less about the mundane details of classroom management and more about their hopes and dreams for the next generation. They start to pay attention to formation of the people they are teaching. So when Savanah Landerholm, a PhD student in Higher Education Studies and Leadership, spontaneously took her freshman leadership class to volunteer at a Waco shelter the day in 2017 after Hurricane Harvey hit Texas, she recognized that the act of helping others in the community was an important part of learning to lead by learning to serve. Stewardship in teaching calls us to a higher purpose, and we think far beyond preparing this class or grading that set of papers as we find ourselves in every day acts of stewardship and formation.

With this list of six tasks of stewardship in teaching, we turn back to our theme: a calling to teach. Calling, formation, stewardship—all good church words for our context, and I think important ideas for us to continue to explore as teachers. I grew up Baptist, and we tend to focus too

11. Personal communication, Michael-John DePalma, Waco Texas, October 12, 2018.

much on individual callings, so when I hear the words of our theme, my default consideration is an individual's calling to teach. As I studied other points of view in my own graduate and seminary experiences, I came to understand the idea of a corporate calling, a *summons* to a congregation, a group of people, or an institution. I hope that Baylor University understands itself to be called to teaching. I believe that we do, and to me the very existence of the ATL and its resources bears witness to that calling.

The alarms signaling the problems with doctoral education are growing louder as the third decade of the twenty-first century approaches. Today, our literature presents fairly depressing views, like that of Leonard Cassuto's *The Graduate School Mess*, doubting that we can salvage what is left of doctoral education.[12] Meanwhile, Baylor continues its journey toward our three-fold calling toward Christ, research, and teaching, with a recent emphasis on becoming a research-focused doctoral university. That goal will lead us to bring even more doctoral students to Baylor. In our corporate calling to value teaching, let's hold each other accountable to continue investing in the formation of the doctoral students who will lead our universities as future faculty. In addition to asking questions about what they will do in the classroom, we will take time to engage them in questions about who they are becoming as teachers, as spouses, as parents, and as followers of Christ. Paying attention to our doctoral students' formation and providing opportunities for them to embrace a higher responsibility as faithful stewards may provide the hope we need for doctoral education and for our academy.

References

Cassuto, Leonard. *The Graduate School Mess: What Caused It and How We Can Fix It.* Cambridge: Harvard University Press, 2015.

Golde, Chris M. "Should I Stay or Should I Go? Student Descriptions of the Doctoral Attrition Process." *Review of Higher Education* 23.2 (2000) 199–227.

Griffiths, Paul. *Intellectual Appetite: A Theological Grammar.* Washington, DC: Catholic University of America Press, 2009.

Hankins, Barry, and Donald, Schmeltekopf, eds. *The Baylor Project: Can a Protestant University Be a First-Class Research Institution and Preserve its Soul?* Notre Dame, IN: St. Augustine's, 2007.

Lovitts Barbara E. *Leaving the Ivory Tower: The Causes and Consequences of Departure from Doctoral Study.* Lanham, MD: Rowman & Littlefield, 2001.

12. Cassuto, *Graduate School Mess.*

Scales, T. Laine. "Dehumanized vs. Holistic Scholars: How Academia Impacts Our Lives." Panel presentation, American Academy of Religion, Atlanta, GA, November 22–24, 2015.

Scales, T. Laine, and Jennifer L. Howell. "Stewardship Reconsidered: Academic Work and the Faithful Christian." In *Christian Faith and University Life: Stewards of the Academy*, edited by T. Laine Scales and Jennifer L. Howell, 1–15. New York: Palgrave Macmillan, 2018.

Schmeltekopf, Donald. *Baylor at the Crossroads: Memoirs of a Provost*. Eugene, OR: Cascade Books, 2015.

Walker, George E., Golde, Chris M, Jones L, et al. *The Formation of Scholars: Rethinking Doctoral Education for the Twenty-First Century*. San Francisco: Jossey-Bass, 2008.

9

Called to Teach the Psalms

A Vocational Reflection

William Bellinger and Rebecca Poe Hays

This essay is reflective in tone and so it is appropriate to begin with a personal comment on vocation. I would articulate my vocation as a teacher-scholar of the Older Testament, as I am wont to label this first and largest part of the Christian Scriptures, in the context of a church-related institution in the academy. One of the hallmarks of that vocation for me is what I would call the rehabilitation of the Older Testament for the church. The Hebrew Scriptures are essentially lost to the contemporary church, to that community's considerable deficit. Brent Strawn has in his recent volume declared that the *Old Testament Is Dying*, with an analogy to a dying language and with comparable suggestions for resuscitation.[1] My work focuses on the worship literature of the Older Testament, beginning with the Psalms, the primary hymnbook and prayer book of the Hebrew canon. Accordingly, I regularly teach an undergraduate course on the Psalms and Wisdom Literature. That course will be the focus of the present reflection.

The course syllabus articulates the primary goal of the course to be enabling students to become better readers of the Psalms. My hope is that students will become better-informed as readers of the Psalms and will grow as persons who want to read these texts. In the modern style, I

---

1. Strawn, *Old Testament Is Dying*.

begin with methodology. How shall we read the Psalms? Modern study of the Psalms begins with Hermann Gunkel and the comparative method in which readers consider vocabulary, literary structure, and religious feeling in order to classify the psalms by type.[2] The major types of psalms are those that plead with God for help in trouble and those that praise and thank God. It is also common to include royal psalms and wisdom psalms in the major types of psalms. These major types usually take a common literary structure. What is more, Gunkel's star student Sigmund Mowinckel argued that those types of psalms and the examples in the Hebrew Psalter derived from the Jerusalem cult, the organized worship of ancient Israel.[3] The poetic form fits its social and religious function. So I badger students to read psalms and tell me what type and structure they see and imagine how the particular psalms related to worship.

Of course, we have these psalms in a book in the Older Testament. What difference does that make? How does Psalm 23 fit in the book of Psalms, and how does it relate to Psalms 22 and 24 (and it does)? This question is a relatively new one; its major advocate was Gerald Wilson, a Baylor graduate, and indeed, this question has tremendous resonance at Baylor in the Religion Department and Truett Seminary.[4]

The other crucial question relates to the fact that these texts are in Hebrew poetry. As we read these texts, students identify repetition, parallel structures, special vocabulary, and poetic imagery and work out how these poetic devices contribute to each poem's articulation of a divine-human dialogue and the life of a worshiping community. William Brown's volume *Seeing the Psalms: A Theology of Metaphor* is of particular help with this teaching strategy.[5]

In a variety of ways in class and on their own as part of papers and projects, students read psalms and answer the questions of type and structure, setting in ancient Israel's social and religious life, the literary context in the book of Psalms, and poetic qualities of these poems. It would be better to have the Hebrew text, but we can work through a good English translation. When I test students, they are asked to answer these questions about psalm texts. Again, my goal is to help them become

2. See Gunkel, *Introduction to Psalms.*

3. See Mowinckel, *Psalms in Israel's Worship.*

4. See Wilson, *Editing of the Hebrew Psalter.* Another Baylor graduate, Nancy deClaissé-Walford, has also contributed significantly to the conversation about the "shape" of the Hebrew Psalter: deClaissé-Walford, *Reading from the Beginning.*

5. See Brown, *Seeing the Psalms.*

better, more educated readers of the Psalms. They read two textbooks on the Psalms, one I wrote that focuses on the types of psalms and their structure and one by Nancy deClaissé-Walford that focuses on the literary context in the organization of the book of Psalms.[6] So we operate from the history of scholarship in the modern study of the Psalms, but I try to do that with attention to the context from which the students enter the study. Students at Baylor often come into the course with an interest in the Psalms as literature of individual piety, perhaps written by an individual such as David or perhaps related to a specific event in ancient Israel's history. What the students often discover is that the psalms are strongly relational literature tied to a worshiping community.

The other side of my goal in the course relates to students becoming motivated to read the Psalms. This goal is, of course, more complicated and perhaps more controversial, but I understand education as transformational, that is, forming persons toward wholeness. I have come to approach this issue with assignments. Students write several brief reflection papers and longer papers that include responding to a final interpretive question with the Psalms: What do we bring to the interpretive process? Walter Brueggemann argues that we have not fully worked at the interpretive process with the Psalms until the language of the text is in conversation with the language of our lives.[7] I basically understand myself in this class to be a teacher of reading and writing while working out of a literary and theological approach to understanding the Psalms.

We spend a lot of time reading texts in my class. I teach reading because reading is a key means of personal growth and development that can broaden our perspective and enhance our community. Students come to see that the Psalms understand the divine-human relationship as an extraordinarily transparent one that weds emotion and intellect, and they come to see that the piety expressed is driven by the articulation of a community's divine-human relationship that includes rapturous joy and hideous enemies, "hallelujah!" and "how long, O Lord?" Those ancient poets become part of our community, and their very different world intersects with ours and enriches ours. Finally, I would say that reading feeds our imaginations. What I am really after is jump-starting our interpretive imaginations. Toni Morrison said it this way: "The words on the

---

6. Bellinger, *Psalms*; deClaissé-Walford, *Introduction to the Psalms*.

7. Brueggemann, *Praying the Psalms*, 16.

page are only half the story. The rest is what we bring to the party."[8] I hope my course invites us to the party. I understand the Psalms to articulate a grammar of faith and ask my students to learn what Peter Candler has called a grammar of participation in which we walk through texts, mapping their literary and theological imaginations and realizing how these intersect with our life imaginations.[9]

When I reflect on teaching the Psalms, I imagine students from the various iterations of this course such as one who is now a sociologist of religion doing ecumenical work in London, who told me recently that the Psalter's transparent honesty intersects with his life and work. Or another student, who insisted that the structure and poetry and worship language of each psalm brought significant meaning and is not enriched much from the broader literary context of the book of Psalms. Her insistence came in the face of my cajoling her to consider how the broader literary context does promise hermeneutical riches. Or the student who has found significant resources in the book of Psalms for her ministry with children.

In the last decade or so, I have had the extraordinary gift of wonderful teaching assistants in this course. They contribute wonderfully to this class and these pedagogical goals. They are especially good at helping me "tune in" to the student context of learning. One of the brilliant ones and recent ones in this remarkable run of doctoral students is Dr. Rebecca Poe Hays.

W. H. Bellinger Jr.
Baylor University

≈ ≈ ≈

The opportunity for "elbow learning" alongside seasoned, top-notch scholars and teachers—the kind of opportunity Dr. Bellinger afforded me by inviting me to be teaching assistant for his undergraduate Psalms and Wisdom Literature class—was one of the primary reasons I came to Baylor for my doctoral work. I came to Baylor to pursue a PhD in Hebrew Bible/Old Testament because of a sense of personal vocation similar to the one Dr. Bellinger articulated: namely, to help the church be better,

8. Morrison, "Reader as Artist."

9. Bellinger, *Psalms as a Grammar for Faith*; Candler, *Theology, Rhetoric, Manduction*, 31.

more informed, and more faithful readers of what my mentor has dubbed the "Older Testament"—in the sense that they actually read it occasionally, if nothing else.

In many ways, the book of Psalms is a perfect place to begin to teach people to read the Older Testament. This collection of prayers is meant to teach us something. The psalms teach us how to pray but also how to view ourselves, God, and the world, and how to operate as part of this world. Apart from the frequent imperative to "Praise the Lord (the Hebrew *hallelujah*)," however, the Psalter contains very little in the way of direct instruction as we find it in places such as the Ten Commandments (Exod 20:1–17, Deut 5:1–21), the book of Proverbs, or, to use a New Testament example, the Sermon on the Mount (Matt 5–7). The poetry of the Psalms forces us to read carefully and to read the whole in order to begin to understand what is being said. Furthermore, the Psalter juxtaposes exuberant affirmations of trust in God with poignant expressions of doubt about whether God is listening or cares. No simple answers to the hard questions of life and faith emerge. The kind of spirituality the Psalms reflects and cultivates in its readers is a mature one: it involves attention and persistence, a sense of justice and of empathy, the boldness both to admit one's own faults and to condemn the wrong one sees in others (including, at times, God), and it involves the willingness to continue the conversation with God through it all. Learning to read the Psalms this way—with tenacity, humility, and an openness of heart and mind—is a good starting point for learning how to read the Hebrew Bible more broadly.

The Psalms are also perhaps the most familiar material in the Older Testament to many people. We regularly hear Psalm 23 at funerals, and the Gideon Bibles in our hotel rooms have the New Testament packaged together with the Psalms (and Proverbs). In my experience teaching the Psalms, this familiarity is something of a two-edged sword. On the one hand, familiarity reduces the fear factor often associated with the Older Testament. On the other hand, familiarity means that we sometimes have a hard time seeing what is actually *in the text* because of our preconceived ideas about what is there—or what we think *should* be there. I have found that a significant part of teaching students to be better readers of the Psalms is teaching them to slow down and read the text as it actually is, on its own terms, before importing anything else.

Two examples come to mind. The first has to do with the different types of psalms Dr. Bellinger mentioned. The Hebrew title for the book of Psalms is "book of praises," and we tend to associate the Psalms with happy "hallelujahs" such as we find in Psalms 29, 100, and 149. The largest number of psalms in the Psalter, however, are actually laments—prayers spoken out of the darkest places of human experience, prayers that will even lay the blame for suffering at God's feet (e.g., Pss 13, 69, 88, 130, 137). As Dr. Bellinger described, much of the Psalms class involves reading through psalm texts together and having the students ask questions about structure, context, and so forth. With lament psalms, a primary question is "What is the crisis? What has gone wrong?" The students tended to do a wonderful job of recognizing when enemies were attacking a city, when the psalmist was sick, when friends had suddenly turned to enemies, and when the psalmist's own sin had brought the trouble. When we came to Psalm 88, however, the students were very unwilling to read the text and accept what it says: namely, that *God* is the problem—not the psalmist, not sin, but God. "God, *you* have put me in the Pit," the psalmist cries (Ps 88:7 [Eng. 88:6])![10] Our students performed all manner of hermeneutical acrobatics to change what the text was actually saying because it stood in tension with their preconceived ideas about what piety and prayer should be. Lament as the Psalms teaches it, however, is part of a more complex, mature spirituality. The Psalms teach us that being angry at God and blaming God for what is going wrong in the world is perfectly acceptable. God can "take it." An important part of teaching students to read the Psalms (and indeed any text they encounter in any context) is to teach them to read what is actually there, even when it challenges us; for those students who read the Psalms as Scripture, teaching them to read what is actually in the text also involves teaching them to accept its lessons even when they challenge students' conceptions of faithfulness. In a world wracked by natural disasters, economic injustice, warfare and those fleeing from war, chronic illnesses, and countless other hurts, learning to lament well—as exhibited in the Hebrew Psalter—is an important and timely lesson to learn.

The second example of how we teach students to become better readers of the biblical text involves equipping students to read the book of Psalms as Scripture without having to do so Christologically in the first instance. This pedagogical challenge is tied to Baylor's institutional identity as a Christian university. Our religion classrooms are by no means Sunday School classes, but most of our students come to the text from a

---

10. All translations are mine.

Christian perspective—whether they currently identify as Christians or not. Part of teaching these students to read the Psalter in more informed, responsible ways is helping them see that faith communities considered the psalms to be inspired Scripture long before the Christian canon came together. While the New Testament certainly points to places in the Psalms as anticipating the coming of Christ,[11] the Psalms already had rich, full, theological significance. One of my major goals as a teacher of the Older Testament is to help Christians realize that God was not just "twiddling his thumbs" until the Incarnation. God was already saving, extending grace, answering prayers, and being God long before Jesus was born in Bethlehem; if the church only attends to God's work through Christ, then the church cannot fully know the God of Christ.

For example, understanding how Israel's kings functioned for the community in the tenth century BCE is an important part of knowing who God is and how God operates. Psalm 2, in which Yahweh proclaims "I have installed my king on Zion ... [the king is] my son, today I have begotten him" (Ps 2:6–7), reflects this royal function and the distinctive relationship between God and God's anointed (Hebrew *meshiah*; Greek *christos*), and many scholars believe the psalm was used as part of coronation ceremonies.[12] Given the ways the faith community read and prayed and worshipped with this psalm in the centuries before New Testament authors would associate it with Jesus (Matt 3:17, Mark 1:11, Luke 3:22, Acts 13:33, Heb 5:5), learning to read Psalm 2 without a Christological lens can teach us important things about the God we also worship.

As teachers of the Psalms, we strive to equip students to engage more honestly with the psalms that challenge their conceptions of spirituality and to attend to how the psalms shape our understanding of God even without Christological applications; as Dr. Bellinger also mentioned, however, we want students to be able to write in ways that reflect the more sophisticated, critically-informed understanding of the Psalter that they acquire in this undergraduate Psalms class. For instance, we want them to be able to write about the Psalms without liberally adding pious "Praise the Lords!" at critical moments of their argumentation in essays—a very real problem with which we have to deal. Again, the

---

11. E.g., Ps 8 as applied in Heb 2:5–9; Ps 110 as applied in Matt 22:41–46, Mark 12:35–37, Luke 20:40–44; Ps 118 as applied in Matt 21:42, Mark 12:10, Luke 20:17, Acts 4:11, 1 Pet 2:7.

12. Weiser, *Psalms*, 109; Brueggemann and Bellinger, *Psalms*, 32; deClaissé-Walford, Jacobson, and Tanner, *Book of Psalms*, 71.

particular challenge of teaching an academic class on the Psalms within the context of a Christian university is that many of our students take the class on the way to seminary or to enhance their own devotional lives. I have found teaching the Psalms to be a good opportunity to introduce students to a kind of spirituality different than that to which many of them have previously been exposed. Doing critical, academic work on a biblical text and writing formal papers does not mean one must divorce oneself from the rich spiritual gifts that come from studying Scripture as a person of faith. I would even argue that we can "Praise the Lord" more deeply if we attend to the work of getting to know God through the kinds of disciplines we teach in the classroom.

Ultimately, this class on the Psalms is an ideal context in which to teach our students what loving God not just with their whole hearts but with their whole minds can look like (Deut 6:5, Matt 22:37, Mark 12:30, Luke 10:27). One might even say that the class on the Psalms is an ideal context in which we as teachers can work to create a caring community within which to integrate academic excellence with Christian commitment—in accord with our Baylor mission:

> *The mission of Baylor University is to educate men and women for worldwide leadership and service by integrating academic excellence and Christian commitment within a caring community.*

As Baylor continues its efforts to attain R-1 status, I believe this course (and others like it) is particularly important for the university not only because of what it does for the undergraduates who learn to approach the biblical text in more informed ways but also because of the opportunity it gives graduate students to learn from world-renowned researchers how to apply their skills to classroom settings.

Rebecca W. Poe Hays
George W. Truett Theological Seminary

BIBLIOGRAPHY

Bellinger, W. H., Jr. *Psalms: A Guide to Studying the Psalter.* 2nd ed. Grand Rapids: Baker Academic, 2012.
———. *Psalms as a Grammar for Faith: Prayer and Praise.* Waco, TX: Baylor University Press, 2019.
Brown, William P. *Seeing the Psalms: A Theology of Metaphor.* Louisville: Westminster John Knox, 2002.

Brueggemann, Walter, and W. H. Bellinger Jr. *Psalms*. New Cambridge Bible Commentary. New York: Cambridge University Press, 2014.

Candler, Peter M. *Theology, Rhetoric, Manduction: Or, Reading Scripture Together on the Path to God*. Grand Rapids: Eerdmans, 2006.

DeClaissé-Walford, Nancy L. *Introduction to the Psalms: A Song from Ancient Israel*. St. Louis, MO: Chalice, 2004.

————. *Reading from the Beginning: The Shaping of the Hebrew Psalter*. Macon, GA: Mercer University Press, 1997.

DeClaissé-Walford, Nancy L., Rolf A. Jacobson, and Beth LaNeel Tanner. *The Book of Psalms*. New International Commentary on the Old Testament. Grand Rapids: Eerdmans, 2014.

Gunkel, Hermann. *Introduction to Psalms: The Genres of the Religious Lyric of Israel*. Translated by James D. Nogalski. Mercer Library of Biblical Studies. Macon, GA: Mercer University Press, 1998.

Morrison, Toni. "The Reader as Artist." *O, The Oprah Magazine*, July 2006.

Mowinckel, Sigmund. *The Psalms in Israel's Worship*. Translated by D. R. Ap-Thomas. 2 vols. Nashville: Abingdon, 1962.

Strawn, Brent. A. *The Old Testament Is Dying: A Diagnosis and Recommended Treatment*. Grand Rapids: Baker Academic, 2017.

Weiser, Artur. *The Psalms: A Commentary*. Translated by Herbert Hartwell. Old Testament Library. Philadelphia: Westminster, 1962.

Wilson, Gerald Henry. *The Editing of the Hebrew Psalter*. Society of Biblical Literature Dissertation Series 76. Chico, CA: Scholars, 1985.

10

Why Study Music?

Laurel E. Zeiss

Why study music? With all the challenges that we face in society today, why should people invest time and energy in learning more about such an ephemeral art? What purpose does it serve?

In response to my opening questions, let me pose some others: Have you heard music today? Yesterday? The day before? At the important occasions of your lives—weddings, funerals, significant birthdays—was music present?

In all probability, you have answered "yes" to one or more of the questions above, which reveals the first important reason why people should study music. We hear music constantly. It permeates our environment. We hear it in the grocery store, at restaurants and sporting events, in films and church services, and while viewing websites. Now admittedly, often music in modern U.S. society serves as a backdrop—sonic wallpaper, as it were. But the fact that it is present in so many contexts merits consideration. What is music's purpose in that particular situation? What is its function? How does its presence influence your experience of that event or of that space? What we are hearing and why are questions worth investigation.

In addition to its ubiquity, there are more tangible, perhaps more practical reasons for children and adults to study music. For purposes of this essay, the "study" of music encompasses listening to music, learning about music as a cultural phenomenon, and participating in music-making through singing or playing an instrument. As numerous research experiments have shown, music-making helps children with verbal skills, language acquisition, and reading preparedness and comprehension.[1] Scientific studies also suggest that studying music as a child leads to greater plasticity and more interconnections in the brain, which in turn may lead to better long-term brain health.[2] Singing in particular appears to engage both hemispheres of the brain.[3] Additionally, music study fosters focused attention, working memory, and fine motor skills which also contribute to better academic performance.[4]

More recent studies suggest that participating in music even as an adolescent or an adult helps people develop and retain listening comprehension skills.[5] One common complaint of older adults is difficulty hearing conversations in crowded, noisy environments. Studies at Northwestern University and the University of Jena have demonstrated that "aging musicians fare better than non-musicians when it comes to distinguishing speech from noise, even when their overall hearing is no better than that of non-musicians."[6] Simply put, musical activities require you to pay attention to sound, and that has long-term benefits. Researchers at

1. For a comprehensive overview of the many benefits of studying music as a young person, see Hallam, "Power of Music," 269–89. The following are representative examples of more specific studies: Forgeard, et al., "Practicing a Musical Instrument in Childhood," 5; Forgeard, et al., "Relation Between Music and Phonological Processing," 383–90; Tsang and Conrad, "Music Training," 157–63; Moreno, Friesen, and Bialystok, "Effect of Music Training," 165–72; Corrigall and Trainor, "Associations Between Length of Music Training," 147–55; Hutchins, "Early Childhood Music Training," 579–93; Slater, et al., "Longitudinal Effects."

2. Hyde, et al., "Effects of Musical Training," 186–89; Habib and Besson, "What Do Music Training," 279–85; Rosenkranz, Williamon, and Rothwell, "Motorcortical Excitability," 5200–5206; Johansson, "Music, Age, Performance, and Excellence," 46–58; Wan and Schlaug, "Music Making as a Tool," 566–77; Bidelman, "Musicians Have Enhanced Audiovisual Multisensory Binding," 3037–47.

3. Gibson, Folley, and Park, "Enhanced Divergent Thinking," 162–69.

4. Forgeard, et al., "Practicing a Musical Instrument in Childhood," 1–8, page 5 in particular; Talamini, Carretti, and Grassi, "Working Memory of Musicians," 183–91; Roden, et al., "Does Music Training Enhance Working Memory," 284–98; Jäncke, Schlaug, and Steinmetz, "Hand Skill Asymmetry," 424–32.

5. Siegel and Hsu, "'Like Brain Boot Camp.'" See also Parbery-Clark, et al., "Musical Experience and the Aging"; Smayda, Worthy, and Chandrasekaran, "Better Late than Never," 734–48; Tierney, Krizman, and Nina Kraus, "Music Training Alters the Course," 10062–67; White-Schwoch, et al., "Older Adults Benefit," 17667–74; Parbery-Clark, Skoe, and Kraus, "Musical Experience Limits," 14100–14107.

6. Siegel and Hsu, "'Like Brain Boot Camp.'" For more on this research see "Brainvolts."

Ryerson University in Toronto are studying whether engaging in singing and commencing musical interval and pitch recognition exercises over the age of fifty helps improve people's listening comprehension. Their preliminary findings are promising.[7] Why should that be? Each person's speaking voice and each musical instrument operate within a customary pitch range and each has a distinct timbre (tone color or tone quality). Timbre or tone color is what allows you to distinguish the sound of a flute from a violin, for example, even if they are playing the same notes. Timbre and pitch together are what make my voice sound different from another person's. It is also partly what makes certain voices so distinctive—James Earl Jones, Ellen DeGeneres, Terry Gross, and Tom Hanks come to mind. By improving a person's ability to track pitch and timbre, that person can more readily focus on and therefore decipher speech sounds in a noisy environment.

Studies with dementia patients and patients with brain injuries have shown that musical memories (particularly songs and hymns learned in youth or heard during important life events, such as a first date) endure longer than verbal or visual ones.[8] Music engages several areas of the brain, but it particularly activates one of the last portions of the brain to atrophy over the course of Alzheimer's disease: the medial prefrontal cortex region.[9] In addition, music appears to decrease agitation in these patients.[10] Therapists and caretakers, including Baylor University's chapter of Music and Memory, are taking advantage of this property of music to help dementia patients and their families.[11] Other studies suggest that singing, particularly singing in a choir, boosts the immune and respiratory systems.[12]

There are other, less quantifiable, reasons to study music. First, music helps create and reinforce community. When we listen to music,

7. Dubinsky, "Seniors Improving Neurocognitive Goals"; Steinberg and Russo, "SMART Lab Singers"; Clason, "Music and Better Hearing?"

8. Jacobsen, et al., "Why Musical Memory Can Be Preserved," 2438–50; Haj, Fasotti, and Allain, "Involuntary Nature," 238–46; Straube, et al., "Dissociation Between Singing and Speaking," 1505–12.

9. Särkämö and Tervaniemi, "Cognitive, Emotional, and Neural Benefits," e69.

10. Sung, Chang, and Lee, "Preferred Music Listening Intervention," 1056–64; Särkämö, et al., "Pattern of Emotional Benefits," 439–40.

11. Music and Memory.

12. "Choir Singing Boosts Immune System"; Kreutz, et al., "Effects of Choir Singing," 623–35; Stegemöller, et al., "Effects of Singing on Voice," 594–600.

frequently our internal bodily rhythms become aligned with that of the music, a process referred to as entrainment. When we do this as a group, we move from individual, personal rhythms or pulses to communal ones. Two studies of choirs, for instance, showed their pulse rates aligned with one another after a period of time.[13] Some scientists argue that is why music is so appealing. Moreover, as Bruno Nettl and other ethnomusicologists have shown, music acts as an identity marker.[14] What music you listen to or participate in makes a statement about the social class, generation, ethnicity to which you belong or with which you identify. It is important to note that our individual responses to as well as our associations with specific sounds are culturally conditioned. These two facets of music—entrainment and music as identity marker—help explain why communal singing is so powerful and has been used by social justice movements in this country and elsewhere. The Civil Rights movement in the 1960s, the independence movement in the Baltics in the 1980s-90s, the anti-apartheid movement in South Africa: all used singing to unite people working towards a common goal.[15]

Admittedly, even though music can bolster a sense of community, unfortunately, the opposite is also true: music can reinforce boundaries between social groups as well. But the fact that it carries this important cultural function is yet another reason to take music seriously and not to remain passive receivers of this art or to remain in our comfortable musical boxes. Studying music other than "our own" can promote global perspectives and respect for diversity as well as a greater understanding of the past. All cultures have music, but which musical elements they emphasize and value varies greatly. Even though musical idioms can sound very different from one another, music often has similar functions or purposes within societies.[16]

13. Morelle, "Choir Singers 'Synchronise Their Heart Beats'"; Vickhoff, et al., "Music Structure Determines Heart Rate"; Müller, Delius, and Lindenberger, "Complex Networks Emerging," 85–101; Haensch, "When Choirs Sing."

14. Nettl, *Study of Ethnomusicology*, 9, 47–51 and 259; Nettl, *Excursions in World Music*, 7.

15. Darden, *Nothing But Love in God's Water*; Sanger, *"When the Spirit Says Sing!"*; Šmidchens, *Power of Song*; Malisa and Malange, "Songs for Freedom," 304–18; Vershbow, "Sounds of Resistance." Currently, singing is unifying pro–democracy protestors in Hong Kong. Brooks, "One United Struggle."

16. Nettl, *Study of Ethnomusicology*, 9–11, 36–51; Nettl, *Excursions in World Music*, 1–8.

In order to demonstrate these points, I will discuss three contrasting examples from three disparate cultures. All three genres use interlocking parts and variations as their basis, but the sounds that result differ greatly. Even though these selections have very different tone colors they all share a similar purpose: that of religious ritual. The first example is mbira music from Shona people in southeastern Africa. Created by small metal keyboards set within large gourds which act as resonators, the purpose of mbira music is to connect the earthly community with the spiritual one; it is *music* that calls the spirits, the ancestral spirits in particular, into this world. An mbira player uses his left thumb and right thumb and forefinger to play a melody and a higher-pitched countermelody, plus an independent bass line. In other words, a few fingers create three separate parts. (That must be good for your brain!) Customarily, mbira are played in pairs. Two performers play similar complementary melodic patterns to which others present may add clapping, singing, and dancing. The musical patterns are repeated extensively and gradually vary over time.[17]

Kecak from the island of Bali in Indonesia serves as the second example. Like mbira, this music has interlocking parts, which are primarily spoken rather than played or sung. Groups of men chant or shout non-lexical syllables in distinctive rhythmic patterns that are layered on top of one another or that abruptly stop and start. At points, the chanting becomes semi-sung and alternates in pitch; solo voices add more sustained lines. The music's rapid pace, rhythmic drive, and loud volume captivate. Although nowadays this music is performed primarily for tourists and is used to portray incidents from the *Ramayana* (a Hindu epic), it originally was part of rituals connected with healing and discernment. The rhythmic chanting was intended to put young women into a trance that would allow them to connect to and then convey messages from the spiritual realm.[18]

The third example is Fugue in A minor BWV 543 by Johann Sebastian Bach. Like the previous two examples, a fugue features multiple, interlocking parts. However, one main melody, referred to as a subject, remains prominent and recurs throughout the piece. Heard by itself at the beginning, the subject is then layered over variants of itself and

17. Berliner, *Soul of Mbira*; Turino, "Music of Sub–Saharan Africa," 161–68; Kaemmer, "Music of the Shona," 761–70. During my presentation I played a selection from Kwenda, *Svikiro*.

18. Bakan, *World Music*, 93, 97–98; Capwell, "Music of Indonesia," 152–53. For streaming audio examples, see Stearns, "Kecak"; "Kepandung Sita"; "Kecak."

with other distinctive melodic lines. The subject also will disappear for a while, only to return at another pitch level.[19] This fugue was composed for the organ, an instrument that many Americans probably associate with churches and sacred music. Many of J. S. Bach's organ works were intended for worship services. For J. S. Bach's contemporaries, however, this fugue might have prompted another association: the music's rhythms are derived from a gigue or a jig, a dance associated in the 1700s with "eagerness" and playful simplicity.[20]

Both the fugue and the Kecak example demonstrate that the function or role of a musical style or an instrument can transform over time. While today many in Europe and North America associate the organ with worship services, during earlier time periods it had other uses. In the 1600s, wealthy Italians often had a small organ in their homes for entertainment, for example, and in the first years of films, organists provided live soundtracks for silent movies.[21] Thus, studying music can demonstrate that present day timbral associations, assumptions, and cultural practices may or may not endure. More importantly, through studying music, people can learn to acknowledge the diversity of cultures (including that of the past), as well as glimpse our commonalities. Music can serve as a mediator.

Lastly, the arts can act as a mirror or serve as a prophetic voice.[22] In other words, the arts may reflect society as it is or reveal how it perhaps could be. During the 1700s, G. F. Handel's operas and their repetitive da capo forms, for instance, mirrored the highly stratified, protocol-driven society that spawned those works. These operas also were written for a culture that acknowledged and respected recurring natural cycles (i.e., morning, noon, night; the seasons of the year, etc.) The musical forms and patterns they contain mimic those cycles.[23] Benny Goodman and his swing band, on the other hand, acted as cultural prophets. Having an integrated band on stage during an era when most venues were legally

19. Two recordings in which you can clearly hear the subject entries are: Otto and Köbler, *J.S. Bach*; and Kujala, *Bach on Porthan Organ*. A recording that brings out the livelier character of the piece is Jacobs, *Paul Jacobs Plays Bach*.

20. Mattheson, *Der Vollkomene Capellmeister*, 186.

21. Arnold, *Organ Literature*, 21–25; Altman, *Silent Film Sound*, 330–331; Fox and Junchen, "Theater Organ."

22. For a good case study of these properties of music, see Byerly, "Mirror, Mediator, and Prophet," 1–44.

23. Berger, *Bach's Cycle, Mozart's Arrow*.

segregated tangibly demonstrated a revised social structure as did the music itself through their improvisations on or new arrangements of standard tunes.[24] Similarly, Mozart's operas portray meritocracies (vs. aristocracies)—realms where honesty, forgiveness, and reconciliation rule rather than revenge and deceit—a vision we are still attempting to live up to today. I would argue that it is not just the plots that communicate this message. Mozart's music, as theorist Scott Burnham has eloquently shown, models interdependence. Each instrument or voice contributes to the whole via distinctive, complementary parts.[25]

To demonstrate this, I would like to discuss an excerpt from one of Mozart's most famous pieces: The Adagio from Wind Serenade K361, also known as the Gran Partita. To me this piece reflects Romans 12:4–8, which states we each have different gifts, together we form one body. In this selection, each instrument or each "member" of the musical body has a different function.[26] The horns, bassoons, and double bass play an introductory fanfare, a call to order if you will, to start the movement. After that, their chief purpose is to sustain the harmony, but they use divergent methods (half notes vs. eighth-note arpeggios) to do so. The inner voices (the clarinets and second oboe) have a different function; their upbeat to downbeat figures create a sense of forward momentum. Over the foundation the lower instruments have laid, the principal oboe glides in. Its long, high note transforms into a descending scale, through which it hands the melody seamlessly over to the first clarinet, who in turn passes it onto the basset horn. On their own these musical components are quite ordinary—arpeggios, scales, a single pitch sustained—but a graceful "sonic community" (to quote Burnham) arises from how they combine with one another and interact.[27]

I believe that "sonic community" extends beyond how the musical sounds interact. Live performances of music, particularly those of large diverse ensembles such as an orchestra, enact cooperation, community,

24. Tackley, *1938 Carnegie Hall Jazz Concert*, 19–25 and 155; Wang, "Goodman, Benny."

25. Burnham, *Mozart's Grace*, 6–26, page 19 in particular.

26. NMA Online—Digital Mozart Edition. Enter K361 in the search box adjacent to the one labelled KV. Click on the link provided. To hear sound, click on the tab titled "Table of Contents." Scroll down to the Adagio of K361 and then select the sound button.

27. Burnham, *Mozart's Grace*, 19. Other examples by Mozart that readily demonstrate this property of the composer's music are the trio "Soave il vento" in *Così fan tutte* and movement 3 of Symphony No. 38 ("Prague").

and interconnectedness in a powerful way. The composer relies on other musicians to transform the notes on the page into tones. In many symphonies and oratorios, over one hundred musicians each contribute to a common goal; each person adds his/her own notes and tone color to the whole. The performers must listen to each other as well as play their own parts to produce an expressive, cohesive sound that communicates to the audience. Engaged listeners in turn enervate and inspire the performers. Every live performance constitutes a temporary community—one that is fleeting and that dissipates but whose vibrations resonate in our souls and, according to scientists, in our bodies and our brains.

So why study music? I hope I have demonstrated there are compelling educational, neurological, and physiological reasons to do so. I also hope I have shown that there are less quantifiable, but perhaps more powerful communal, theological, and cultural reasons to do so as well. That is why I continue to honor my call to teach this art that I love.

References

Altman, Rick. *Silent Film Sound.* New York: Columbia University Press, 2004.

Arnold, Corliss Richard. *Organ Literature: A Comprehensive Survey.* Vol. 1, *Historical Survey.* 3rd ed. Metuchen, NJ: Scarecrow, 1995.

Bakan, Michael B. *World Music: Traditions and Transformations.* New York: McGraw-Hill, 2007.

Berger, Karol. *Bach's Cycle, Mozart's Arrow: An Essay on the Origins of Musical Modernity.* Berkeley: University of California Press, 2007.

Berliner, Paul. *The Soul of Mbira: Music and Traditions of the Shona People of Zimbabwe.* Berkeley: University of California Press, 1978.

Bidelman, Gavin M. "Musicians Have Enhanced Audiovisual Multisensory Binding: Experience-Dependent Effects in the Double-Flash Illusion." *Experimental Brain Research* 234.10 (2016) 3037–47. https://doi.org/10.1007/s00221-016-4705-6.

"Brainvolts." Auditory Neuroscience Laboratory. Northwestern University, https://brainvolts.northwestern.edu.

Brooks, David. "The One United Struggle for Freedom." *New York Times,* August 27, 2019.

Burnham, Scott. *Mozart's Grace.* Princeton: Princeton University Press, 2013.

Byerly, Ingrid. "Mirror, Mediator, and Prophet: The Music *Indaba* of Late-Apartheid South Africa." *Ethnomusicology* 42 (1998) 1–44.

Capwell, Charles. "The Music of Indonesia." In *Excursions in World Music,* 2nd ed., edited by Bruno Nettl, et al., 152–153. Upper Saddle River, NJ: Prentice-Hall, 1997.

"Choir Singing Boosts Immune System Activity in Cancer Patients and Carers, Study Shows." ScienceDaily, April 4, 2016. www.sciencedaily.com/releases/2016/04/160404221004.htm.

Clason, Debbie. "Music and Better Hearing: What's the Connection?" Healthy Hearing, July 20, 2017. https://www.healthyhearing.com/report/52768-Music-and-better-hearing-what-s-the-connection.

Corrigall, Kathleen A., and Laurel J. Trainor. "Associations between Length of Music Training and Reading Skills in Children." *Music Perception: An Interdisciplinary Journal* 29.2 (2011) 147–55.

Darden, Robert. *Nothing But Love In God's Water: Black Sacred Music from the Civil War to the Civil Rights Movement.* Vol. 2. University Park: Pennsylvania State University Press, 2016.

Dubinsky, Ella. "Seniors Improving Neurocognitive Goals through Song (SINGS): Teaching Your Brain to Hear Better While Learning How to Sing." SMART Lab—Science of Music, Auditory Research, and Technology, Ryerson University, June 2015. https://smartlaboratory.org/our-choirs/our-hearing-impaired-choir.

Forgeard, Marie, Gottfried Schlaug, Andrea Norton, Camilla Rosam, Udita Iyengar, and Ellen Winner. "The Relation between Music and Phonological Processing in Normal-Reading Children and Children with Dyslexia." *Music Perception: An Interdisciplinary Journal* 25.4 (2008) 383–90.

Forgeard, Marie, Ellen Winner, Andrea Norton, and Gottfried Schlaug. "Practicing a Musical Instrument in Childhood Is Associated with Enhanced Verbal Ability and Nonverbal Reasoning." *PLoS ONE* 3.10 (2008) 1–7. https://doi.org/10.1371/journal.pone.0003566.

Fox, David H., and David L. Junchen. "Theater Organ [Cinema Organ]." *Grove Music Online/Oxford Music Online,* October 16, 2013. https://doi-org.ezproxy.baylor.edu/10.1093/gmo/9781561592630.article.A2252521.

Gibson, Crystal, Bradley S. Folley, and Sohee Park. "Enhanced Divergent Thinking and Creativity in Musicians: A Behavioral and Near-Infrared Spectroscopy Study." *Brain and Cognition* 69.1 (2009) 162–69.

Habib, Michel, and Mireille Besson. "What Do Music Training and Musical Experience Teach Us About Brain Plasticity?" *Music Perception: An Interdisciplinary Journal* 26.3 (2009) 279–85.

Haensch, Anna. "When Choirs Sing, Many Hearts Beat as One." NPR, July 10, 2013. https://www.npr.org/sections/health-shots/2013/07/09/200390454/when-choirs-sing-many-hearts-beat-as-one.

Haj, Mohamad El, Luciano Fasotti, and Philippe Allain. "The Involuntary Nature of Music-Evoked Autobiographical Memories in Alzheimer's Disease." *Consciousness and Cognition* 21.1 (2012) 238–46. https://doi.org/10.1016/j.concog.2011.12.005.

Hallam, Susan. "The Power of Music: Its Impact on the Intellectual, Social and Personal Development of Children and Young People." *International Journal of Music Education* 28.3 (2010) 269–89.

Hutchins, Sean. "Early Childhood Music Training and Associated Improvements in Music and Language Abilities." *Music Perception: An Interdisciplinary Journal* 35.5 (2018) 579–93.

Hyde, Krista L., Jason Lerch, Andrea Norton, Marie Forgeard, Ellen Winner, Alan C. Evans, and Gottfried Schlaug. "The Effects of Musical Training on Structural Brain Development." *Annals of the New York Academy of Sciences* 1169.1 (2009) 182–86. https://doi.org/10.1111/j.1749-6632.2009.04852.x.

Jacobs, Paul. *Paul Jacobs Plays Bach (an unedited release).* JAV JAV145, 2004. https://www.youtube.com/watch?v=bgjMkhy5yOU.

Jacobsen, Jörn-Henrik, Johannes Stelzer, Thomas Hans Fritz, Gael Chételat, Renaud La Joie, and Robert Turner. "Why Musical Memory Can Be Preserved in Advanced Alzheimer's Disease." *Brain* 138.8 (2015) 2438–50. https://doi.org/10.1093/brain/awv135.

Jäncke, Lutz, Gottfried Schlaug, and Helmuth Steinmetz. "Hand Skill Asymmetry in Professional Musicians." *Brain and Cognition* 34.3 (1997) 424–32. https://doi.org/10.1006/brcg.1997.0922.

Johansson Babro B. "Music, Age, Performance, and Excellence: A Neuroscientific Approach." *Psychomusicology* 18 (2002) 46–58.

Kaemmer, John E. "Music of the Shona of Zimbabwe." In *Garland Encyclopedia of World Music*. Vol. 1: *Africa*, edited by Ruth M. Stone, 761–70. New York: Routledge, 1997.

"Kecak." *Music for the Gods: The Fahnestock South Sea Expedition: Indonesia*, Smithsonian Global Sound for Libraries, Mickey Hart Collection, 1994, streaming audio. https://search.alexanderstreet.com/view/work/bibliographic_entity%7Crecorded_cd%7C1754541.

"Kepandung Sita." *The Bali Sessions: Living Art, Sounding Spirit*, Smithsonian Global Sound for Libraries, Mickey Hart Collection, 1999, streaming audio. https://search.alexanderstreet.com/view/work/bibliographic_entity%7Crecorded_cd%7C1754536.

Kreutz, Gunter, Stephan Bongard, Sonja Rohrmann, Volker Hodapp, and Dorothee Grebe. "Effects of Choir Singing or Listening on Secretory Immunoglobulin A, Cortisol, and Emotional State." *Journal of Behavioral Medicine* 27.6 (2004) 623–35.

Kujala, Susanne. *Bach on Porthan Organ*. Alba ABCD424, 2018, www.NaxosMusicLibrary.com.

Kwenda, Forward. *Svikiro*, Shanachie 64095, 1997. CD.

Malisa, Mark, and Nandipha Malange. "Songs of Freedom." In *The Routledge History of Social Protest in Popular Music*, edited by Jonathan Friedman, 304–18. London: Routledge, 2013.

Mattheson, Johann. *Der vollkomene Capellmeister* (1739). In *Music in the Western World: A History in Documents*, 2nd ed., edited by Piero Weiss and Richard Taruskin. New York: Thomson/Schirmer, 2008.

Morelle, Rebecca. "Choir Singers 'Synchronise Their Heartbeats.'" BBC News. BBC, July 9, 2013. https://www.bbc.com/news/science-environment-23230411.

Moreno, Sylvain, Deanna Friesen, and Ellen Bialystok. "Effect of Music Training on Promoting Preliteracy Skills: Preliminary Causal Evidence." *Music Perception: An Interdisciplinary Journal* 29.2 (2011) 165–72.

Müller, Viktor, Julia A.M. Delius, and Ulman Lindenberger. "Complex Networks Emerging During Choir Singing." *Annals of the New York Academy of Sciences* 1431.1 (2018) 85–101.

Music and Memory. www.musicandmemory.org.

Nettl, Bruno. *Excursions in World Music*. Upper Saddle River, NJ: Prentice Hall, 1997.

Nettl, Bruno. *The Study of Ethnomusicology: Twenty-Nine Issues and Concepts*. Urbana-Champaign: University of Illinois Press, 1983.

NMA Online—Digital Mozart Edition, edited by the Internationale Stiftung Mozarteum, Salzburg. https://dme.mozarteum.at/en/nmaonline-2.

Otto, Hans and Robert Köbler, organists. *J.S. Bach: Organ Music on Silbermann Organs*, Vol. 7, Berlin Classics 0093672BC, 1998. www.NaxosMusicLibrary.com.

Parbery-Clark, Alexandra, Dana L. Strait, Samira Anderson, Emily Hittner, and Nina Kraus. "Musical Experience and the Aging Auditory System: Implications for Cognitive Abilities and Hearing Speech in Noise." *PLoS ONE* 6.5 (2011) e18082. http://journals.plos.org/plosone/article?id=10.1371/journal.pone.0018082.

Parbery-Clark, Alexandra, Erika Skoe, and Nina Kraus. "Musical Experience Limits the Degradative Effects of Background Noise on the Neural Processing of Sound." *Journal of Neuroscience* 29.45 (2009) 14100–107.

Roden, Ingo, Dietmar Grube, Stephan Bongard, and Gunter Kreutz. "Does Music Training Enhance Working Memory Performance? Findings from a Quasi-Experimental Longitudinal Study." *Psychology of Music* 42.2 (2013) 284–98.

Rosenkranz, Karin, Aaron Williamon, and John C. Rothwell. "Motorcortical Excitability and Synaptic Plasticity Is Enhanced in Professional Musicians." *Journal of Neuroscience* 27.19 (2007) 5200–6. https://doi.org/10.1523/JNEUROSCI.0836-07.2007.

Sanger, Kerran L. *"When the Spirit Says Sing!" The Role of Freedom Songs in the Civil Rights Movement*. New York: Routledge, 2015.

Särkämö, T., and M. Tervaniemi. "Cognitive, Emotional, and Neural Benefits of Musical Leisure Activities in Stroke and Dementia." *Annals of Physical and Rehabilitation Medicine* 58S (2015) e69. https://doi.org/10.1016/j.rehab.2015.07.169.

Särkämö, Teppo, Sari Laitinen, Ava Numminen, Merja Kurki, Julene K. Johnson, and Pekka Rantanen. "Pattern of Emotional Benefits Induced by Regular Singing and Music Listening in Dementia." *Journal of the American Geriatrics Society* 64.2 (2016) 439–40. https://doi.org/10.1111/jgs.13963.

"Shona Ancestral Spirit Song, 'Nyama Musango.'" In *Garland Encyclopedia of World Music*. https://search.alexanderstreet.com/lti/view/work/383980.

Siegel, Robert, and Andrea Hsu. "'Like Brain Boot Camp': Using Music to Ease Hearing Loss." NPR, May 31, 2017. https://www.npr.org/sections/health-shots/2017/05/31/530723021/like-brain-boot-camp-using-music-to-ease-hearing-loss.

Slater, Jessica, Dana L. Strait, Erika Skoe, Samantha O'Connell Elaine Thompson, and Nina Kraus. "Longitudinal Effects of Group Music Instruction on Literacy Skills in Low-Income Children." *PLoS ONE* 9.11 (2014) e113383. https://doi.org/10.1371/journal.pone.0113383.

Smayda, Kirsten E., Darrell A. Worthy, and Bharath Chandrasekaran. "Better Late than Never (or Early): Music Training in Late Childhood Is Associated with Enhanced Decision-Making." *Psychology of Music* 46.5 (2017) 734–48. https://doi.org/10.1177/0305735617723721.

Šmidchens, Guntis. *The Power of Song: Nonviolent National Culture in the Baltic Singing Revolution*. Seattle: University of Washington Press, 2017.

Stearns, Michael. "Kecak" (field recording from Bona, Bali at the Ganung Kawi Temple), *Baraka*. Varese Sarabande 3020671602, 2012. www.Naxosmusiclibrary.com.

Stegemöller, Elizabeth L., Hollie Radig, Paul Hibbing, Judith Wingate, and Christine Sapienza. "Effects of Singing on Voice, Respiratory Control and Quality of Life in Persons with Parkinson's Disease." *Disability and Rehabilitation* 39.6 (2016) 594–600. https://doi:10.3109/09638288.2016.1152610.

Steinberg, Saul Moshé, and Frank Russo. "The SMART Lab Singers: Improving Age-Related Hearing Difficulties Through Choir Lessons." SMART Lab—Science of Music, Auditory Research, and Technology, Ryerson University, June 2015. https://smartlaboratory.org/our-choirs/our-hearing-impaired-choir.

Straube, Thomas, Alexander Schulz, Katja Geipel, Hans-Joachim Mentzel, and Wolfgang H.R. Miltner. "Dissociation between Singing and Speaking in Expressive Aphasia: The Role of Song Familiarity." *Neuropsychologia* 46.5 (2008) 1505–12. https://doi.org/10.1016/j.neuropsychologia.2008.01.008.

Sung, Huei-Chuan, Anne M Chang, and Wen-Li Lee. "A Preferred Music Listening Intervention to Reduce Anxiety in Older Adults with Dementia in Nursing Homes." *Journal of Clinical Nursing* 19.7–8 (2010) 1056–64. https://doi/epdf/10.1111/j.1365–2702.2009.03016.x.

Tackley, Catherine. *Benny Goodman's Famous 1938 Carnegie Hall Jazz Concert.* New York: Oxford University Press, 2013.

Talamini, Francesca, Barabara Carretti, and Massimo Grassi. "The Working Memory of Musicians and Nonmusicians." *Music Perception: An Interdisciplinary Journal* 34.2 (2016) 183–91.

Tierney, Adam T., Jennifer Krizman, and Nina Kraus. "Music Training Alters the Course of Adolescent Auditory Development." *Proceedings of the National Academy of Sciences* 112.32 (2015) 10062–67. https://doi.org/10.1073/pnas.1505114112.

Tsang, Christine D., and Nicole J. Conrad. "Music Training and Reading Readiness." *Music Perception: An Interdisciplinary Journal* 29.2 (2011) 157–63.

Turino, Thomas. "The Music of Sub-Saharan Africa." In *Excursions in World Music*, 2nd ed., edited by Bruno Nettl et al., 161–168. Upper Saddle River, NJ: Prentice-Hall, 1997.

Vershbow, Michela E. "The Sounds of Resistance: The Role of Music in South Africa's Anti-Apartheid Movement." *Inquiries Journal* 2.6 (2010). http://www.inquiriesjournal.com/a?id=265.

Vickhoff, Björn, Helge Malmgren, Rickard Åström, Gunnar Nyberg, Seth-Reino Ekström, Mathias Engwall, Johan Snygg, Michael Nilsson, and Rebecka Jörnsten. "Music Structure Determines Heart Rate Variability of Singers." *Frontiers in Psychology* 4 (2013). https://doi.org/10.3389/fpsyg.2013.00334.

Wan, Catherine Y., and Gottfried Schlaug. "Music Making as a Tool for Promoting Brain Plasticity across the Life Span." *The Neuroscientist* 16.5 (2010) 566–77. https://doi.org/10.1177/1073858410377805.

Wang, Richard. "Goodman, Benny [Benjamin David]." *Grove Music Online/Oxford Music Online*, 2001. https://doi.org/10.1093/gmo/9781561592630.article.11459.

White-Schwoch, Travis, Kali Woodruff Carr, Samira Anderson, Dana L. Strait, and Nina Kraus. "Older Adults Benefit from Music Training Early in Life: Biological Evidence for Long-Term Training-Driven Plasticity." *Journal of Neuroscience* 33.45 (2013) 17667–74.

11

Nurturing Spiritual Intelligence

BURT BURLESON

THERE ARE SPIRITUAL CAPACITIES that are within us, and these spiritual capacities can be developed. That is the working premise of this essay, and it is the teaching of the Christian spiritual tradition as well. These capacities are simply within us, we believe as Christians, because we are "imago dei," in God's image. As human beings, we are spiritual and made for maturity and maturing, but what we know is that soul maturity and maturing does not always—or we might say on lots of days—take place.

And that is apparent to us every day; if we're even half-awake, we see and sense it, although there are moments, too, when we see that divine image made known, that divine-like capacity expressed. When someone acts in a compassionate way. When someone's consciousness is raised in an "ah ha" moment. When someone weeps for the beauty of something. When wisdom flows from someone. We know in those moments that there is a soul manifesting its purpose.

But that said, what we also witness day by day is that a human being will not only express compassion but cruelty as well. We know that consciousness can go up, but it comes right back down—and a kind of "soul amnesia" forgets the new meaning it understood for a time or maybe for a fleeting moment. We know that so many of us walking the planet seem sadly to have no ability to be amazed by anything—we are unfazed by a sunset or a sonata. And we know that ours is just not a wisdom culture. We are a bumper sticker, tweeting culture, and we have spiritual appetites satisfied by "fast food faith."

Though we might affirm that we all long for and are made for spiritual maturity, actually maturing is not a given. (There's no giant "mother-may-I" step forward.) They are there, these capacities, and yet they must be developed. If not, they will only be manifested in our journeys in random or sporadic ways, if at all.

This has been the consensus of the Christian spiritual tradition. We have a heart—but it can be hardened or divided or darkened. We can think—but our thinking can become mechanical, and we have "bothered" minds that furiously spin like caged hamster wheels. We have natural, God-given drives—but they are highjacked by immaturity and off we go onto some sinful, broken path. We have will and intention and attention—but all three are often enslaved, captive to lesser rule. We are in a culture that captivates us day by day; our busyness, our climbing, our complexities, our technology, all our stuff???? There are many "masters to serve."

Our inner lives are disturbed; the waters inside are choppy so that we cannot see ourselves or the world clearly, as we might if we were peering into still waters. There a True Self—but a smaller self on auto-pilot—takes us predictably into compulsive behavior that betrays how stuck we are in immature spiritual states.

All this surrounds us and, as St. Paul says, "so easily entangles us" (Heb 12:1, NASB). And there we are, entangled spiritual beings, by fall and by default, by slothful sin and by what the world has done to us, not living fully as those made in God's image.

Spiritual Intelligence

Danah Zohar and Ian Marshall entitled their latest book, "Spiritual Intelligence."[1] In it they make the case that in addition to intellectual and emotional intelligences, IQ and EQ, there is also SQ, our Spiritual Quotient. They, and the research they use, are pointing to what we intuit and that spiritual traditions have always taught. We are endowed, gifted spiritually, but the gift within us must be *stirred*, as St. Paul says. This essay is not framed by that research but does assume the same premise and, from a pastoral perspective, also draws on the Christian spiritual tradition. The essay does not speak to the pedagogies that might nurture spiritual intelligence but does offer five capacities that are named and considered here.

1. Zohar and Marshall, *Spiritual Intelligence*.

Awakening

This capacity is within us and, in so many ways, seems to grow naturally in various stages of our lives. That said, most of us are astonished (perhaps in these times especially) at all those in the world around us who are sleepwalking. (There is a reason zombie films continue to emerge.)

Although our cognitive growth and the journey we make create the possibility of awakening, there seems to be some choice or agency on the part of the individual to awaken to the dream that we are in. So, we somehow "pinch" ourselves in the midst of our dream. We can choose consciousness. We can consent to God's work in us. Spiritually mature individuals are always awakening to who they are (self-awareness) and to what "is"—what is true about the world (a truer worldview)—and they are beginning to understand the relationship between those two.

This spiritual intelligence, the capacity to awaken, helps us to discern, helps us "connect the dots" of our existence. In the healthiest journeys, as this capacity grows, it transcends but also includes what has been seen and known before. (Awakening to deeper truth does not by necessity involve rejecting what has been previously imparted.)

As we awaken, our perspective can change. We have "eyes to see" and "ears to hear," as Jesus says over and over. Through curiosity or compassion, or because of experiences and encounters, our angle on our relationship to the world changes, and then we can even choose to take two steps sideways, on purpose, "and see ourselves over there seeing the world." Yes, there is cognitive development taking place but also something more essential as human beings and as Christians.

All this, though exciting and lifegiving, also requires some vulnerability. Being self-critical or letting go of tribal-identities or of the self we came to be (in and because of middle school) is likely to be threatening. And out of fear, many, as is clear, will "batten down the hatches" on the smaller container that previously held their world.

But that is not what we're made for, and this is "why it is said," as Paul wrote in Ephesians 5:14 (NIV), "Wake up, sleeper, rise from the dead, and Christ will shine on you." Jesus is always looking at his disciples, then and now, and saying, "Stay awake with me" (author's paraphrase). This is what disciples do—they awaken and stay near to God's heart.

Finding Purpose

Having purpose in our lives flows from our God-given ability to envision, to imagine, how life might unfold. Clearly we are made for this kind of imagination and it is why we were all asked that question, "*And what do you want to be when you grow up?*"

Made for motion as we are, this spiritual instinct is in us all and its manifestation in our lives certainly matures. One moves from pretending to be a super hero, to dreaming of being a secret agent, and then to being point guard for the New York Knicks, and then perhaps to being a youth minister, and on our envisioning evolves. Although that sort of envisioning happens naturally in so many lives, this spiritual capacity considers questions more significant than "What do I want to be or do?" or "How will I spend my time 8:00 to 5:00?" It is within us also to ask, "What's my purpose? Why am I on the planet? What is emerging in front of me or beckoning to me?" This developed intelligence can wonder, "What do my desires mean? What does the world need of me? Does it matter where I go and how I live? Who am I? Whose am I?"

This search must and will go way, way beyond a student choosing a major and landing a job after graduation that she or he will enjoy. At some point, if we develop spiritually, we begin to sense that our life is not our own and, though we are blessed to make choices, we're not really driving things. As Gregory Mayers says in *Listen to the Desert*,

> The longer you live, the more you learn that you cannot control your life very much. The more you realize this fact, the more likely you will enjoy life, the natural ecstasy inherent in life itself . . . It means you cease judging life . . . The religious traditions call this "living the will of God." Then something happens, something indescribable. We are living in the Mystery, or perhaps to say it better, the Mystery is living us.[2]

Walking Humbly

The third intelligence has to do with our ability to see ourselves amidst a larger creation and because of that *to be humble*. And it does not take long teaching at a university to know that some students have more difficulty getting to this virtue, expressing this intelligence, than others.

2. Mayers, *Listen to the Desert*, 31.

At Baylor University in the last chapel session each academic year, we always do the same thing. With the small group of students who are there because they have no more absences to use, we have a dialogue, which is driven by the question, *"When you go home for the summer and your friends ask you, 'What's it like being at a Christian University? What's it like being at Baylor?,' what do you tell them?"*

For the most part we hear really encouraging things about their experience with faith at Baylor—and this from students who may not have been excited about chapel, evidenced by the fact that they have no more absences and have to attend the last day. Almost every response is affirming of Baylor's mission and how it is being expressed. Some are amazing and belong on the admissions website:

> So, coming from a very Christian background and a very Christian town, a mostly Baptist town up in north Texas, I know that question is something I'm going to get asked . . . and I can honestly say (to them) that I've learned . . . I learned how much I did not know about what I believe, just being surrounded by the people here on campus and by my professors . . . I've learned how much I did not know about the things I believe. And so, it's kind of transformed . . . what I believe . . . So, I guess that something I can say (to them) is, "there's so much we don't know and . . . even if you've been raised in the Christian faith, there's still so much to learn."

This student is echoing Job, who says from the ashes in response to having heard a very long Divine poem, "I spoke about things I do not understand/too wonderful for me to know" (Job 42:3, author's paraphrase). There is a move, as singer-song writer Carrie Newcomer puts it in one of her songs, from "certainty to mystery." And as we make the move, our capacity for awe and reverence grows. We become, in our humility, open and curious. We hold what we hold less defensively and convictions are expressed with an ironic certainty about our uncertainty.

The theologians in the early centuries of the Church spoke of this as a movement from "kataphatic" knowing to "apophatic" knowing. These were two important ideas in the Patristic era. Kataphatic (with images) is that need to name and that capacity to discover and to say "this is what is"—certainly a good thing, but most of these early teachers also taught us that, when it comes to knowing God, we can know that once we have named it we have missed it. That is "apophatic" knowing or the "apophatic way," the way of humility.

What is infinite cannot be handled by the finite. It is transcendent—beyond us. And knowing this and resting in it, even as we search, is a mark of spiritual intelligence. It changes how we engage in conversations about the truth and keeps us from hurting the world. As Jesus said in John 9 to angry leaders in the synagogue, "because you think you see, your sin remains" (author's paraphrase).

Being Present

We have the capacity *to be present*—to actually be where we are and attend to what is before us. This intelligence has always been held in the spiritual, contemplative tradition as an important aim and always something with which "frail creatures of dust" struggle. However, we know that snap-chatting post-millennials will struggle even more to be present. Sociologist Jean Twenge has thus dubbed them "iGen," those who have had held smart phones all of their lives.[3] It is a cognitive problem, but the cognitive limitation is likely to have significant spiritual implications because God is in this moment—now—in between, amidst, within. HERE is where God is . . . right here.

In the tradition of Desert Spirituality, koan-like teachings were passed on and passed down, and in these days of appreciation for those early centuries and the saints who were seeking God, many of these ancient teachings are available to us. This one lures us into considering the significance of being where you are:

> An old man was asked, "What is necessary to be saved?" He was making a rope and without looking up from the work he replied, "You are looking at it."[4]

What you need, is right here. All of God there is to enjoy is right here; that has been our Christian confession, but our thoughts and behavior betray a different and lesser "conviction." We do not really believe God is going to be here in this moment—with this friend, in this conversation, in this classroom, in this lecture, with this book, doing this thing that I would rather not do . . . right here, "making this rope."

We do not seem to think that *this place* is the holy place—but it is. Salvation is now. The Kingdom of God is at hand, but the kingdom of

---

3. Twenge, *iGen*.

4. Cited in Mayers, *Listen to the Desert*, 105.

smart phones and "altars of entertainment" are in the way, so presence is downright impossible. Attention, intention, follow-through, engagement, focus, prioritizing, choosing—these are spiritual matters, but the capacity for them is developed as we give our attention to anything, including whatever a student is called to be studying.

Persevering

Those who were around in the early 1980s will remember Scott Peck's best-selling book, *The Road Less Travelled*. We all bought it and read it, and most of us could quote the first few lines back then:

> Life is difficult. This is a great truth, one of the greatest truths.
> It is a great truth because once we truly see this truth, we transcend it.[5]

The fifth intelligence involves our *capacity to persevere*. All through scriptures God's people acknowledge that life is difficult, faith is difficult, faithfulness is difficult, remaining committed is difficult, being patient with our own and others' brokenness is difficult. Life is difficult—and yet, there is a spiritual disposition that helps us move beyond the malaise and complaint-ridden state in us that difficulty often deposits.

People who are resilient, who know they must bear suffering, are able to be honest with life and they have a courageous seeing of what is real. However, those with Spiritual Intelligence do not cynically name this as "the cold cruel world" that one "just better get used to." Rather, it has a kind of hopeful intuition about the nature of suffering and the vulnerability that this world insists upon and where all that might lead us.

Remember reading Frankl's, *Man's Search for Meaning*? There was meaning in the midst of Auschwitz. Remember the Apostle Paul saying, "Jesus was made perfect through his suffering"? Remember the invitation to a path, "take up your cross and follow me"? There is more going on in our suffering, especially when suffering is borne consciously.

Pastors, and others seeking to help, have to be careful with this theology and have to be careful how to enter this wisdom when with those who are suffering. But good pastoral practice acknowledged, the saints know the hard stuff is taking us someplace and that grace, like water, has

5. Peck, *Road Less Travelled*, 13.

a way of pooling up in the low places of our lives, as many saints have noted.

Christians have different convictions on the matter of who or what is behind the "hard stuff." We all have some convictions about the problem of pain. However, the conviction that something is being worked out in the midst of it, that something is being formed in the midst of us, that something is being redeemed, this perennial conviction, bears witness to a spiritual capacity that can mature in God's children.

Conclusion

Five spiritual capacities: awakening, purpose, humility, presence, and perseverance. We could name many more: our capacity for community, our capacity for healthy rhythms in life, our capacity to . . . be at peace, to make peace, to be prophetic, to live from a truer self, to trust, to create, to love (the "others" and one's enemies), to hold mystery. These are the marks of and the spiritual fruits that flow from spiritual maturity, they are capacities that the classroom can develop in our students.

REFERENCES

Mayers, Gregory. *Listen to the Desert: Secrets of Spiritual Maturity from the Desert Fathers and Mothers.* Ligouri, MO: Ligouri/Triumph, 1996.

Peck, M. Scott. *The Road Less Travelled: A New Psychology of Love, Traditional Values and Spiritual Growth.* London: Arrow, 1978.

Twenge, Jean M. *iGen: Why Today's Super-Connected Kids are Growing Up Less Rebellious, More Tolerant, Less Happy—and Completely Unprepared for Adulthood.* New York: Atria, 2017.

Zohar, Danah, and Ian Marshall. *Spiritual Intelligence: The Ultimate Intelligence.* London: Bloomsbury, 2000.

Part 3

COMMUNITY

12

The Teaching Vocation as Sharing Life

Reflections from a Faculty-in-Residence[1]

CANDI K. CANN

It is grace, nothing but grace, that we are allowed to live in
community with Christian brethren.

—Dietrich Bonhoeffer[2]

Notice how we are perpetually surprised at Time. ("How time
flies! Fancy John being grown-up and married! I can hardly
believe it!") In heaven's name, why? Unless, indeed, there is
something in us which is not temporal.

—C.S. Lewis[3]

---

1. I am indebted to the generous support of the Louisville Institute, which helped
fund graduate student assistance, and to the Louisville Institute's 2018 Winter Seminar, whose walking labyrinth helped me to reflect more on sacred time and space.

2. Bonhoeffer, *Life Together,* 20.

3. Lewis, *Collected Letters,* 76.

Introduction

I HAVE ALWAYS LOVED living in community, and I believe that, as Christians, we are called to live with others in kinship and humility. In fact, with the exception of his forty days alone in the wilderness, Jesus conducts his entire ministry alongside others, living in community. I believe that living in community—and not always communities of our choosing or those in which we feel most comfortable—is part of what makes us accountable and allows us to grow. After graduating from college, I taught English in the People's Republic of China at Hua Nan Women's College—the first private women's college in China—and lived in a residence with nine other foreign women who were also employed as teachers. We each had our own bedroom, shared a bathroom, and congregated in the common room and dining room where we ate our meals cooked by the chef, who made semi-approximations of Western food for our homesick hearts. It was hard living in community—and we had our share of disagreements, shared reflections, petty moments, and also poignant times as we spent that year together in a foreign country. At the height of the Cold War, every movement was monitored, our mail opened and phones tapped, so the community was imposed (though still appreciated) and was a time filled with growth. I most appreciated our diversity in age, since three of us were young and the others were retirees from various places in the world, and our perspectives and experiences were quite different.

The second intentional community I lived in was at Harvard, where I was a residential fellow in the Center for the Study of World Religions (CSWR). There, I had my own apartment but attended regular gatherings and festivities with other residents in the community—all of us from different faith traditions and backgrounds. I loved living there and expanded my understanding of other faiths and people. I became friends with Italian scholars who studied Japanese Buddhism, an Israeli family who studied Chinese Buddhism, a German Lutheran pastor from a seminary in Tubingen, and a few Orthodox Jewish friends who called on me for help when they were observing the sabbath and needed help getting into the electronic doors. Living there in the CSWR expanded both my mind and my perspective. I saw people from all over the world interested in other faiths and cultures, living with like-minded people and practicing in real-time what diversity looks like. The CSWR residents didn't just talk about tolerance and respect; they practiced it on a daily basis, as we shared our love for each other as residents and co-learners.

And now at Baylor University, I live in community again as a Faculty-in-Residence (FIR)—one of fifteen faculty members at Baylor who live in residence halls with undergraduate and graduate students. Every residence hall except one at Baylor has a FIR, and the academic interests and family structures of the various FIRs vary widely. I am a scholar of religion, and a single parent with a twelve-year-old child. The residential community of North Village is home to three different communities, and Texana House—the hall I live in—is home to approximately 150 women, consisting of about 40 percent upper-class students and about 60 percent first-year students. I live in a fourth-floor apartment with my family, have no private entrance, and interact with students daily. The staff at Texana is small. We have a residential hall chaplain who resides in Texana, but serves three different residential halls, a graduate student who serves as our residential director and lives on the first floor, and four community floor leaders—one for each floor—who are largely responsible for planning programming for the residents on their floor, the hall, and ensuring that students follow protocol. I love living in Texana House. Through this experience, I have grown a lot as an individual, but even more as a teacher; and I believe it has made me a better professor both in the classroom and outside of it. Living and working at Baylor, we are called to follow our Christian mission to educate men and women for worldwide leadership and service by integrating academic excellence and Christian commitment within a caring community. Since Baylor's commitment to its Christian identity is a large part of why I work at Baylor, I see living on campus as a FIR as a part of my calling in teaching and service. I want to model Christian living and community by living and working in fellowship with Baylor students.

A Brief Meditation on Time

When I was first asked to write about how my experience as a FIR has informed my teaching, I initially thought about the more obvious topic—space—and how we are informed by our spaces, and how living in close proximity to students shifts the way we teach,[4] but I wanted to move away

4. I often refer to classroom layouts here and the ways in which they influence how we interact with students and even teach out classes. Auditoriums with fixed seating,

from the more obvious and instead began to think about time and how living in community can shift the ways in which community influences and affects how we experience time. Time shapes human experience— our days, our years—and we rely on it to tell us when we are to begin or end—our work, our play, our interactions, and even our lives. Time is the common referent we rely on to relate to and with one another, but time is also constrictive and confining, shaping our experience of learning through both the definitions it gives to our days and the ways in which we think about academic years and school calendars. Joining and being a part of the academic community of a university or a college means entering the residential life of the university and belonging to academic time.

Adjustment to a residential space is an obvious rite of passage for many new students, as they embark on their preparations for their new living spaces in their academic communities. They are given recommended shopping lists of things they will need as they embark on their scholarly journey—extra-long twin sheets, a mini-refrigerator, a shower caddy to carry their belongings to and from the bathroom. But many students don't recognize the unspoken and unwritten contract between themselves and the academic calendar. Academic time sculpts the syllabi that define the course content and expectations laid out for every student, it defines the beginning and the end of each academic year, and time takes on new meaning as some see breaks as time for rest and relaxation, while others view them as extended study periods. As teachers we rely on the academic calendar-skeleton to shape how we will structure our courses and manage student learning, assigning midterm exams and papers before fall/spring break, and giving final exams at the end of the term. In short, time in the form of the academic calendar shapes our lives, our learning, and the ways in which we interact with each other, both in the residential hall and in the classroom.

Sacred Time and Calendars

In reflecting on my last two years living at Texana, I have thought a lot about space and time—the ways in which our living spaces inform and create community—and how we think about time in terms of the school

for example, always assume a top-down model of learning with teachers as the knowledge bearers and students as the knowledge receivers, while classrooms with movable desks and chairs allow for a more flexible student-based model of learning that is more egalitarian.

calendar and how academic time intersects with religious understandings of time. Because a large part of Baylor's identity is its mission as a Christian school, I believe it's important to be intentional about the ways in which the secular academic calendar and the religious calendar intersect. In fact, in many ways, Baylor's school calendar mimics the liturgical one, so I want to focus on the notion of Christian Time, and how living in community calls us, as Christians, to think about our time in the classroom in sacred ways.

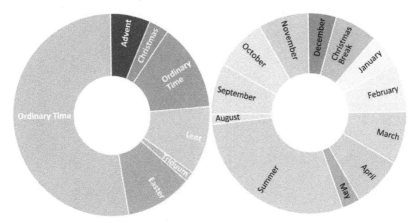

These two charts represent liturgical time (the Christian religious calendar) on the left, and the academic calendar on the right.[5] The liturgical calendar begins during the month of November on the First Sunday of Advent and consists of six different "seasons": Advent, Christmas, Lent, Triduum, Easter and what is known as "Ordinary Time." I highlight this, because as employees working at a Christian university, I feel it is important to note the similarities and overlaps of the liturgical calendar with the university one. The second pie chart depicts the school calendar, which in many ways overlaps Holy Time, or the Christian liturgical calendar. The similarities between the two depictions of time reflect even more the importance of our work as Christian scholars and educators. I feel called to live my life in "God-time," and the school calendar gives me just that opportunity. To illustrate this, I've overlapped the two calendars below, and in this chapter, I'm going to go through some highlights of the school year at Baylor, suggesting how we might think about our lives among students in the classroom in God's time while also noting how

5. All charts have been expertly designed and executed by Tyler Mowry and James Mowry and are used with permission.

these experiences interact with space. I argue that shifting the notion of how one constructs the syllabus to be mindful of the ways we might include sacred time can help students to view the world we live in as a holy one.

Academic Time

Moving In

Students arrive in mid-August and move on campus during the season known as Ordinary Time in the liturgical calendar, but this is, for them, no ordinary time. Students are preparing to share their lives in an academic setting and willing to open themselves up to educational and spiritual transformation, beginning a four-year journey with both educators and other students in the community. Every year, I help students on move-in day. I watch them say goodbye to one phase of their lives and prepare to start a new one. I had never been a part of move-in before I became a FIR, and it has helped me to grow as I see the bravery these students have, and the transformation they make from child to adult. Part of my job on these days is to meet and converse with the parents, listening to their worries and concerns as they leave their young adults in my stead, and in the hands of the university. Move-in day marks not only a shift in landscape, but a marked shift in time, as parents and children acknowledge their changing roles. In many ways, Baylor's transformational education starts here at move-in as students say good-bye to their old lives and prepare to embark on new ones.

Roommate Contracts

Then students start classes. In terms of space, their feet travel new paths; many get lost, go to the wrong building, and figure out a new landscape. They struggle with the choice they've made to come to Baylor, while going to classes, choosing a major, thinking about their future selves, and encountering disappointment and excitement. Time also makes itself felt: roommate contracts are usually due about three weeks after moving in. In the roommate contract, students will outline their expectations of each other and define their living community through written agreements signed by everyone in their suite. By this time, newness has worn off, homesickness has set in, classes are feeling routine, conflicts are emerging with others and the community that initially felt exciting begins to feel more oppressive than fun at times. The roommate contract deadline was helpful to me as a professor, since it's often when students would begin to feel *ennui* or look and act overwhelmed. While not all universities have the same schedule, this time period is about three or four weeks after the start of the semester—when the decision to participate in this four-year journey begins to seem routine and the reality sets in that the change is permanent. As I initiated conversations with my students based on these deadlines in the residential hall, my students in my classroom began to talk with me about their feelings regarding shifting expectations, worries, concerns, and disappointments. Time and space can interact in helpful ways. In my class at this time, I found that changing the class setting and holding class in a coffee shop opened space and time to acknowledge their feelings, which went far towards establishing a rapport with the students in the classroom. Students felt seen and heard and felt confident in confiding with me. But it also helped them see that their experiences were normal and okay. Roommate contracts mark community through mutual agreement—one might even say that roommates enter into a covenant with one another through these contracts, agreeing on shared expectations and assumptions to move through their educational journey with one another.

The Social Fit Period

After the roommate contracts are due, some students begin the rush season, while others start joining clubs, intramural sports teams, and academic leadership, etc. I label this time the Social Fit period, and it's mostly, in my mind, about students finding their place, or their people. Some students feel enormous pressure from parents to join or not join these sororities and fraternities, and I found this period ran parallel to students trying to establish independence without relying on their parents (which I've found can be quite difficult on the parents; I have received emails and phone calls from parents in this time, as they sometimes struggle with their children seeking independence). As a FIR, I've found it key in this period to validate the many feelings and frustrations of students as they search for their place. I think here of Jesus in the Gospels as the disciples seek him out and develop a community. The disciples all have very different personalities, yet they form a community; and so it is with the students. We are still in Ordinary Time here, but the Sacred Time is coming!

Thanksgiving and the Advent Season

The liturgical calendar marks the beginning of Sacred Time with the Advent season, which usually begins at the end of November. This corresponds with the students' return from Thanksgiving Break. The return from Thanksgiving Break is truly one of the more interesting periods for me as a FIR. Students return home excited to once again spend time with their families and sleep in their old room only to see how much they have changed—they feel both homesick and yet out of place. They have changed, yet their families often still treat them the same, and this is frustrating. Students miss their new school routines, their rooms at Baylor and their new friendship circles, and often return to Baylor eager and relieved to be back. When they return, though, students enter an intense last push and testing period for grades and wrapping up the semester. As a FIR, I observe lots of anxiety regarding school performance, and this period, which marks the start of the liturgical calendar, and the beginning of the Advent Season, is easily eclipsed by the school calendar, often to the detriment of the students, and spiritual reflection.

Incorporating Sacred Time into the First Semester

University faculty often place much of the course's grade weight in the last two weeks of the class, with final papers worth twenty percent of students' grades and/or final exams worth twenty to forty percent due at the end of the term. It is difficult to think about incorporating Sacred Time into these couple of weeks when most of us are used to thinking about the school calendar through a secular lens. As a FIR, it's easy to counterbalance this trend with intentional programming that re-centers students on the Advent season and the coming of Christ, but in the classroom, I think it's more difficult to do, and this is something that I think a university that wants to be intentionally Christian, could do better. What does this mean for spiritual growth? For us as mentors? Advent and Christmas promises Christ's faithfulness in the midst of everyday world concerns. How can we, as teachers, build this promise into our syllabi through an acknowledgement of Sacred Time? How do we bridge our vocation as educators with our calling as spiritual mentors? Some brief suggestions here (and this is by no means an exhaustive list), to address this disconnect are as follows:

- To more evenly distribute the weight of a course so that the bulk of student performance isn't placed in the last part of the class

- To incorporate Christian values and virtues as a part of the course (this could be done through relevant learning exercises such as journal reflections, contemplative practices, and/or community learning exercises, and can be done in a non-exclusive manner)

- To celebrate Advent with students, rather than to simply celebrate the end of the class

Incorporating sacred time through practice need not (and indeed, should not) alienate non-Christians, either, but reflect an acknowledgement of what is unique about studying at a Christian university—that sacred time informs secular time as Christians, and therefore should be incorporated into it. For example, I teach World Religions, and though I am a practicing Christian, I deeply value integrating practices such as Tai Qi, yoga, and meditation into my course structure, using those practices as ways to demonstrate how we can incorporate the sacred into our everyday routines. By constructing the course syllabus with a thoughtful reflection on how one views and interacts with the world, we can broaden our spiritual practices and internalize learning. If one is exhausted and resentful about an exam and does not see it as an interesting interactive and reflective exercise through which to grow and expand one's learning, then the exam doesn't do much beyond measuring one's ability to ingest large quantities of information and effectively regurgitate it. Constructing a syllabus in light of this can have lasting and meaningful repercussions for both learning and the way we approach learning. In short, learning is a holy task, and could be approached as such. The birth of Christ is an opportunity to view the world through different eyes and through a promise of redemption from God. In the same way, syllabi that are sensitive to the promises learning can hold for students can incorporate the hope that educational transformation brings, rather than simply assessing learning as an evaluative tool.

Spring Term

While university faculty and staff spend the Christmas season with their families, most students, of course, go home for Christmas, but they return early in January, ready for the spring, the Lenten season, and the Easter holiday (or Triduum). Last year as a FIR, I observed that generally, students returned for the spring semester with confidence, ownership, and a sense of belonging, ready to rejoin their Baylor community and eager to be back. I believe this is also the fruit of the liturgical calendar as we move through Sacred Time, as students become confident in their new lives as young adults and Baylor students. But there are a few specific highlights of the spring term that I want to discuss. Not long after students return to campus, in January, those who have been rushing the Greek system receive an invitation to join a particular sorority or fraternity and are sent gift baskets proclaiming their acceptance. This is an exciting time for some students who have found new friends and a community, while a few others either do not choose to join the Greek system or may realize they have not been invited to join, and that they need to look elsewhere for their community. Returning from home where they no longer belong in the same way they did before, some students return to realize that the community they had sought is not interested in having them as members. This can be a difficult transition back to school after a holiday in which old friends have changed, parents have somewhat adjusted to their students' absences, and students now seem to not fit in two places (home and school), rather than just one.

Reflection and Vocation

Additionally, over the holidays, students received their first term grades, and some realized that their self-selected majors were, in fact, not a good fit. I believe this is where the Lenten model of solemn reflection and the promise of resurrection at Easter can serve as a hope for students who feel lost in their second term while their colleagues seem to have it all figured out. I think it is important for us as professors to invite students to reflect why they have chosen particular majors, and to contemplate the notion of calling. For me, calling involves listening: God calls, and we must hear him in order to respond. I've found it particularly helpful as both a FIR and instructor to deconstruct the notion of "vocation" or "career" for students so that they don't feel compelled to "have it all figured out" by the second semester of their first year. I have found that many American Christians are quite good at prayer, but not at listening, or waiting. I like to practice contemplative exercises in my class (usually meditation), introducing it as one way in which we can learn to listen, and to wait. My students find the concept of listening to God discomfiting, and usually come to my class with little practice in listening or waiting. While I have the advantage of teaching a religion class, I think any exercises that stress the value of listening to others, and to waiting, rather than guiding the discourse can be helpful practices for students as they learn to listen not only to God's voice, but to the quiet hunger of their souls. Getting rid of the many distractions of daily life is a valuable task for students—and not one to assume they already know how to do.

Syllabi Honoring the Sabbath

As a FIR and a professor, I try to encourage students through contemplative practices built into my syllabus, or reflection questions in journal assignments that will encourage students to think beyond their own expectations. It is important to me to challenge traditional norms of success that are either unrealistic or socially constructed. We can construct the syllabus to consider God's time and the liturgical calendar. Including assignments and practices that encourage spiritual growth and incorporating concepts like the sabbath and God's command that we rest are all, for me, an important part of teaching in the classroom. So, for example, in order to encourage students to honor the sabbath, we might think about constructing syllabi in such a way as to honor the need for rest. I like to make sure that calendar breaks serve as time for family and not as a time utilized for catching up on work. It's a lot harder than it sounds, and I'm not always successful, but I think letting students know how I feel about God's time is important. One of my favorite illustrations to explain the importance of the sabbath is through musical rests. Musical rests function as the punctuation of good music—like a period or a comma—and help shape the music and give it definition. The sabbath needs to do this for us, in our lives. Practically, this means intentionally constructing a syllabus that honors the sabbath and these breaks. Offering quizzes midweek, rather than directly after a weekend or a holiday, or having due dates that are not largely dependent on the last couple weeks of class are a few ways to logistically do this. And while other classes may not operate with a similar mindset, it will offer students a reprieve that is intentional, thoughtful, and opens up reflective discussion.

In my World Religions class, for example, when we discuss Buddhism, I have the students try a variety of meditation practices; I encourage them to *hear* and to make time to be still so they can listen. When we discuss Hinduism, we do a short yoga practice every class. When we study Daoism, we practice Tai Qi, while discussing the importance of maintaining balance. I also encourage students to create projects that speak to their passions and possibly their vocations—rather than simply doing papers. I give students the choice over what type of grade assessment they would like to partake in over the term—a paper, or a project—and I let students vote over the exam date and type. This gives students ownership over their learning, while investing them into their outcomes. Over the years, I've had students build meditation huts in a local park, write and perform a rock song duet about a Shinto wedding, paint a Daoist landscape watercolor, create a board game that involved various stages of enlightenment and Buddhist bardos, film a half-hour video on the beef industry in Argentina, cook and serve empanadas in class, and create short stories set in the time period of my history class. Seeing the students' passions come alive is invigorating and exciting and helps students connect their learning to their real-world interests. They are also much more interesting to grade.

The Cycle of Sacred Time and the Return to Ordinary

Spring is a time of renewal, both educational and spiritual, while also serving as a time of thinking about the future. Situating learning in sacred time and thinking about the ways the resurrection can inform our Christian vocation of teaching are important parts of the classroom for me. The resurrection offers us a promise of eternal renewal, in which God's promise to us is made manifest, similar to the ways in which education offers a promise to transform our lives and give us new beginnings. The end of the spring term roughly coincides with the end of Sacred Time, and the shift back to Ordinary Time, as students prepare to move back home for the summer, embark on summer travels and adventures, or graduate and enter the workforce. Time and community both shift and change with the end of the school year, and summer becomes characterized by another kind of time entirely. The return of summer and Ordinary Time pull us out of the deep reflective work of the liturgical calendar. Summer, or Ordinary Time, seems to have few expectations and offers a reprieve from work, sacred or educational, and the cycle begins again. Being a FIR has helped me to think about education from the perspective of spiritual practice and building community, shifting my views of both sacred space and time and how I interact with them to create transformational education.

REFERENCES

Bonhoeffer, Dietrich. *Life Together and Prayerbook of the Bible*. Dietrich Bonhoeffer Works 5. Edited by Geffrey B. Kelly. Translated by James H. Burtness and Daniel W. Bloesch. Minneapolis: Fortress, 1996.

Lewis, C. S. *Collected Letters Volume Three: Narnia, Cambridge and Joy 1950–1963*. Edited by Walter Hooper. San Francisco: HarperCollins, 2009.

13

Embracing Diversity through
Cultural Humility

Differences and Inclusion

A COLLEAGUE ONCE SAID to me, "When I go into my classroom, I don't
see color. I see everyone the same." I pondered a moment before responding. Yes, I thought, we were taught to treat each other the same without
regard to color, race, ethnicity, and so on. It was the Christian thing to
do, after all. Differences were to be tolerated with a benevolent spirit. To
be color blind was the right thing to do. Difference was not the norm,
mainstream, or the default.[1]

But differences are important. There are individual differences,
learning preferences, personality, and life experiences. Then there are
group differences, class, ethnicity, faith, gender, etc.[2] Yet, we think that if
we treat everyone the same, then we are being equal. In truth, sameness
is not fairness. There is the story of three boys trying to look over the
fence to see a baseball game. The first boy was tall enough to look over
the fence without any trouble. The second boy could almost see over the
fence but needed a small box to stand on. Finally, the third boy, who also
happened to be the shortest, found a large box, stood on it, and happily

1. Andrews, "Rejecting Culture-Blindness."
2. American Association of Colleges and Universities, "Vision for Equity."

saw the game. The fence remained the same height, but the boxes were what made the difference for the boys reaching their objective. Equality would have been for the boys to stand behind the fence regardless if they could see or not, no special treatment. Equity occurred when boxes of different sizes were used to fit the needs of the young boys, allowing them to see over the fence. What the boys needed was equity, not equality. I know it sounds suspiciously similar, but equity is meeting students where they are.

We tend to throw the word "diversity" around in terms of training, professional development, strategic planning, campus climate surveys, etc. The term *diversity* is simply naming difference—numbers, statistics, indicating differences in a specific space or group. In our classroom, diversity implies that our students vary in color, backgrounds, gender, cultures, and abilities. But that is just the beginning of the process of inclusion, appreciation, and celebration of difference. Diversity itself doesn't denote welcoming, engagement, understanding, or connectedness. It simply is difference. When we refer to diversity at Baylor, we refer to our minority students making up 38% of student body. They simply are different. So now what?

If one *is* to recognize the differences in their classroom, that would mean that indeed, you do see color, shapes, sizes, gender, abilities, etc. To dismiss these attributes is to dismiss your students' individuality, their unique ideas, styles, and cultural nuances. When we dismiss our students' differences, we use mainstream methods of teaching rather than learning from our students and finding innovative ways to teach. For instance, when we rely on traditional lectures, we miss the opportunity to develop relationships with our young scholars. Most of us teach the way we learned. At times it may be described as the "shotgun" approach. We will fling our information across the classroom and hopefully most of our students will "catch it."

The tradition of teaching in U.S. higher education began with homogenous classrooms, specifically white males. Eventually, women and minorities were allowed into the academy, filling our classrooms with diverse perspectives, experiences, questions, and challenges. In the traditional manner, professors were experts in their disciplines and were to "profess" their knowledge and wisdom to their students. Classrooms were centered on the content rather than the learner.

Today, much has changed. Professors are not only expected to bring their knowledge and research from their specific disciplines, but also to understand the students they teach. Students today bring with them diverse perspectives of thought, values, faith, and much more. We need to understand how students learn and how culture influences the teaching and learning process. Inclusion is the active, intentional, and ongoing *engagement with diversity*. For education, this happens in the classroom, in the curriculum, in the co-curriculum, and in communities (intellectual, social, cultural, geographical) with which individuals might connect, in ways that increase awareness, content knowledge, cognitive sophistication, and empathic understanding of the complex ways individuals interact within systems and institutions.[3]

When Baylor faculty, staff, and students participated in our first ever campus climate survey several years ago, the most common concern at Baylor was the lack of diversity among faculty. Faculty readily noted that there were few faculty of color and/or women in their departments. Students repeatedly through surveys and focus groups expressed their desire to have faculty that reflected the student body.

Faculty of color enhance not only the success of students of color, but their White counterparts as well. We know that if students can see themselves reflected in their professors, they are more apt to succeed academically. Student engagement and retention increase. Students can interact with professors with diverse perspectives, teaching styles, research interests, and life experiences. White students have reported that having a faculty of color better prepared them for the "real world." Diverse classrooms are essential as well, as they broaden the scope of classroom discussions and strengthen the quality of learning.

As institutions seek to improve all students' success, the inclusion of people with diverse backgrounds, ideas, and methods of teaching and learning is an educational imperative. Such inclusion simultaneously (1) creates more equitable opportunities for students from marginalized groups to participate in higher education, and (2) promotes the kinds of outcomes for all students that employers and society need, such as complex thinking skills, the ability to work across difference, increased civic participation, and decreased prejudice.[4]

Faculty members often recognize that inclusion is key to learning. Even students who have matriculated into universities and colleges with the necessary qualifications have felt excluded from the full college

3. American Association of Colleges and Universities, "Vision for Equity."
4. American Association of Colleges and Universities, "Vision for Equity."

experience.[5] To create an inclusive learning environment throughout the academy, all faculty members should consider how they are incorporating diversity into their courses and how they can be more inclusive in their teaching.

Cultural Humility

Cultural competence is not attained in a workshop or seminar, or even by reading a book. It takes time and the right approach. That is where *cultural humility* factors in. Cultural humility is a humble and respectful attitude toward individuals of other cultures that pushes one to challenge their own cultural biases, realize they cannot possibly know everything about other cultures, and approach learning about other cultures as a lifelong goal and process.

Cultural humility was established due to the limitations of cultural competence. Some professionals, like social workers, medical professionals, or educators, believed themselves to be culturally competent after learning some generalizations of a particular culture. Cultural humility encourages an active participation in order to learn about a student's personal, cultural experiences. In the pursuit of cultural humility in the context of higher education, the following concepts can be crucial:

- *Cultural Self-Awareness.* Culture—the sum total of an individual's experiences, knowledge, skills, beliefs, values, and interests—shapes educators' sense of who they are and where they fit in their family, school, and community.

- *Value of Diversity.* Educators should accept and respect differences—different cultural backgrounds and customs, different ways of communicating, and different traditions and values.

- *Dynamics of Difference.* Educators must know what can go wrong in cross-cultural communication and how to respond to these situations.

- *Knowledge of Students' Culture.* Educators must have some base knowledge of their students' culture so that student behaviors can be understood in their proper cultural context.

---

5. Hurtado et al., *Enacting Diverse Learning Environments*, 25–26.

- *Institutionalization of Cultural Knowledge and Adaptation to Diversity.* Culturally competent educators, and the institutions they work in, can take a step further by institutionalizing cultural knowledge so they can adapt to diversity and better serve diverse populations.

Aspects of Inclusion in Teaching

Incorporating and engaging diversity in one's teaching takes time and depends on the specifics of the situation (who is teaching which students, and in what context). It requires intentionality in reading assignments, discussion, examples, experiential learning, and more. Faculty require training, mentoring, and support from their chairs, deans, and provost to be successful in creating an inclusive classroom.

Purposes and Goals

A course's purposes or goals represent its intended outcomes. With inclusive goals, the aim is for students to gain the knowledge, attitudes, and skills necessary for participation in a diverse society. With less inclusive goals, the aim is for students to gain knowledge, skills, and attitudes sanctioned by the mainstream, with little inclusion of diverse perspectives.

Content

Course content deals primarily with the subject matter to be covered but manifests also in the manner in which it is presented and the assignments that reinforce learning. In courses that include some diversity, the content includes subjects that are ignored in traditional courses or alternative perspectives on traditional subjects. In more inclusive courses, the content reflects the experiences of multiple cultural groups from their own as well as other perspectives.

Foundations and Perspectives

The background characteristics of students and faculty affect their understandings of events (e.g., Columbus's voyages), issues (e.g., domestic violence), and concepts (e.g., justice). A course that includes diverse foundations or perspectives draws on theories that help explain how human differences influence our understanding of a course topic.[6] As a course's foundations become more inclusive, the number of perspectives and depth of understanding increases, and the foundations and perspectives themselves generally become a part of the course's content.[7]

Learners

At the non-inclusive end of the spectrum, student characteristics (e.g., race, gender, class, skill level, and developmental needs) are not taken into account. At the inclusive end, these characteristics are assessed and explored so that other course elements can be designed and adjusted to fit students' learning needs.[8]

Instructor(s)

In more inclusive classrooms, the individuals charged with planning and facilitating a course investigate their own identities, biases, and values and how these may influence the way they operate in the classroom. Inclusive instructors also learn about identities, biases, and values that are different from their own so that the course can rely on multiple perspectives.

Pedagogy

In addition to classroom processes and teaching methods, pedagogy includes the theories and scholarship (e.g., theories of student development and learning) that inform these processes and methods. More inclusive pedagogies account for the fact that not all students are the same, but rather have varied learning needs. At its most inclusive, pedagogy will demonstrate a focus on the learning of diverse students through the interplay of theory and instructional process at a highly developed level.

6. Banks, "Improving Race Relations in Schools," 607–14.

7. Bell and Griffin, "Designing Social Justice Education Courses," 44–58.

8. Bell and Griffin, "Designing Social Justice Education Courses," 44–58; Schoem et al., *Multicultural Teaching*.

Classroom Environment

The classroom environment is the space where a course takes place as well as the interactions that occur within that space. It consists of the values, norms, ethos, and experiences of a course. When highly inclusive, the environment should be empowering,[9] reflective of the diverse backgrounds of students and instructors,[10] and structured to support student learning.[11]

Assessment and Evaluation

Instructors should use a variety of methods, both formal and informal, to assess student characteristics and learning and should also be aware of potential biases in their techniques.[12] More inclusive evaluation methods are more sensitive to the various backgrounds of students and the diverse ways students can demonstrate understanding.

Adjustment

In any course, instructors may need to change their plans as assessments reveal new information about students, as student desires or frustrations assert themselves, as incidents occur in class, or as activities require more time than allotted. An instructor who capitalizes on new information can adjust other elements of a course to enhance student learning.[13] Inclusive adjustments are sensitive to students' diverse learning needs and aligned with course goals. Adjustments made despite student needs (e.g., to cover a predetermined amount of material) are non-inclusive.

This framework can be applied in a variety of areas, including course design and assessment. In the area of course design, for example, the framework encourages instructors to question and make decisions about the inclusivity of each element when designing or making adjustments to

---

9. Banks, "Improving Race Relations in Schools," 607–14.

10. Schoem et al., *Multicultural Teaching*.

11. Bell and Griffin, "Designing Social Justice Education Courses," 44–58.

12. Banks, "Improving Race Relations in Schools," 607–14; Lattuca and Stark, *Shaping College Curriculum*.

13. Bell and Griffin, "Designing Social Justice Education Courses," 44–58; Lattuca and Stark, *Shaping College Curriculum*.

a course. The framework allows for flexibility in which elements a faculty member chooses to address, and in which order (as decisions about one element will affect decisions about the others).

At the end of the day, we are all responsible for our own learning. It is upon us to seek information, interact with those who are different than us, to try to understand the *other*, and to engage in and appreciate knowledge through cultural humility. How do you become culturally engaged through cultural humility?

1. Understand it is a life-long journey.

2. Attend workshops and conferences in this area and in your discipline.

3. Collaborate with your colleagues.

4. Ask your chair, dean, provost for support.

5. Make use of campus resources.[14]

REFERENCES

American Association of Colleges and Universities. *A Vision for Equity: Results from AAC&U's Project "Committing to Equity and Inclusive Excellence: Campus-Based Strategies for Student Success."* Washington, DC: 2018.

Andrews, Dorinda Carter, "Rejecting Culture-Blindness: Toward Cultural Competence in STEM Undergraduate Teaching." Presentation, Michigan State University, November 6, 2014. https://www.aacu.org/sites/default/files/files/tides/Cultural%20Competence%20in%20Undergraduate%20STEM%20Teaching%20for%20AACU.pdf.

Banks, James A. "Improving Race Relations in Schools: From Theory and Research to Practice." *Journal of Social Issues* 62.3 (2006) 607–14.

Bell, Lee Anne, and Pat Griffin. "Designing Social Justice Education Courses." In *Teaching for Diversity and Social Justice: A Sourcebook*, edited by Mauianne Adams, Lee Anne Bell, and Pat Griffin, 44–58. New York: Routledge, 1997.

Hurtado, Sylvia, Jeffrey Milem, Alma Clayton-Pedersen, and Walter Allen. *Enacting Diverse Learning Environments: Improving the Climate for Racial/Ethnic Diversity in Higher Education*. San Francisco: Jossey-Bass, 1997.

Lattuca, Lisa R., and Joan S. Stark. *Shaping the College Curriculum: Academic Plans in Context*. San Francisco: Jossey-Bass, 2009.

Schoem, David., Linda Frankel, Ximena Zúñiga, and Edith A. Lewis, eds. *Multicultural Teaching in the University*. Westport, CT: Praeger, 1993.

14. For instance, Baylor's diversity website: https://www.baylor.edu/diversity. Baylor is also an institutional member of the National Center for Faculty Development and Diversity, https://www.facultydiversity.org.

14

Of Fireflies, Skeletons, and the Abbot's Pew

Ineffable Distinctives within the Teaching Tradition at Baylor

Elizabeth Vardaman

THIS IS A PERSONAL journey—musing on what I would argue has been and is the soul of teaching both as I experienced it in my student days in the early 1960s and as I have seen it lived out during my tenure as a faculty member these past forty years.

Fireflies

I encountered a master teacher in every sense of the word (before Baylor began to identify and honor such skills through formal titles). Professor Elizabeth Smith (later Githens) taught modern poetry in the English Department, commanded a student's attention because modern poetry was serious, and expected the class to be focused on the text, her explication of it, and the classroom discussion. (Context: I was not a sophisticated learner, and I did not have words for what I was seeking, but I am certain I understood what awe was—and that was a felt presence in Professor Smith's classroom.) One day was definitive for me. Professor Smith began to read a poem by Gerard Manley Hopkins, "The Windhover." Under her masterful teaching, I was mesmerized and somehow I lost myself in the hour, in the falcon, flying and then crumpling to earth only to turn into something even more amazing, a phoenix that would rise from embers.[1] We discussed the poem within the context first of Hopkins' life as a priest and poet and then in terms that allowed the sonnet to be seen solely as a text that stands alone—its sprung rhythms, accent marks, line breaks, and each carefully chosen word on the page. We pondered the subtitle Hopkins had given the poem, "To Christ Our Lord."

I did not know exactly what had taken place. But looking back on that hour throughout my life, I know I changed that day from one kind of person into another. Perhaps it was the professor's magnetic reading, the beauty, the symbols, that artist's craft—for Hopkins indeed had made that falcon fly and then break into fire as it buckled to earth. Until Professor Smith cast a spell on me, I had had no words with which to tell my life or my inner sanctums. But because of her excellence in teaching, the modern poets became my voice. They had found the words and shared them. They could and did speak for me. I memorized "The Windhover" and determined I would commit to memory as many more of the poems in that text as I could. And I did. *A College Book of Modern Verse* remains to this day the dearest book I own.

In later years, I have often turned to the image of "fireflies" to describe the gasp of recognition a student might feel as he or she encounters wonder and mystery and kinship within an academic experience. But in truth, the first memory I have of such a seismic shift in my worldview was produced by an incandescent falcon. The point, of course, could be served by the metaphor of firefly or falcon, by an astonishing scientific curiosity, by a realization that an author such as Richard Brookhiser has just revealed the soul of George Washington to you through words on a page in a thrilling biography, or any number of other encounters that connect a student with bodies of knowledge that lead to deep questions, to truths, and to illumination. Whatever the medium, that pulsing encounter with ideas and texts and questions that causes a student to hear new voices in herself, to begin new conversations with himself, or to experience the beauty in an idea or an art-form that delights the soul—I believe such things happen here at Baylor in ways that are not necessarily replicated at many universities.

1. Hopkins, "Windhover," 30.

Indeed, I would argue that our calling into the teaching profession, whatever our expertise or subject, and specifically into a life of offering up a liberal arts education, is exactly what Baylor has always seen as its signature voltage. I would also want to argue that here, creating those carefully planned moments when lights seem almost magically to ignite and students are stunned at the conversation with themselves that a teacher has provoked or inspired—in my view these can well be regarded as sacred acts, ways in which we, as professors, do our best to live out our faith commitment to and in Christ.

Professors here, having studied deeply the texts, theorems, principles of uncertainty, opposing positions that are grounded in intellectual and philosophical thought, feel compelled to present those materials thoughtfully, not didactically. I would hope fewer of our professors than at many institutions locate their value most fully within their own egos or use their classrooms as platforms for evangelizing their own points of view. Rather they are raising questions and showing contrary positions in such a way that students are engaged and invited to examine evidence. Such critical thinking leads to new questions and more investigation of the materials, whether those be in literature, history, political science, or any other discipline. These kinds of encounters may also lead students to come to our offices to ask further questions. Mentoring, likewise, has always been a point of pride at this institution.

Our responsibility is to keep the focus on the materials and on the students so that they can see and experience what is, as it were, glowing in the dark of their own minds and on the printed page. And, as a professor, I have to say that some of the most privileged moments I have had with students have been those when the student's face kind of morphs into something new and you realize he or she may have just experienced a "glimmering" (to use Seamus Heaney's term). It is an exchange between the self and reality, in Christopher Wiman's phrasing;[2] or in our more prosaic wording, a light or recognition begins to shine in a student's eyes.

We know many of our students are asking the question of themselves that Andrew Delbanco articulates in his important book, *College: What It Was, Is and Should Be*. "[F]iguring out what's worth wanting," Delbanco says, is central to the work of a student in college.[3] He adds from a student manuscript he found (written in 1850): "Oh that the Lord

2. Wiman, *My Bright Abyss*, 93.
3. Delbanco, *College*, 14.

would show me how to think and how to choose." Then he expounds upon that thought:

> That sentence, poised somewhere between a wish and a plea, sounds archaic today . . . And yet I have never encountered a better formulation . . . of what a college should strive to be: an aid to reflection, a place and process whereby young people take stock of their talents and passions and begin to sort out their lives in a way that is true to themselves and responsible to others.[4]

We are sometimes privileged to be in the room or at least tangential to their lives when students come to realize: "This, yes, is fascinating. I must have the skills to delve further into this issue, this landscape, this field of dreams."[5]

At Baylor, we believe it is an honor and an obligation to foster students' encounters with texts and theorems, with things seen and unseen, and with themselves. We want our sojourners to know and experience the best and most noble things. We want them to have the sciences, and the arts and the social sciences; we hope they will make connections across these vast rivers of knowledge. We pray they will think and read and live deeply . . . and feel the fires going off in their minds as they find ways and community through which to secure (must have, will have) insights or in some way to process every jolt.

---

4. Delbanco, *College*, 15–16.

5. Examples: I will treasure always the day a student called me from Russia to say, "This is the place. This is the thing I am supposed to be doing." For another, it was realizing that she does not want to be a doctor, even though there are compelling reasons to be one. For another, it was recognizing that he did not want to be an accountant who wears a suit every day, but an accountant who runs a fitness center and can wear shorts every day. For another, it was about figuring out a way to love mathematics but also love a way to put complex science to work to address social issues. She became fascinated with analyzing cell-phone data to see how contagion or epidemics move or solar power works. For another, it was bidding for a public health degree because a brother was turned down for health care when they were children, and this student never wants anyone who comes to him to be turned down for health care again. I was privileged to watch a student come to terms recently with a tension that was going on within her about whether she wanted to be a public health professional focused on work in the US or a public health nurse serving in Latin America. And I am still watching one who is interested in international development and agriculture but also has an abiding love for the French language, and for Africa, and for theatre. Will he become a professor? A farmer? An ambassador? A teacher in Rwanda? At Baylor? Or all of the above!

As faculty, we take seriously that quest and do our best to help students note where the light is pulsing and aligning their skills, interests, aptitudes, values—and joys. We have always been famous for that. We always will be. It is a covenant we renew in the life of this university each day.

That is to say, in my view, primarily and forever, Baylor is an undergraduate institution that values its students' search to find themselves and the questions and texts that become as important as air. Faculty here watch for these things and know it is part of our responsibility to help students notice and claim insights that can seem mysterious or fleeting but that also (as Seamus Heaney has so wonderfully expressed) "catch the heart off guard and blow it open."[6]

Skeletons

As marvelous as it would be to link our responsibility as professors almost solely with the incandescent and often introspective self that is essential to a student's college life, a quick glance at the morning news argues that a university student must also confront the realities that historically have culminated in injustice, sorrow, crime, tragedy, and heartbreak. We know in our bones that error is inextricably bound up with the pursuit of truth and that perseverance is a quality our students must obtain. Richard Wilbur sets a scene that exemplifies the dualities we all face in life in his poem "Love Calls Us to the Things of This World." His speaker awakens early in the morning and sees, just beyond his window, freshly washed clothes and bedsheets wafting in a breeze. After enumerating the wonders of these fresh things, flying like angels, he realizes he cannot lie there all day: "The soul shrinks / From all that it is about to remember,/ From the punctual rape of every blessed day." And the waking man cries out his lament for a world eternally filled with clean laundry! Nevertheless, he knows reality is more complicated than that and will require him to pay attention, every hour of every day. So he really must climb out of bed and get ready to go to work.[7] Likewise, Gilbert and Sullivan's Buttercup abjures in *H.M.S. Pinafore* that we all recall, "Things are seldom what they seem. / Skim milk masquerades as cream." So as professor-teachers

6. Heaney, "Postscript," 111.

7. Wilbur, "Love Calls Us to the Things of This World," 307.

at Baylor we are charged with being real and presenting a world that, warts and all, is standing in the need of prayer.

When I was in graduate school, I read a book by Erik Erikson on the psychological development of adolescents. It was pretty dull stuff in my view and had no poetry in it whatsoever. But there was a statement in the preface that has haunted me ever since. Erikson provides an anecdote about George Bernard Shaw's life, and indeed Shaw uses this metaphor in his 1930 novel *Immaturity*. Shaw's point was (and I am paraphrasing here), that almost all families have skeletons in their closets, as he would concede were in his own, but he had found a way "to make the skeletons dance." Clearly whatever challenges or dark times had confronted Mr. Shaw, he was able not only to overcome but transform them, ultimately contributing greatly to the world through his plays (*Pygmalion*, for example). No one could argue that Shaw had not found value in facing some difficulties from his past and then spinning that straw into gold. His story became deeply meaningful for me, possibly winning the day over the whole thesis project itself.

So when my students lament having gone down the wrong path or spun out of control in this way or that for this reason or that, I do my best to acknowledge their pain—because I know it is real. Then at some point, I may concur that they had made serious mistakes, become lazy or confused, violated policy, or just done something stupid. Many professors at Baylor stand ready to assure those in our charge they are much more awesome than they think they are. Many faculty members show grace and extend mercy; we do what we can to help students regain direction and move forward on the path to academic redemption, if needed.

More than a few times I have been reminded of another professor here at Baylor who was working with me to help a scholarship applicant refine his prose for an essay for the Rhodes Scholarship. The applicant had made some fairly egregious grammatical mistakes as we chatted, and my colleague and I possibly both winced over his use of objective pronouns where subjective ones should go. When we corrected this remarkable young person's grammar, we inadvertently embarrassed him. I was afraid the student was going to walk out on our session or perhaps the whole scholarship process. My colleague recognized the situation and said, "Okay. We are going to learn noun/pronoun usage rules. They are not impossible. We are sorry we knocked you down. We didn't mean to embarrass you. But you got knocked down in football, too. So, get up. We have work to do." And the student did. He finished strong, even though he did not ultimately prevail in the Rhodes competition. I feel certain our student felt the love and support we and others were offering him throughout the process. I am also fairly sure he never used the grammatical construct again that had plagued him before. "Me and Sammy," I suspect, never did anything together, ever again.

We hope our students come to terms with the world while they are here. There are politics, and troubles, and Title IX. There are the "ends of things." And there is value in understanding that doors open and close. Some of this awareness comes with age. But some is purposefully integrated into our belief as an educational institution—leaning on the Everlasting Arms—that we can become beacons of grace, burying some things that need to be buried and where possible finding ways to change dry bones to light.

So, in my view, a teacher at Baylor is charged not only with helping students "find themselves" but also with encouraging students to discern what issues they care about so deeply and what beliefs are so much larger than themselves that they can lose themselves into those issues, agencies, visions. I came to those "twin ontological needs" via Ernest Becker's *Denial of Death*, in which Becker explains that on the one hand we are "impelled by a powerful desire to identify with the cosmic process, to merge [ourselves] with the rest of nature. On the other hand [we] want to be unique, to stand out as something different and apart."[8]

For some of us, teaching meets Becker's criteria. It is larger than ourselves, reaching toward the transcendent. But of course we also want to stand out, to be individuals, too. And we are eager to see both of those ontological motives realized in our students. We hope college will give them a sense of what reality is and what they can contribute to it. In order to do that, we want (among many other things) for our students to be able to discern when something is dead or—also very important to critical thinking skills—when someone is talking "rot" to them.[9]

So Baylor should also be a place where our graduates have not only earned degrees but have also left behind naiveté. We want them to have contemplated with Hamlet (whose soliloquy is usually performed

---

8. Becker, *Denial of Death*, 151–52.

9. Delbanco, *College*, 29. Here he quotes an Oxford professor from one hundred years ago, John Alexander Smith, to drive home this point, but he also adds, "Americans tend to prefer a two-syllable synonym, bullshit, for the one-syllable Anglicism, rot—and so we might say that the most important thing one can acquire in college is a well-functioning bullshit meter. It's a technology that will never become obsolete."

interacting with a skull) the decision "to be or not to be," and to have chosen "Life and that abundantly!" We hope they will have become burdened to make a difference in their societies. To help instill that ballast of soul and sense of responsibility, our faculty provide structure and guide those in their charge toward communication skills, a desire to be of service as citizens, humility, critical thinking, and a grasp of the tenets of Christianity. Our faculty know the stories of the heroes in their intellectual fields and they tell stories of those who have faced war, conspiratorial forces, death and dismay and have found ways to keep on keeping on. Their stories are legendary and inspirational.[10]

This is the reality. Good people may die young or long before they have finished being lights in the darkness for us. People who seem to be made of stuff and nonsense may live forever, or at least they are not accident prone. We must have the courage to live the questions and as faculty embody a kind of humility that affirms a degree of uncertainty as a way of life. For we are all standing in the need of prayer, and often we and/or others must carefully rethink our stance on issues. As Oliver Cromwell

---

10. Dr. James Vardaman gave this portrait in words of Dr. George Truett, pastor of First Baptist Church in Dallas, during a graduation ceremony at Truett Seminary, August 2017. He says, "A devastating tragedy occurred early in Dr. Truett's ministry at the First Baptist Church of Dallas. He was a member of a group from his church that had formed a hunting party and they were climbing through a barbed-wire fence when, as Dr. Truett made his passage, his weapon discharged. The fatal shot struck his friend, Bob Welsh, who was then Chief of Police in Dallas. As a result, Welch died. Truett was shattered. He descended into the Valley of the Shadow of Death. The Germans have a word for what Truett now suffered: *Anfechtung*. It is a powerful designation—indeed it is often used to describe Martin Luther's horror during his quest for but inability to find assurances of salvation while a monk in Wittenberg. He, too, like Truett, was utterly wretched, lost, filled with despair, anguish, and desolation. I'm not sure the English language has an equivalent term to describe his stark condition. Truett slowly and desperately emerged from this miasma. He resumed his duties, but his life would never be the same. Henceforth, he established almost clinical self-control—rather like his namesake, George Washington, who was sober, steady and calm, regardless of all obstacles. Truett was careful never to say or do anything that could possibly lead to a repetition of such heart-rending sadness and loss. Love became his trademark. If one met him, one could almost feel his capacity for love. However, along with such love, his heart contained a core of steel. There was no gushing or back-slapping, no flippant conversation, no excess verbiage. One would never hear the rampant, flame-thrower discourse that has become commonplace from pulpits and podiums today. Indeed, I cannot recall Dr. Truett ever laughing or even smiling. Life had become a very serious issue for him. To sum him up: love of his God and his fellow-struggling mankind was his vision and commitment in this dark and challenging world. He did his duty through unstinting care and concern every day he lived."

said in a letter to the general assembly of the Church of Scotland in 1650 (and which my husband frequently quoted to his classes), "Is it therefore infallibly agreeable to the Word of God all that you say? I beseech thee in the bowels of Christ, consider you may be mistaken." So students—and indeed all of us—get down and then, with the help of God's legions and angels, we get up again. The Baylor community does not, of course, agree on a variety of important issues. But as teachers, we encourage dialogue, introspection, scholarly research, and the use of many critical tools as we walk together, pondering and often disagreeing on wide-ranging, complex issues great and small. This takes courage, discipline, and prayerful contemplation and reflection throughout our sojourn as professors here. The standard for who we are and whose we are is set high indeed.

And our students—both in their search for themselves and for their place to serve in the world—have a tremendous impact on all of us who work here. They renew us, and we stand amazed in their presence. They are the future. Some of them know it. And Baylor continues to draw these searching, inspiring students to our sphere and then sends them out into a real world with ideals intact, but also with sobered experiences with loss and sadness and many unanswered, unresolved questions. Thanks be to God.

The Abbot's Pew

Of course, Baylor is not a church. But we identify through all that we do with being as faithful to God's messenger and exemplar, Christ, as we can be. "For Christ plays in ten thousand places/ Lovely in limbs, and lovely in eyes not his/ To the Father through the features of men's faces."[11]

In the late 1970s, throughout the 80s and into the 90s, my husband directed a summer Baylor in the British Isles program in London. And where we lived did feel quite a lot like a church because our program was housed at Westminster School, inside the Westminster Abbey compound. We were privileged to hear the Westminster Choir Boys practice daily as we stepped over ancient tombs and through hallowed archways to go to our meals. We also listened to Big Ben bong the hours night and day and stood in awe of the Victoria Tower on Parliament that was lit each night over the roofs and chimney pots of our "home." Jim and I became friends during those years, incredibly, with The Very Reverend

---

11. Hopkins, "As kingfishers catch fire," 51.

Michael Mayne (served 1986–1995) and his wife, Alison. One night after we had enjoyed supper with them in their kitchen, Dean Mayne led us up a stairway to a door on the second floor of their home. He stopped and smiled at us, then opened the heavy wooden door. We walked into one of the spaces above Westminster Abbey that very few people know about—the Abbot's Pew. This space is only accessible through the private living quarters of the Dean of the Abbey or from the Jerusalem Chamber, but it is also public to a degree in that, if you are down below, touring the Abbey and standing by the Tomb of the Unknown Warrior, you can look up and see its exterior, a little like a balcony or box seats in a theatre just to your right and high above. It was built in the early sixteenth century. From there, the Dean may survey the Abbey at any hour.

Dean Mayne had words of Boethius[12] inscribed around the walls of this holy space (in Helen Waddell's translation):

> To see Thee is the end and the beginning,
> Thou carriest me and thou dost go before,
> Thou art the journey and the journey's end.[13]

Like the Abbot's Pew, Baylor has spaces/gardens/rooms/chapels where our students may move into the "holy of holies" and refocus, redefine, repent, renew. I often like to define what we are with words Philip Larkin used for the church—a serious house on serious earth.[14] And we mean to be about the Lord's business in every interaction. As professors or staff, we are often in that space where we can see the holy and draw strength from it, but we turn back also into the world of work and duty from there. We can look both ways.

And so, never saying this place is a perfect place—for we are always standing in the need of prayer—nevertheless, Baylor is a place where many people understand the terms of their contracts. That obligates us as a university to be a still point in our students' life journeys as they learn who they are, learn how to serve in the world, and discern how to stand out as individuals. Here they garnered real skills, paid respect to the texts and the narratives of those who have gone before them, and/or are learning to recognize when someone is talking "rot." We hope to model for our students how one can always cling to the steps of the throne of God,

12. Boethius was born in Italy around 482. He wrote *Consolations of Philosophy* and died a martyr's death in the sixth century.

13. Waddell, trans., *More Latin Lyrics*, 113.

14. Larkin, "Church Going," 59.

claiming wonder and mystery and grace. For we believe God takes what we bring to Him and gives us radiance, grit to go at it, and sometimes transformation.

That my husband and I were given the privilege of studying here as undergraduates and then spending our careers here, helping others find the value of a Baylor education, was astonishing and life-defining for us both. I could close with lines from T. S. Eliot's "Little Gidding" because Jim and I went to Little Gidding to kneel where prayer has been valid. And I have a lot to say about that. But then I also wanted to tell you about our trip to Ronald Blythe's home in England and the fields of tulips we saw when we were leading Baylor's program in Maastricht. Instead I'll lean on a poet (thank you again Professor Smith!), whose art provides the words I need. Christian Wiman, in "My Stop Is Grand," describes an encounter he and other travelers on an underground train, the "El" in Chicago, have with a "lone, unearned loveliness" (an array of multicolored sparks that are produced when iron strikes iron in the darkness). For an instant, all the astonished travelers appear to have become one being in the panoply of rainbow-colored fire. Then they roar on through a subterranean world under a bustling, impersonal metropolitan city. The poem's speaker disembarks at Grand Street to walk on toward his office. Yet that dazzling experience, as years pass, stays with him. And even now he sometimes reflects on the memory or vision "through which I walked / teeming human streets, / filled with a shine / that was most intimately me / and not mine."[15]

Yes, that's it. The stop, from undergraduate years to now, was grand. And the resulting shine has been and always will be linked to the "lone unearned loveliness" that happened for me because of Baylor.

REFERENCES

Becker, Ernest. *The Denial of Death.* New York: Free Press, 1973.

Delbanco, Andrew. *College: What It Was, Is, and Should Be.* Princeton: Princeton University Press 2012.

Heaney, Seamus. "Postscript." In *Selected Poems, 1988–2013*, 111. New York: Farrar, Straus & Giroux, 2014.

Hopkins, Gerard Manley. "As kingfishers catch fire, dragonflies draw flame." In *Poems and Prose*, 51. London: Penguin Classics, 1985.

———. "The Windhover." In *Poems and Prose*, 30. London: Penguin Classics, 1985.

15. Wiman, "My Stop Is Grand," 53–54.

Larkin, Philip. "Church Going." In *Collected Poems*, edited by Anthony Thwaite, 58–59. New York: Farrar, Straus & Giroux, 2011.

Robinson, James K., and Walter B. Rideout, eds. *A College Book of Modern Verse*. Evanston, IL: Row, Peterson, 1962.

Waddell, Helen J., trans. *More Latin Lyrics from Virgil to Milton*. Edited by Dame Felicitas Corrigan. London: Gollancz, 1976.

Wilbur, Richard. "Love Calls Us to the Things of This World." In *Collected Poems, 1943–2004*, 307. Orlando: Harcourt, 2004.

Wiman, Christian *My Bright Abyss: Meditation of a Modern Believer*. New York: Farrar, Straus & Giroux, 2013.

———. "My Stop is Grand." In *Once in the West*, 53–54. New York: Farrar, Straus & Giroux, 2014.

15

Teacher Authority and the Student-Teacher Relationship

Searching for the Golden Mean

Byron Newberry

Student-Teacher Relationships

Despite having much to learn when I first started teaching, I feel fortunate because from the outset I managed to forge good connections with students. I didn't fully understand the significance of this early on; I was too busy just learning how to lecture, how to write and grade exams, and how to do myriad other chores associated with keeping the trains running on time in my classes, not to mention attending to research and service work. But as my career progressed, I came to realize that my interactions with students enhanced and underpinned all the other teaching skills I was developing. What I had previously taken for granted and treated as incidental to my teaching, I eventually came to see as a distinct and vital component of teaching, and one amenable to reflection and improvement. So, in more recent years, I've spent time thinking critically about the student-teacher relationship. As a result, in this essay I seek to outline what I believe is a useful way to think about the student-teacher relationship, and that is through the lens of *teacher authority*.

By relationship, I mean more than just the casual exchange of social niceties. Rather, I am talking about a complex interaction that is vital to our goals as educators. No one term captures the scope of such relationships: rapport, friendship, guidance, trust, respect, collegiality, role modeling, intellectual affinity, scholarly exchange, mentorship. And there is no unique relational blueprint. Some teachers are formal, some are familiar. Styles are as plentiful as human personalities. You might be tempted to assume, as I did early on, that the student-teacher relationship is primarily what happens when you're face-to-face with a student. But this is only the tip of the iceberg. Great relationships can exist even in cases where there is little or no direct interpersonal interaction. Good teachers will undoubtedly have former students who sat in the back of the auditorium, whose names the teachers never knew, and whose faces the teachers wouldn't recognize, but who today, unbeknownst to the teachers, count those teachers among their great influences. Most of the student-teacher relationship building happens below the surface, and often without the teacher realizing it, as students quietly observe the teacher's behavior, note the teacher's interactions with other students, hear the emotions conveyed in the teacher's voice, deconstruct the comments the teacher wrote on their papers, and experience epiphanies when the teacher makes an offhand comment that causes the final piece of some puzzle to fall into place in their minds. Everything a teacher does, says, or writes in view of students contributes to building the relationship, whether intended or not!

So, what are the common denominators of good relationships? Imagine if students are thinking the following kinds of thoughts about a teacher:

- He knows what he's talking about.
- She cares about whether I'm learning.
- She takes time to answer my questions.
- He makes the subject interesting.
- I feel encouraged to express my ideas.
- I always learn new things from him.
- I feel like I know where I stand in her class.
- She makes me excited about my choice of major.
- He grades my work fairly.
- She believes in me.

If a student is thinking such things, the teacher is building a good relationship. Suffice it to say that the best student-teacher relationships, whatever the particular dynamic, are ones that maximize the potential for student learning, that inspire and motivate students, that give students guidance and feedback, and that provide students with a sense of purpose and belonging.

To accomplish these things, teachers need to become influential to their students; that is, capable of strongly affecting their behaviors and beliefs. And teacher influence should come by virtue of being *authoritative*, by which I mean: credibly viewed by students as knowledgeable, accurate, reliable, honorable, and worthy of heeding. As a teacher seeks to cultivate such authority and influence, two important facts must be kept in view: (1) student-teacher relationships are not symmetric; and (2) student-teacher relationships are not neutral. Teachers are in a position of leverage because they control the prize students seek—access to education and educational credentials. And, teachers have an agenda: they literally get paid to transform students.

Of course, teachers shouldn't seek to transform students by force; rather, students should want to pursue their own transformation, and even to work hard for it. So the authority teachers seek is not the *hard* type, in which a prison guard has authority over the inmates; rather, I'm referring to a *soft* type of authority, of the kind possessed by a mountaintop sage, who might inspire someone to make an arduous climb just for the sake of knowing.

Teacher Authority

One classic model defines five types of authority that a person can acquire: formal, expert, referent, reward, and coercive.[1] Teachers use *formal* authority when they write a syllabus, develop lesson plans, lead classes, give exams, assign grades, and enforce policies—in short, when teachers carry out the official tasks associated with the managerial role of being a teacher. Teachers also need to have *expert* authority, which stems from possessing extensive subject-matter knowledge. But expert authority isn't had by just being knowledgeable; as I will elaborate on later, it also depends on students valuing and seeking that knowledge. Teachers attain *referent* authority when they successfully engender towards themselves

1. French and Raven, "Bases of Social Power," 150–67.

feelings of trust, affinity, respect, or admiration from students; this is a powerful form of authority that allows teachers to be especially influential if they are successful at cultivating it. It is what can lead a teacher to becoming a trusted advisor or mentor. The final two types of authority, *coercive* and *reward*, are about the power to wield sticks and carrots, such as criticism and praise. These overlap with formal authority in the case of grading, which is both a formal task as well as a powerful form of coercion and reward. But there are many other informal ways in which students can be coerced or rewarded. A simple rewarding remark like, "Mary, this is one of the most insightful essays I've ever read on this topic," can be deceptively powerful, even when made offhandedly—it can genuinely alter a student's life.

While many aspects of formal authority are inherent in the job of being a teacher, most types of authority are not automatic. They must be earned. Cultivating them is a process. Having expertise, for instance, does not in and of itself confer expert authority, which also depends on there being others willing to trust in, rely upon, or seek out that expertise. An expert whom no one consults has no authority. Similarly, referent authority is only had by developing relationships. One cannot be a mentor without first establishing trust and respect.

With this in mind, I will now explore what healthy teacher authority might look like. I will focus on *formal*, *expert*, and *referent* types, but similar arguments could also extend to *coercive* and *reward* authority as well. My approach will be to employ Aristotle's notion of the "golden mean" as a tool of analysis, whereby one hopes to gain clarity about the ideal to which one aspires by considering the consequences of its excesses and deficiencies. In this way, these authority types can be seen not only as categories, but as the effective exercise of the qualities of formality, expertise, and authenticity.

Formal Authority

Formal authority refers to a teacher's administrative role in the classroom, which includes constructing a learning environment and then managing the activities that occur within it. So how does one do that well? Consider the following contrast. One teacher creates an exhaustive syllabus with detailed policies, schedules, rubrics, outlines. Every moment of every class session is carefully planned and executed, and students are never in doubt about where they stand or what they are expected to do. Another teacher has only a perfunctory syllabus. Topics, assignments, due dates, and methods of assessment are all ill-defined and fluid. Class sessions are likely to go on unexpected tangents, and students are often unsure what might come next. Is one of these an exemplar and the other a failure of formal authority? Not necessarily. Either could be an excellent course in which students thrive. Either could be a nightmare experience.

The key to the "golden mean" of formality—that is, to be rightly viewed as a successful classroom manager—is not determined by the size of one's syllabus or the orthodoxy of one's class activities. Syllabi, classroom policies, lectures, exams, homework, textbooks, schedules, rubrics—these are all just tools; they are means to ends, not ends in themselves. Not one of these things is sacred or indispensable. The actual ends of a particular course—in fact, the ends of any individual class session, of the curriculum overall, and of the entire university experience—are all the same in one important sense: students should be different when they finish than they were when they began. But not just randomly different; they should change in very specific, tangible ways that reflect educational objectives, either writ large as a university mission, or writ small as a single class lesson plan. On the grand scale, students should emerge from their educational experience thinking more critically, or communicating more effectively; on the small scale, students should walk out of class knowing how to solve a new equation, or how to conjugate a new verb in another language.

The proper exercise of formality means creating and managing a learning environment—with appropriate instructional activities, guidance, and feedbacks—that enables such changes to be manifest and lasting. This can happen using very traditional classroom techniques. It can also happen with unconventional or even radically iconoclastic pedagogies. But either way, the teacher must have a well-considered plan for what to do and must execute it effectively. Ends don't just achieve themselves. Even in the most chaotic and freewheeling classroom, students should have confidence that a teacher has the course well in hand, and the students' best interests in view, while steering the class through the semester.

If such confidence in the teacher's management is not justified—if the students are confused, not because the teacher gave them something difficult to think about or pushed them out of their comfort zones, but rather because the teacher has neglected proper planning and organization—then that is evidence of a deficiency. We could call this deficiency of formality *dereliction,* as it represents cases in which teachers fail to carry out important formal obligations attached to their roles. In spending time around students over the years, I've heard them vent frustrations about teachers who didn't return graded assignments or exams for weeks, or sometimes never; who were often late and unprepared for class; who abruptly cancelled classes for insubstantial reasons; who were inconsistent in enforcing policies; who treated students unevenly; who gave confusing or contradictory instructions; who didn't follow their own syllabi and schedules; or who were impossible to find for help. I've overheard students say, "He's nice, and smart, but . . ." What follows the "but" is usually an expression of disappointment and frustration. A chronic inability to carry out core functions of class administration is deadly for student confidence in teachers. If students don't trust a teacher to use class time wisely, to provide the feedback they crave, or to follow through on promises made, it diminishes the influence the teacher is able to have. Teachers, like most everyone else, are very busy, and will inevitably have a few bad days of being behind or unprepared. But, bad days notwithstanding, it's crucial for student-teacher relationships for teachers to responsibly carry out the duties of course management.

Can there be excessive formality? If teachers wield their administrative power in counterproductive ways, then yes. Such cases can arise when teachers focus more on policy than on learning and tend toward what I would characterize as an *authoritarian* control of the classroom. That's not to say that process and policy are not important, and there are times when it's essential to dot all the i's and cross all the t's. But students can sense when a teacher is being overly imperious. "If you don't like my rules, then drop my course." That's not a statement that helps a student with a legitimate concern. "I don't care if your essay does solve the problem of evil, if the margins aren't 0.9 inches all around, it's an F!" Research shows that when teachers assert their formal authority in persnickety, bureaucratic ways, it results in diminished student learning and decreased motivation.[2] Persnickety behavior by a teacher may arise because, well, the teacher just has a persnickety streak. But it can also happen when teachers are put on the defensive. Whether from lacking confidence or feeling overburdened, a teacher who feels beset by student questions, concerns, or challenges may erect a rigid wall of policy to

2. Finn, "Teacher Use of Prosocial and Antisocial Power Bases," 67–79; Richmond et al., "Power in the Classroom VII," 1–12.

deflect from having to address issues one-by-one. Students will rightly grow frustrated if they believe they are being nitpicked or stonewalled; and if the students' secret nickname for a teacher is *Professor Inspector Javert*, that's probably not a good sign.

Expert Authority

"My professor is super smart. Probably too smart to be teaching *this* class. Nobody can keep up!" Such a statement from a student illustrates what I call *loftiness*, the excessive case of expertise. The teacher seems to be operating on a higher level, and may be oblivious to, or even contemptuous of the intellectual gap separating the teacher from the students. Students recognize the teacher's expertise, and even admire it abstractly, but they don't see it as being useful to them; it seems remote and out of reach. Worse, it may cause them to doubt their own ability to succeed in the subject. Of course, there may always be some students in any classroom who feel lost. But if most students, including the best students, are wondering if they somehow missed taking several necessary prerequisites, there could be a problem. This situation, if it occurs, may be indicative of an otherwise well-meaning teacher who simply lacks a knack for sensing student comprehension, or has difficulty seeing the world through the students' eyes. Or it could be that a busy teacher does not spend the time to adequately think through how best to frame topics at the appropriate level and just misses the mark. Less charitably, perhaps a haughty teacher just revels in displaying a superior level of erudition. In the former cases, teachers who consistently overshoot their students' ken may be unaware of the disconnect they've created. In the latter case, they may blame the disconnect on the poor quality of students, which will lead to mutually-assured frustration. Whatever the reason, the less students feel able to translate a teacher's knowledge into their own learning, the less expert *authority* the teacher will have, regardless of actual expertise.

Teachers exhibiting the "golden mean" of expertise don't know any less than lofty experts, nor do they dumb down the material or shy away from challenging their students. Rather, they know how to make their expertise accessible. They can comfortably walk a mile in their students' cognitive shoes; they frame ideas in ways that are relevant to students and that build upon the students' pre-existing mental scaffolding; they sense levels of student understanding, pick up on subtle misconceptions, and provide instructive clarification; they engage students in lively subject matter discussions; they connect the dots between the classroom and the world outside; they model how one learns in the discipline; students find it fruitful to ask questions and to seek help from such teachers; and students can imagine themselves one day knowing what their teachers know. If these things hold true, the teacher will be very influential. Some teachers have an instinct for knowing which keys will unlock a student's understanding. But all teachers can learn techniques to better explain material and better gauge student comprehension.

I hope it's rare that a college teacher lacks expertise. But expert authority requires two additional ingredients beyond just knowing the subject. Teachers must mentally organize it (what main points to make, the order to make them, which examples to use, and so forth) and they must physically prepare (write notes, create visual aids, print handouts). From the students' perspective, it doesn't much matter which of these ingredients is lacking. Poor expertise, poor organization, or poor preparation can all lead to the same conclusion: "This teacher doesn't seem to have mastery of the material." I would call such deficiency of expertise, whether real or apparent, *ineptness*.

All teachers must teach a course for the first time, and many have been asked to teach courses outside their comfort zone; either of these cases can make expertise appear shaky. I have certainly suffered my share of deer-in-the-headlights moments when student questions outpaced my preparation. Even with courses I routinely teach, there have been times when I was busy and naively said to myself, "I've given this lecture before, I can just wing it this time," only to wind up tying myself in knots in front of the students. We're all going to have off days, when a lecture goes horribly wrong and actually decreases the sum of human knowledge. But these should be exceptions and not the rule. Unfortunately, I've heard students make statements like, "The professor didn't seem to know the material, and spent half of each class period trying to correct his own errors." When these things happen repeatedly, students lose confidence, and may eschew interacting with the teacher. I've heard one student advise another, "Don't bother going to that class; you'll learn more watching YouTube videos." Since expertise is the foundational qualification for college teaching, a lack of expert authority is particularly devastating for the student-teacher relationship. Assuming teachers actually know their own subjects, the cure for a deficiency of expertise is usually straightforward—put in the effort needed to organize their thoughts and prepare their teaching materials.

Referent Authority

Referent authority seems most natural to associate with student-teacher relationships, involving, as it does, students identifying personally in some way with a teacher. They may come to respect and admire the teacher, even if from a distance, and perhaps will see the teacher as a mentor and role model. A teacher high in this type of authority can have a great, motivating influence upon students. A wonderful comment I once heard a student say about a colleague was, "She expected a lot from us, which made us work hard to fulfill her expectations. We wanted to do well in order to impress her." There are several reasons a teacher might develop referent authority like this, including when students perceive that the teacher cares about them and takes a personal interest in their learning; or when they think the teacher believes in them and has high expectations of them; or when the teacher seems truly committed to teaching and is enthusiastic and joyful about the class and passionate about the subject matter; or when the teacher simply comes across as genuine, down to earth, and relatable. One might suppose that having referent authority is easier if one is naturally blessed with magnetic charm, a high social IQ, boundless energy, and an endearing wit. Thankfully, however, these traits are not prerequisites for referent authority. As counterintuitive as it might seem, even demanding, hard-bitten teachers, legendary for inducing fear in students, can possess high referent authority, provided students can sense that behind the intimidating exterior lies, not a demon that slakes its thirst on the tears of students, but an idealist with a commitment to learning, a passion for excellence, and a desire to push the students to achieve more than they imagined possible. Likewise, shy, awkward teachers with monotone voices can find subtle and creative ways to engage, inspire, and motivate students without the need of spellbinding orations. The key ingredient for referent authority, what I might call the mean, is *authenticity*. When a teacher actually does care deeply about students, or truly does believe students are capable of great achievement, or actually is quite passionate about the subject matter, or really is a relatable, down-to-earth person, that message will usually find its way through.

We must be careful to distinguish between authentic referent authority and simply becoming the students' friend in a more casual sense, the
excess case which I'll call *familiarity*. It's possible for a teacher to socialize
with students in ways that might create a facade of referent authority,
but which actually undermine the power of being a teacher. The saying,
"familiarity breeds contempt," is apt here, inasmuch as friendships that
are too close and casual can erode a necessary measure of mutual respect
that should exist between a teacher and students. In addition, such familiarity can impair the ability of teachers to make (sometimes critical)
objective judgments about students. That's not to say that it isn't good to
develop meaningful friendships with students, just that care must be tak-
en. Interactions with students should always be tempered by professional
obligations toward them. I imagine having a control knob on the side of
my head. Whenever I find myself in the company of students, I turn the
knob to "Professor Mode," which is a bit like the eco-friendly setting on
the dishwasher—the dishes still get clean, but with more self-restraint
and social awareness. A teacher who ignores professional boundaries and
develops more symmetric social friendships with students may become
well-liked in a casual sense, but at the cost of diminished authority, and
possibly worse.

A teacher deficient in authenticity—and so also lacking referent authority—could be called *detached*. This teacher can have trouble engaging
students' interests or motivating them. The teacher might run a tight ship
in the classroom and be a competent explainer of the subject, yet may
still be seen by students as dry or indifferent. Poor referent authority can
suppress the student motivation and interest that might otherwise turn
a mundane class into a favorite one. A teacher might have a particularly
reserved personality. Or perhaps the class is one that the teacher finds
terribly uninteresting. Or maybe research and other commitments make
the teacher feel there is no time for doing much more than phoning it in
in the classroom. Or, to a teacher with many large classes, making connections with individual students seems impossibly daunting. Whatever
the reason, if students don't see a way to forge some type of personal
connection with their teacher, even if at a distance, or they aren't able to
draw from their teacher some spark to ignite their interest, the teacher's
influence on them will necessarily be attenuated. The good news is that
most teachers can learn to increase their referent authority. There is a
body of literature on techniques for enhancing what is known as "teacher

immediacy," which is a term that describes the state in which students feel closer and more connected to a teacher.[3]

Coda

I'll end with a brief recap and a silly metaphor. Teachers need to effect changes in their students. To effect changes in students, they need to have influence. To have influence, students need to see teachers as being authoritative. Therefore, student-teacher relationships revolve around this interplay between authority, influence, and change. Good relationships involve the confluence of the right amount of authority, strong positive influence, and substantial desired change. Formal authority is what gives teachers the power to create and structure the environments in which learning can occur. Expert authority is the power teachers have to share with the students their knowledge and experience and to model learning. And referent authority is the power teachers have to excite and motivate students and to make the learning feel personal. Excesses or deficiencies of the qualities that make up these types of authority weaken the influence teachers can have, and limit teachers' abilities to cause the changes they seek in their students.

And now for the silly metaphor: formal authority is the kettle in which teachers cook, expert authority is the meat and potatoes that provide sustenance, and referent authority is the seasoning that adds flavor and spice. Without the kettle, students just have an uncooked mess. Without the meat and potatoes, students get no calories. And without the seasoning, the food just doesn't taste good. If teachers become good chefs by seeking the golden mean characteristic of each type of authority, they can cook nutritious and appetizing meals, and students will enjoy dining at their tables.

References

Finn, Amber N. "Teacher Use of Prosocial and Antisocial Power Bases and Students' Perceived Instructor Understanding and Misunderstanding in the College Classroom." *Communication Education* 61.1 (2012) 67–79.

3. McCroskey and Richmond, "Increasing Teacher Influence," 101–19; Malouff et al., "Use of Motivational Teaching Techniques," 39–44.

French, John R. P., and Bertram Raven. "The Bases of Social Power." In *Studies in Social Power*, edited by Dorwin Cartwright, 150–67. Ann Arbor: University of Michigan, 1959.

Malouff, John M., Lena Hall, Nicola S. Schutte, and Sally E. Rooke. "Use of Motivational Teaching Techniques and Psychology Student Satisfaction." *Psychology Learning and Teaching* 9.1 (2010) 39–44.

McCroskey, James C., and Virginia P. Richmond. "Increasing Teacher Influence through Immediacy." In *Power in the Classroom*, edited by Virginia Richmond and James McCroskey, 101–19. New York: Routledge, 1992.

Richmond, Virginia P., James C. McCroskey, Patricia Kearney, and Timothy G. Plax. "Power in the Classroom VII: Linking Behavioral Alteration Techniques to Cognitive Learning." *Communication Education* 36, no.1 (1987) 1–12.

16

Integrating Christian Faith and Social Work Practice

Students' Views of the Journey

JON SINGLETARY, HELEN WILSON HARRIS, T. LAINE
SCALES, AND DENNIS MYERS

MUCH HAS BEEN WRITTEN about excellent teaching, both inspirational and technical.[1] The role of the teacher, indeed the faculty, is central to the student's transformational experience. As educators, we are called to "greater reflection, dialogue, and commitment to uncover and inhabit this vital and renewable heart of higher education."[2] The journey of the teacher is inextricably connected to the journeys of the students we teach. Our call to teach is not just about content and discipline but more importantly about continued generational investment in the teacher-learner relationship. So, excellent teaching begins with understanding the motivation, drive, and call of the student. For some, this understanding informs helping students discover their vocation, that deep call to purpose and meaning. For others, the teacher's role is to help students connect their motivation and call to critical thinking and new knowledge discovery

1. Fink, *Creating Significant Learning Experiences*; Jones, Noyd, and Sagendorf, *Building a Pathway for Student Learning*; Nilson, *Teaching at Its Best*; Palmer and Zajonc, *Heart of Higher Education*; Reeves, *Where Great Teaching Begins*; Svinicki and McKeachie, *McKeachie's Teaching Tips*.

2. Palmer and Zajonc, *Heart of Higher Education*, x.

that is at the center of real education. As faculty, our call is to nurture the sparks of inspiration and fan the flames of vocation. We become fellow travelers, and in many cases sherpas, on our students' journeys.

Perhaps you remember family vacations that included road trips across the country, trips that started with the unfolding of a map on the dining room table or an internet search for driving directions. You found your current location on the map or through your GPS, then found your destination on the map and only then began the exploration of various routes to get there. The journey really started before the map was secured or the computer was booted up. It very likely started as you considered your destination and the purpose of your trip. Once you knew where you were going, your focus could move to the "how to" of getting there.

In this chapter we will share several student views of one of the most challenging journeys for Christians in social work: the journey toward integration of faith and social work practice. We are a group of four social work faculty members at a Christian university, Baylor University in Waco, Texas. We spend a lot of time pondering this journey toward integration. We think about Christianity and social work very personally, in relation to ourselves and our callings both to the profession and to the academy. We talk about this often with other faculty members on retreats or in meetings. Most importantly, we explore this topic with students in advising, in classrooms, and over the course of more than a decade, in a research project with several of our students. We have been intentional in our exploration of this topic because of our call to teach and because we have been deeply affected by our own responses to the question "Where am I on the journey toward integrating Christian faith and social work practice?"

Our purpose in writing this chapter is three-fold. First, we want to share with you the fulfillment of our vocation in capturing the stories from Christian students at our university who have been on this journey toward becoming a social worker. We collected interviews from students and alumni during three different periods across their journeys, as students and as alumni, beginning in 2004, again in 2011, and in 2019. All participants were seeking or had completed one of three programs: Bachelor of Social Work, Master of Social Work (MSW), or in some cases, our dual-degree program, in which they sought the MSW from the School of Social Work and the Master of Divinity from Baylor's George W. Truett Theological Seminary. Our second purpose in writing is to comment on the various themes emerging from the students' reflections as they shared stories of seeking God's plan, dealing with obstacles, and seeking companionship for their vocational journey. Finally, we will invite you to join with other Christian travelers and educators as we figure out together various ways to integrate Christian faith and social work practice.

We are addressing our comments to students, faculty members, social work practitioners, and others who may read this chapter. Our hope is that the stories of these Baylor students will prompt you to reflect on your own journey. We expect that for our readers, these conversations about calling have been and will continue to be a central part of the dialogue concerning Christians in social work: a dialogue involving other students, advisors, supervisors, teachers, families, and friends. This chapter is grounded in our data analysis but is not presented as a standard research article. We refer you to those findings in another, earlier publication.[3] Instead, this is a personal sharing of selected quotes from students turned alumni that we hope will serve as information and inspiration as you consider your calling and your pilgrimage. We invite you to travel with us.

The Road Trip of a Lifetime

For the Christian student, one of their most compelling questions is "Where am I going?" It is frequently easier for Christian students to talk freely about their eternal destination while struggling significantly with determining the course of their life journeys. Which of the many career paths available shall we take? What is it we are to "do" with this life we have been given? We look at the "life map" of possibilities and consider our options while many voices, from parents to mentors to detractors, offer opinions. Shall we travel major highways with large loops that let us travel quickly and efficiently but that help us or make us skirt around the inner cities where the bustle of life and pain of others is almost palpable? Shall we travel the back roads of life where the pace is slower and the interactions more measured and deliberate? Will our travels take us through many small adventures or will this journey center on one or two defining highways?

For the Christian social worker, there is a real sense that God serves as a Navigator who helps chart our path, who created us with particular gifts and talents, and who works with us to accomplish the purposes of a

3. Singletary et al., "Student Narratives," 188–99.

good and beautiful creation. But understanding the message and instructions of the Navigator that guide our journey is often the challenge. Has God called me to a specific work? And if so, how will I "hear" the call and know the path? We find ourselves asking, "What are the roads or pathways that will get me to the work and then sustain me through the work to which God is calling me?"

Students who understand that they have been "called" to social work describe that time of hearing the Navigator's voice in a variety of ways. Becoming a social worker is a process, a journey that may begin from any place at any time. Some social workers can trace the beginning of their travels to childhood: parents who modeled for them the giving of self in service of others and encouraged the journey of helping. For some, the journey toward social work may have begun later in life, after several apparently false starts down roads that were blocked or just seemed to be the wrong direction. Eventually they realized that in the midst of these unsettling destinations, the Navigator provided directional signs toward new pathways for strength-building, clarity, and focus.

While all social work students may be on a journey, for Christians in social work, the paths toward mature life as a Christian and toward professional social work are often traveled simultaneously. Even a student who has been a Christian for many years may be walking a path of deepening faith. Therefore, Christian students in social work explore questions such as these: "How does my journey as a Christian intersect with, compliment, replicate, or diverge from travel along my journey toward professional social work? Will I be confronted with the choice between two roads, one representing my faith journey and the other representing my professional journey? Or is there truth in the statement that social work and Christianity really are quite compatible with one another? Is it possible that we have been called by God to forge a new road that brings our path across the most vulnerable, the most wounded, those needing a guide to get back to the road?"

Several of our students, now alumni with fifteen years of practice experience, are able to tell us that the road is long, the path is not always clear, and that the journey is the destination. One alumna reflecting on her practice talks about the adventure and explains "that it comes down to a few simple things . . . being genuine, being intentional and most importantly being a sojourner for those whom I encounter. As a social worker, these encounters often happen with my clients, but having these moments in my daily life are just as important." Each day represents another step on the road trip of a lifetime.

Why Social Work Education?

Our students' stories remind us that all journeys must begin somewhere, even though the map has not been secured or the destination is not in view. Some students are very comfortable with wandering. Some are taking a leisurely journey that may be spontaneous and filled with last-minute decisions about destinations and activities. In some instances, students may enter social work to check it out and decide along the way what is interesting. In contrast, other students are on a carefully defined path to a very specific destination. They have a particular vocational goal in mind and their social work education is an intentional arrival point on their map. One student described where she hopes to be in ten years:

> I want to have started a nonprofit [agency] for doing job training for women. For impoverished women—that's what I would like to be doing in ten years. To get there, I think in two years I am going to be working at an agency doing very micro work . . . I really need to have that perspective.[4]

One can imagine this student viewing social work classes as a predetermined route with sign posts that lead to the ten-year goal.

In some cases, students found their way to social work after developing a commitment to a particular population. For example, one young woman knew that she was gifted in working with children, so she planned to pursue teaching in a school setting. In conversation with her own teachers she began to broaden her view of careers in which she might work with children. Soon she was imagining social work as an option. In her own words, "I would have more job options [in social work] and if I'm a school teacher, then that's what I do with kids, I just teach them, but with social work I could do a whole bunch of different things and I liked that."

---

4. This and all other quotes are from Baylor University Institutional Review Board approved interviews conducted in 2004–2005, with follow-up interviews in 2011 and 2019, with Baylor University students and alumni. We present interviewees' responses with minimal editing in grammar, syntax, etc. To protect their confidentiality, names will not be cited. See Singletary et al., "Student Narratives."

Another student began social work in order to work with children and adolescents, but, through experience in internships and classes, opened her mind to consider work with additional populations:

> I always thought I was going to work with children. And it's switched a lot. Our society's changing as well, so Alzheimer's and caregivers are going to be big needs our population is going to have. I definitely could see myself in that kind of field . . . I have lots of options.

Another student's ultimate goal was ministry, but this student intentionally sought a social work education to gain particular skills and information. Encountering other travelers with social work competencies motivated this student to walk with them:

> I want to connect to people and really help them work through these issues that they've got. I thought that I could do that in seminary, but when I got in there—that's where the catch was— when I started asking questions, the only two people in the room that knew were social work students, that was what really did it for me. This is some information that I have always wanted to know. How do I get this information? And social work has that information with it.

While the student quoted above wanted to join the social workers to gain particular knowledge or skills, another student wanted to journey alongside social workers because she appreciated the value base of the profession:

> The first draw in my mind was that I thought social workers worked with the poor, that was the initial lead in. But also, helping the oppressed and the poor in justice issues from a biblical basis and seeing that as a value of the social work profession . . . So social work values are definitely places that attracted me as a means of vocation or a job where I live out the values.

As our alumni look back, their social work education is just as meaningful fifteen years later. One offers, "I don't think it's possible to overstate the positive impact my social work education, as well as my relationship with other social workers, have had on my life and my sense of calling."

Another talks about how her education gives meaning to each area of her life:

While my [view of calling] has drifted from professional work to my private relationships, the education and social work perspective have given me insight and understanding I often notice are not present in many of my non-social work peers. I feel this has led to the development of healthier, more fulfilling relationships and stronger peer networks.

Clarity of Calling

For some, social work education expands students' view of calling. One says,

Growing up, being "called by God" meant church. Through the experiences I had in graduate school, I started to see that God's calling was so much bigger than this. I began to recognize that my calling was not to ministry in the traditional sense, my calling was to show Christ's love to everyone I encountered.

Another young alumna expresses the breadth and depth of her calling:

My calling is to hug someone who feels untouchable because he just found out he is HIV positive. My calling is to sit with a suicidal client being admitted in to a mental health facility because he has no one else who can. My calling is to be honest with my clients having those hard conversations about living wills and advanced directives. My calling was to sit with my eighty-two-year-old client as he died because he had no other family. My calling is walking alongside a couple, really wanting a second child, while also understanding their risks . . . and then celebrating with them when their daughter was born HIV negative (she is now eight years old). My calling [is] also being able to celebrate with my client as he begins his fifth year of sobriety.

Even when there is this rich sense of purpose, our alumni know that faithfulness to their calling is needed to sustain them in light of the profession's challenges, "When people ask me what I do, I already know what their reaction and response will be, 'Wow, that must [be] so hard.' Of course, it is hard but there is nothing else I would rather do. This is my calling."

Another alumna looks back on how she understands her vocation as a way of following God in the fullness of her life's journey. She says, "My understanding of vocation is that it is a seamless thread by which I understand my life's journey, who I am, and what I am called to do that both pervades and transcends not only my work life, but also my life as a wife, a mother, a friend, a neighbor, and a child of God."

Where Am I Going?

In contrast to students who had a clear picture about why they chose social work education and what their calling means, other students were wandering, seeking clarity on the journey. One student was simply lost and stated bluntly "I have no direction on my future at this point." Another traveler expressed outwardly a feeling of confidence that she would find the way as she goes, but at the same time, admits an "uneasy feeling" as well:

> To me, at this point, it's all very unclear. I'm learning that there are so many options out there and that I have to give it time to know things will develop, and I'll find it as I go. So I'm doing my education to help give me some more options and some more places, but I can't see down the line right now. And it's kind of an uneasy feeling, not knowing which direction or any of the options that are available—in either direction.

We may know that good things can happen along the way and that the path will be there when we need it; however, the uneasiness described above leads to a natural question for students: will we really like what we find along the way? And, perhaps a more troubling question: when we arrive at our destination, will the satisfaction we find be worth the time and effort we have invested?

Sometimes it is easier to see where we are on the path by looking behind us, at where we have been. This student reflects on the calling to social work as a process; looking back as a young alumna, she can see that there were signposts of confirmation on her journey:

> I don't think it was one instance, like one minute, all of a sudden, I was like," I'm called to social work." I think it was a process . . . the constant affirmation. I believe when people are walking with God, and in His word every day, and are really seeking Him, then He'll lead you in a certain direction, and so as I've been seeking Him throughout college, my college experience and life, I've felt confirmed over and over again to continue in the path of social work. And more so every day, even today, more so than yesterday.

Am I on the Right Road?

One of the lessons we learned from the students we interviewed was that entering and staying on the path to a vocation in social work can be an uncertain and complicated task. Their experiences made us more aware of the unexpected turns, intersections, and detours that accompany most who travel this way. These honest reports of the terrain will alert you to the possibility that you may encounter obstacles in the pathway—you or others in your life may question the direction you are going, the accuracy of your map, and the worth of your destination. You will discover that others have traveled the path that you are now on or that you are thinking of entering. They have much to say about the challenges you face and about how God keeps them on the path and helps them make sense of the journey.

Some students told us that, in the beginning, they didn't want to be on the path toward a career in social work. It seems that God's plan for their life's journey was very different from the life map they envisioned. This reflection illustrates how God's plans may not be our plans:

> I remember a point where I sat there and I said, "I don't want to go this direction." I remember praying, "God, you got something confused here. You got the wrong plan for the wrong girl." There was a point where I really remember just about screaming my head off going, "God; you're just off, here! I don't understand why you're doing this!"

Another student described the experience of misinterpreting God's plan:

> I think, for me, I misinterpret God, definitely because I am a selfish person and have my own agenda and my own plans that aren't necessarily in conjunction with His, so I do get a little confused and can't see the line—but I definitely know that from my experience, He's used other people and is just planting a seed in my heart, or maybe a desire or maybe just a little interest.

It seems that once these students reluctantly entered the path of God's plan for their Christian vocation, confirmation that they were in the right place reassured them. Students reported confirmation from a number of sources:

> I really think, looking back, it was nothing other than God saying, "We're going to have to take major steps to intervene on this

girl's life, because she is not listening to anything I'm saying to her! I've put this desire in her heart, I've put this internal factor in her that is driving her towards social work, and she is just abandoning it!" So, that's why I think that God definitely had a huge part in that.

One student described the sense of peace that confirmed the chosen path:

> I think it's completely natural for me to be in social work. And if I try to pursue other things, it really doesn't give me that sense of peace, it gives me more of a sense of like I don't belong there. That's really the role that social work plays and that's how I feel as far as my calling, when I know that when I'm doing something that God doesn't want me to do, I don't have that peace. And when God wants me to do something and that's where I should be, and that's where I am, I have that sense of peace and I'm fine with it even if it makes me uncomfortable, but I feel just natural to be there.

Looking back as alumni, these young professionals know the value of the journey in and of itself. We do not often know if we are on the right road, at the right time, or even if we have landed at the right place. One alumna put it this way:

> I have found reorientation of how I view my own calling and perceive the calling of others; being called by God is less about finding a "perfect" path and more about being willing to be led on a journey for the purpose of becoming, belonging, and contributing. This can take place in spite of finding the "perfect" job, relationship, or experience. In fact, the pursuit of these perfect situations can often keep us paralyzed from moving forward.

Encountering Obstacles

After overcoming their resistance, and then heading out on to the social work path, some students reported that they encountered unanticipated obstacles along the way. Some of these challenges, such as the family members who questioned their choices and the public perception of social work, affected their decisions to begin the journey while others, such as a loss of professional destination, created a temporary disorientation.

Family Concerns

Confusion or concern may be the response of parents and family members to students who choose social work as a career. Family members may want to understand the motivation and reasoning that underlie this sometimes controversial decision. These two quotes from students reflect the concerns that some family members may have about the choice of social work as a career:

> No matter what I do, there is [from my parents] this, "ok what is your reasoning behind this?" I think that is a real big key thing, to see where my motivation is coming from, and what makes me do this, to make sure I am doing it for the right reasons. Also, I think, part of it is for bragging rights, so that when people ask them, [parents] can say, "well, she's doing it because she wants to dah, dah, dah." I get a kick out of that—that that's one of the things that they do.

Another student described a negative reaction to the career path from family:

> Oh, well, they definitely have not influenced me to be called to—I mean, they are—my grandparents still are in denial that I am a social work major. I mean, no one in my family wanted me to be a social work major. So, they really have not done anything to encourage me to do that. But I think they just really wanted me to do business. But, I don't know.

Public Perception of Social Work

Professional prestige and societal recognition may affect career choice. This was not an often mentioned concern in these interviews but there were at least several references to this potential obstacle. One student described a narrow perception of social work when initially considering the profession, asking "Aren't they just CPS [Child Protective Services] workers? That was my whole idea of social work." Another student suggested that "social work isn't that glamorous of a profession." He described the questions others ask: "'Is social work a real profession?' People look down on social workers. They don't think it is a real thing. In court, they don't listen to their testimony, they don't think it's real, but that's just how it was with Jesus."

Obstacles as a Path to New Directions

Obstacles can detour the traveler in a direction that actually leads to God's intention for the social work student. Consider this observation:

> I wish I could say I was that trusting and that easy to influence, but one of the characteristics I have is being stubborn. I am someone who's not very easy to move and it seems I keep getting hit from different directions until I'm finally going, maybe I'm being told something here. That includes some of the people that I know. I'm wanting to go on this path and I keep getting stumbling blocks that are really actually people who are kind of going, "you might want to consider doing this, you're fitted for this."

All of these social work students were seeking a path that would lead them to a place where they could ethically live into their vocation and their faith. The stories provide maps for travelers that aspire to the same destination. The pathway can be clearly marked with signs of confirmation and direction. We also have seen that, along the way, social work students who embrace Christian faith may encounter unanticipated obstacles that may disorient and even cause them to lose their way. Amazingly, the God who called them to the journey is also able to set their feet on the life-long path of service and Christian vocation. And, fortunately, Christian social workers do not ever have to walk alone.

Fellow Travelers

Social workers know perhaps better than most that no one successfully journeys alone in this life. As you learn how to walk alongside the people you serve, you also may begin to wonder "Who will travel with me? Family, faculty, supervisors, student colleagues, God?" You may experience the presence of God calling in many ways; some direct and some indirect, but a part of God's calling is found in the voices of those who go with you on the journey.

Students in our program discussed their understanding of God's call through the influence of other people. We heard about direct and indirect influence of family members, co-workers, social workers, faculty, or others who helped students understand social work as an option for responding to God's call. Interpersonal relationships helped students discern God's call to the profession of social work and to know that there was someone on the journey with them. And, as alumni, relationships are no less important. These professionals continue to recognize the need for support on the journey, for friends and colleagues who can walk alongside them in the conversations prompted along the way. One alumna states:

> I find relationships are significant for me in keeping a right mind and heart when I think about my vocation and calling . . . I have found having relationships with people who are willing to hold me accountable, calling out places of needed development and acknowledging moments of growth, are helpful so that I am not only walking in my own judgment.

Here we highlight some of these relationships on the journey.

Who Will Guide My Journey? God.

In trusting God's presence in our midst, we heard students describe the meaning of this for their journeys. One student said that God's "hand was there and just kept guiding me through." Another student offers, "the calling for me is just following what God wants me to do and where God is leading me to." And also, "With me, I feel like God really, strongly directed me towards this." Finally, an alumna looks back in recognition of God's guidance, "God calls us, not just me, to shine and show love for his creation. This creation includes everything and everyone. In other words, we're all called to take responsibility for God's creation."

Who Will Go with Me? Family and Friends.

The most common travelers alongside students were their family and friends. Sometimes these loved ones question the turns we make on the journey. Sometimes, they aren't sure how to support us along the way. Looking back on years of family strife, a student reflected on her family's role in her journey, saying, "I don't know if my family necessarily, in a positive way, influenced my decision for social work."

Yet, other students had different experiences as families ventured forth with them: "I knew that by choosing a profession where I would be helping people," said one student, "I would be understood by my family and they would support that decision because that's what I wanted to do." Another student also voiced the encouragement of family traveling with them, "I think that there is an experience where your family, they are helping me through a lot of this. That's one thing I feel very blessed with, is that they have been very supportive." And in hindsight, an alumna says, "Belief in me by others whose opinions I value and trust has played a vital role in affirming my sense of call."

One alumnus we talked to is married to a social worker-turned-minister who reflects on vocation with him. He says,

> My wife has had an impact on my sense of calling. As an ordained minister, she has her individual calling. However, we do not see our calling apart from one another. In other words, in order to do the work that we're called to do, we both have to be called. That is, our mutual support is crucial to doing what we're called to do.

Who Will Go with Me? Social Workers Such as Faculty, Classmates, and Field Supervisors.

Significant relationships are influential in helping you make your way down the road into professional social work practice. There are many others who travel alongside you in the adventure of becoming a professional, and social work education offers students unique and practical experiences in developing strength for the journey. Students spend a great deal of time with classmates, faculty, and field supervisors, who are a part of their journeys of discernment. They often recognize right away the importance of these relationships.

One new student described one of her attractions to the program: "I knew the faculty was very friendly and very interested in their students succeeding."

Students commented on the relationships faculty intentionally developed with students on this journey. "I think it's pretty much invaluable," said one student, "At least if it's set up properly, because you can draw on the experience of your professors, who have years of experience in the field, as well as the experience of the people who are even writing the textbooks." Professors are described as mentors in students' lives as they walk alongside them, "they really push to a high standard, but they're also there to, not hold your hand, but support you, encourage you, and I just got a really strong sense of community, and support."

And as the years go by, an alumna is mindful of colleagues and faculty who continue to shape her journey:

> Colleagues from the social work program past and future, as well as colleagues in my broader higher educational institution have certainly played an important role in shaping my sense of belonging and have been influential. There is no question that one of the greatest privileges I feel is having the support and encouragement of my former professors to lean into.

Faculty understood the importance of engaging with students and alumni. After a weekend of discussions about our own vocational journeys, faculty in our program wrote about the role they envisioned for themselves in walking alongside students: "My assessment is that sharing about our journeys and aspirations enabled us to see and appreciate the complexity and richness of the fabric of our collective relationship," offered one professor. Another added her reflections:

> My renewed awareness of my own calling and what has contributed to living it out has made me more aware of the potential significance of every interaction I have with students. I find myself asking my advisees and other students more open-ended questions about their purpose and urging them to see their inner promptings and long-held dreams.

As students, you also have supervisors guiding you while you learn, preparing you for the road ahead: "I talk to my supervisor constantly about what is going on with this client," said one person we interviewed. "She lets me do the work, but she is there for advice and consultation. This is uncharted territory for me, but I am learning so much." Students express appreciation for the learning that comes in supervision. One offers, "It was tremendously helpful to me that my supervisor went out on an assessment with me. I was able to discuss advanced practice with her and it was really good to have her feedback from the assessment." And another echoes the support on the journey of learning: "In the middle of the crises of moving the clients I was on the phone with my supervisor. I wasn't sure what to do, and she talked me through it. But she also let me do it on my own, for which I am now thankful. It was a great experience."

Who Will Go with Me? Clients.

In social work education, you will have opportunities to reflect upon and then practice traveling with your clients. Whether you are in generalist practice, direct practice, or practice with larger systems, you will be asking how to accompany your clients and how they will accompany you on this journey.

Our students may be aware of where they have stumbled along the way, but they are not sure that the people they serve understand the challenges of their journeys. "Sometimes, it's harder to meet people's needs because sometimes you have to convince them they have needs, or they don't realize they have needs," said one interviewee. What this suggests is that students are learning the reciprocal nature of walking alongside others. They walk with clients in hopes of making a difference in their journeys. One student said, "If you can intervene and somehow help them realize that they are worth something and they have true potential, I feel like it changes so many things." After a similar experience with a client, another student said, "That made me feel good because I didn't force anything on him, I just lived right and tried to treat him like I treat anybody else."

As students on the journey into the profession walk with clients, they want to help them, but we know they also learn to "have the clients be the expert of their experience," as one student put it. In this, the clients also walk with students. They help students move further along the journey.

Integration of Christian Faith and Social Work Practice

Now we have come to the heart of what we learned from our interviews. If you are reading this, you probably have some interest in exploring the integration of Christian faith with a passion for service. Maybe you are faculty members, like us, who have thought about this for years. Maybe you are a student, who is exploring various aspects of what it means to travel this road. Social work students who embrace Christian faith seek a path leading to places where they can integrate professional values and ethics with their religious beliefs. The journey down this path usually creates a unique set of opportunities, challenges and blessings.

Opportunities

sFor some students, Christian faith adds an extra measure of compassion to their work. This student articulated how faith integration may allow the worker to understand the client more completely:

> My faith shapes who I am—kind of like my thought processes
> . . . as I'm in social work, I'm learning to evaluate situations and
> just know who I am and what my beliefs are, but then to see that
> person for who they are and to work with them in where they're
> at. So . . . I think how I approach situations may be different. I
> may be a little more compassionate than somebody else would
> be.

Another student explored a similar theme, acknowledging that her own Christian values are a lens through which she sees the world, but this lens does not prevent her from valuing the different perspectives of her clients:

> I'm at peace, I guess, as far as, I'm able to discuss with clients
> about their own views and their own wants and desires for
> whom—for who they are. Without imposing my own values.
> Because I realize that my values are, maybe, different from
> theirs. But that doesn't mean that I cannot help that person.

Looking back, an alumna offered a similar response, "Social work education prepared me to fully engage individuals who are different from me and to help them even if I do not agree with them. In other words, the task is to serve regardless of my own values and beliefs."

Perhaps most significantly, a number of students reported the important interplay between their faith and their professional identity and practice. This student described this as "accountability":

> Another great blessing I have had is that it [social work] has
> made me,—it has held me accountable to my faith. But it has
> made me more genuine in my faith. It has really made me exam-
> ine what it means to be a Christian—what it means to minister.
> The word "ministry" to me just means doing good social work.
> The profession has held me more accountable to my faith, and
> my faith has held me more accountable to my profession.

Challenges and Dilemmas

For some of the students we interviewed, the potential dissonance between faith and practice created significant, but not overwhelming, concerns along the way. For one student this blend was a "dangerous" idea:

> I think that calling and social work sometimes can be dangerous words to associate together for the social work profession because you don't want to minimize the professionalism of social work. And classifying social work as a ministry is very dangerous. I think that it does take out the element of professionalism. At the same time, you need to know how to effectively balance faith and practice, because you are never going to be just a social worker. I am going to be going somewhere as a Christian, with the title social worker. And I think it's a wonderful blessing to have that opportunity, but it can be very dangerous because you are representing two amazing things. I think that's why so many people are so afraid of having faith in practice, and those two words together are like an oxymoron to so many people. I think it's sad, but I think there is a delicate balance there.

Other interviewees, preparing for ministry roles, echoed the potential dissonance between the role of social worker and the role of minister:

> I like the fact that in social work, you know—there are certain things you can do that you can't seem to do in ministry. And there's the other catch where there are certain things you can't do in social work that you can in ministry. For example, with a pastor, they can openly go in and say, this is what I believe and all of this. In social work, it's not really—that's kind of frowned upon.

Students admitted that learning to do this integration was a process; one that sometimes involved some "hard knocks." One student, who described the process of integration as "a little confusing," told us about a learning experience:

> For the most part, it's just a hard issue. You take it case by case. I had a hard experience this past semester in my agency where I did an intake and I asked my client if she ever prayed and it helped our conversation and I didn't regret doing it but my supervisor and I had to talk a long time about why that would have been a bad idea and it was hard. In the end I really saw where he was coming from. I just want to know what is best for the client. I just want to be led by the Holy Spirit and not necessarily by

the [NASW] Code of Ethics. It's just really hard for me, but I am
learning a lot and I am open to learning a lot more.

Some students reported that trying to reconcile the values of the
social work profession with Christian values presented a major obstacle
for them. One felt frustrated stating, "I don't know that I have been able
to integrate it [faith and social work] to the point that I feel that it works;
I feel really torn." Another student described in more detail:

> I think that there are major conflicts with how I was raised
> and element of faith in my life. Something I struggled with a
> lot in undergrad is kind of taking on my parents' values and
> the things that I learned in the church, you know things that I
> was supposed to do and how I was supposed to act, and what I
> needed to do I felt like conflicted greatly with social work, and
> that troubled me.

These are the dilemmas that students mention as they embark on
a journey that fully embraces the authentic integration of social work
and Christian faith. While the struggles are significant and formative,
there are also encounters with blessings and opportunities that mark the
journey.

Blessings

In spite of encountering challenges, the students we interviewed reported
a wide array of blessings and opportunities associated with the blending
of Christian faith and professional identity. At a deeply personal level,
students indicated that their intentional efforts at integration resulted in
"the feeling of inner harmony," "freedom and flexibility," and helping "me
realize more of who I am and making me understand . . . what I want to
do." Sometimes the reward is a feeling of comfort and joy as reflected in
this statement: "I prayed about it, and I feel great about it."

One frequently mentioned outcome of the intentional integration
of faith and practice was that faith was strengthened in the process. For
example, "my social work education has shaped my faith and has made
me—it's kind of really helped me be a better Christian." These words
echoed this same conclusion—"it [social work] has made me more
genuine in my faith." This kind of integration may also have the power
to change important assumptions. One student described herself as "a
Christian wearing the hat of a social worker," with training that "is going

to be shaping how I speak to people, even though it [professional education] may not have changed everything how I feel, but it has changed how I think."

The process of blending faith and practice seemed to have beneficial consequences for interactions with clients. Consider this observation: "I think that's my biggest thing that I've enjoyed . . . it's what pulled me into it is being able to identify a need and to be aware of needs more than probably the average person is." One student counted among her blessings: "I have gotten to work with people who I never would have ever talked to or met . . ." While there may be dilemmas and challenges related to an intentional quest to integrate Christian faith and social work practice, you may also find blessings and opportunities to discover and claim along the way. Whatever you encounter, please know that you do not have to travel alone.

The Journey Leads Home

As we follow up with alumni who continue to reflect on their education and the profession, on obstacles they encounter and on those who travel with them, as they consider the role of faith, a consistent theme is both the metaphor of calling as a journey and the sense of home they feel on the journey. We heard one remark, "When I think of my calling at this stage of my journey, I physically feel a sense of calmness; I feel I have finally found my home." Another shares a similar thought, "Calling feels like coming home. It's having a better understanding of who you are, and how that connects to understanding what is your purpose in this world." One more reflection on this theme:

> I am in a space in my life today where my sense of call is pretty solid. In my spirit through prayer, through worship, through conversations with colleagues with a shared love of teaching, I feel God's affirming "Yes. Yes, my child this is where you are at home, and where I want you."

And what is this place called home? It is clear that they have found a home in faithful service, a home in following in the way of their faith, and a home in the profession of social work.

Conclusion: The Journey Matters

The scripture is replete with journey metaphors that help us understand that our relationship with God and our response to God's call is about the day-to-day living out of our faith rather than rushing headlong toward a destination. Moses, called to deliver the people, died after a life of leadership with the discovery that his ministry was about the journey, not about the destination. Saul was out looking for donkeys when Samuel found him and communicated God's call for leadership. David was tending sheep when God called him to lead an army and eventually a nation. Jesus' ministry occurred from village to village as he traveled, preached, healed, and loved. He called to his disciples (who were not sure where he would take them), "Come, follow me" (Matt 4:19, NIV). He invited them to participate with him in ministry rather than to arrive at a particular destination.

Our response to God's call to teach and guide our students is a model for those students in following their call to the profession. The journey for them is about the lives of their clients and the ministry that is professional helping.

We know from the life and ministry of Jesus that the journey is not always easy or without challenges. To be called to teach and do compelling research while honoring one's faith experience demands fidelity to truth-seeking rather than doctrinal agreements and to student growth rather than student compliance. It is an honorable journey. Further, the words of our students confirmed that in spite of challenges, they found strength to continue, by faith, as followers of Jesus, to travel with him as he equips them and leads them to the hungry, the poor, the broken in body and spirit, the dying, the rejected and lonely, the least of these. We commit then to journey on together, to talk with them, and listen to them, and reflect with them, bound by the call to be fellow travelers with the one who taught us best about the ministry of presence.

We end our chapter with a prayer offered up for social workers by our founding dean Dr. Diana Garland. It is our intercession on behalf of you who are joining us on the journey.

> We are grateful, Lord God, that when you call us on this journey,
> You don't call us to walk it alone.
> We thank you for one another to share the journey,
> To comfort and encourage one another.

Hold us together, Lord; hold our hands and steady us on the way. Show us just the next steps to take—
We don't need to see all the way, for we trust the destination to you.
Give us courage to go, step by step, with one another and with you.

References

Fink, L. Dee. *Creating Significant Learning Experiences: An Integrated Approach to Designing College Courses.* San Francisco: Jossey-Bass, 2013.

Gillard, Richard. "The Servant Song." In *The Baptist Hymnal,* edited by Wesley L. Forbis, 613. Nashville: Convention, 1991.

Jones, Steven K., Robert K. Noyd, and Kenneth S. Sagendorf. *Building A Pathway for Student Learning: A How-To Guide to Course Design.* Sterling, VA: Stylus, 2014.

Nilson, Linda B. *Teaching at Its Best: A Research-Based Resource for College Instructors.* 4th ed. San Francisco: Jossey-Bass, 2016.

Palmer, Parker J., and Arthur Zajonc, with Megan Scribner. *The Heart of Higher Education: A Call to Renewal.* San Francisco: Jossey-Bass, 2010.

Reeves, Anne R. *Where Great Teaching Begins: Planning for Student Thinking and Learning.* Alexandria, VA: ASCD, 2011.

Singletary, Jon, Helen W. Harris, Dennis Myers, and T. Laine Scales. "Student Narratives on Social Work as a Calling." *Aretê* 30.1 (2006) 188–99.

Svinicki, Marilla D., and Wilburt J. McKeachie. *McKeachie's Teaching Tips: Strategies, Research, and Theory for College and University Teachers.* 14th ed. Belmont, CA: Wadsworth Cengage, 2014.

Epilogue

D. Thomas Hanks

My prologue for this epilogue is itself an epilogue: please consider the last four lines to Robert Frost's poem, "Two Tramps in Mud Time":

> Only where love and need are one,
> and the work is play for mortal stakes,
> Is the deed ever really done
> For Heaven and the future's sakes.[1]

Before this epilogue begins in earnest, let me ask that you consider reading it with an eye to writing down, after you finish it, what will come to be the *real* epilogue for this collection. In some fashion, that practice will change this essay—necessarily a monologue—to a dialogue, at least in a limited sense. As you read, look for the two "most important" thoughts, or practices, or observations, that come to you as you read. As the epilogue ends, I will ask you to write down those two items and then to decide on the *single most important* thought or practice or observation that you want to take with you from this collection. There will perhaps be several, but I will ask you simply to state—not to develop, not to explain, but simply to write down—what you consider the single most important element from this collection that you want to take with you for further thought or practice or—University Chaplain Burt Burleson's term—your further awakening.

---

1. Frost, "Two Tramps in Mud Time," 277.

Stories

I open now with a few challenging thoughts. The first is inspirational and comes from physician and philosopher Lewis Thomas, two-time National Book Award winner, former Chancellor of the Sloan-Kettering Cancer Center in Manhattan, and frequent contributor to the *New England Journal of Medicine*: "It is in our genes to understand the universe if we can, to keep trying even if we cannot, and to be enchanted by the act of learning all the way."[2]

The second thought doesn't start out being inspirational, but hang on. It comes from Noam Chomsky, now ninety years old and still writing about linguistics and philosophy in equal measure. Chomsky might almost be responding to Thomas on our students' genetic desire to understand our universe. He poses this challenge to how teachers from pre-kindergarten through graduate study *profess* their/our calling to help students understand their world:

> Most problems of teaching are not problems of growth but helping cultivate growth. As far as I know, and this is only from personal experience in teaching, I think about ninety percent of the problem in teaching, or maybe ninety-eight percent, is just to help the students get interested. Or what it usually amounts to [is] to not prevent them from being interested. Typically they come in interested, and the process of education is a way of driving that defect out of their minds. But if children['s] . . . normal interest is maintained or even aroused, they can do all kinds of things in ways we don't understand.[3]

I want to turn to stories. I teach literature and writing; I like to talk about stories. Professor Bob Baird begins the story approach early in this collection, as he discusses Baylor's blended Christian and secular teaching heritage. He opens with a story about how his life here was shaped by an encounter with a teacher at Ouachita Baptist University. More shaping happened right here at Baylor, with Professors Ralph Lynn, Glenn Capp and Jack Kilgore, the latter of whom led him to read John Stuart Mill's "On Liberty." That essay insists that "mere accident has decided which . . . is the object of [a Christian's] reliance, and . . . the same causes which make him a [Christian] in London, would have made him a Buddhist or a Confucian in Beijing."

2. Lewis, "On Science and Uncertainty," 59.
3. Chomsky, "Creation & Culture," part 2, 22:02.

Next consider a longer story about teaching, one that appears in Charles Dickens's 1854 novel *Hard Times*, Chapter 1. The chapter is titled, "The One Thing Needful" and tells of Sissy Jupe and her education at the hands of Mr. Gradgrind, her teacher. Dickens opens the chapter with these words, delivered by an administrator to one of his teachers:

> Now, what I want is, Facts. Teach these boys and girls nothing but Facts. Facts alone are wanted in life. Plant nothing else, and root out everything else. You can only form the minds of reasoning animals upon Facts: nothing else will ever be of any service to them. This is the principle on which I bring up my own children, and this is the principle on which I bring up these children. Stick to Facts, sir![4]

Now here is the rest of Dickens's little story beginning *Hard Times*. It shows the value of sticking solely to the facts. You will be pleased to read that Mr. Gradgrind uses the Socratic question-and-answer approach to teaching. [Yes, that is my ironic comment . . .]

> "Girl number twenty," said Mr Gradgrind, squarely pointing with his square forefinger, "I don't know that girl. Who is that girl?"
>
> "Sissy Jupe, sir," explained number twenty, blushing, standing up and curtsying.
>
> "Sissy is not a name," said Mr Gradgrind. "Don't call yourself Sissy. Call yourself Cecilia."
>
> "It's father as calls me Sissy, sir," returned the young girl, in a trembling voice and with another curtsey.
>
> "Then he has no business to do it," said Mr Gradgrind. "Tell him he mustn't. Cecilia Jupe. Let me see. What is your father?"
>
> "He belongs to the horse-riding, if you please, sir." Mr Gradgrind frowned, and waved off the objectionable calling with his hand.
>
> "We don't want to know anything about that here. You mustn't tell us about that here. Your father breaks horses, don't he?"
>
> "If you please, sir, when they can get any to break, they do break horses in the ring, sir."
>
> "You mustn't tell us about the ring here . . . Very well then . . . Give me your definition of a horse."
>
> (Sissy Jupe thrown into the greatest alarm by this demand.)

4. Dickens, *Hard Times*, 2.

"Girl number twenty unable to define a horse! . . . Girl number twenty possessed of no facts, in reference to one of the commonest of animals!" . . .

The square finger, moving here and there, lighted suddenly on Bitzer . . .

"Bitzer," said Thomas Gradgrind. "Your definition of a horse."

"Quadruped. Graminivorous. Forty teeth, namely twenty-four grinders, four eye-teeth, and twelve incisive. Sheds coat in the spring; in marshy countries, sheds hoofs too. Hoofs hard but requiring to be shod with iron. Age known by marks in mouth."
. . .

"Now girl number twenty," said Mr Gradgrind, "you know what a horse is."

She curtsied again, and would have blushed deeper, if she could have blushed deeper than she had blushed all of this time . . .[5]

Dickens describes Sissy's teacher:

Thomas Gradgrind, sir. A man of realities. A man of facts and calculations. A man who proceeds upon the principle that two and two are four, and nothing over, and who is not to be talked into allowing for anything over . . .

[He] . . . [sweeps his] eyes over the inclined plane of little vessels then and there arranged in order, ready to have imperial gallons of facts poured into them until they were full to the brim . . . [H]e seem[s] a kind of cannon loaded to the muzzle with facts, and prepared to blow them right out of the regions of childhood at one discharge. He seem[s] a galvanising apparatus, too, charged with a grim, mechanical substitute for the tender young imaginations that [are] to be stormed away.[6]

You realized as you read that Gradgrind is teaching biology: the study of life as it appears in its various forms. This form is labelled "horse." Gradgrind gives us one model for teaching science, then. We may find it dismaying. Even more dismaying: we may recognize it from our own experience.

A physician and philosopher who did find Gradgrind's model dismaying was Lewis Thomas, mentioned above. In a 1982 essay in the *New York Times* which later appeared in the journal-magazine *Science*

5. Dickens, *Hard Times*, 5–7.
6. Dickens, *Hard Times*, 4–5.

and has now become easily available on several web sites, Thomas writes about teaching STEM subjects in terms that apply just as clearly to the way you, I, and most of our global colleagues may have taught—may still teach—subjects ranging from psychology through organic chemistry or medieval English literature to twenty-first century work on Artificial Intelligence. Thomas describes it thus, and you will hear the pleased humming of Mr. Gradgrind as you read an excerpt from his 1982 editorial in the *New York Times*:

> . . . we have been teaching the sciences [or Latin, or history] as though they were the same collection of academic subjects as always, and—here is what has really gone wrong—as though they would always be the same. Students learn today's biology, for example, the same way we learned Latin when I was in high school long ago: first, the fundamentals; then, the underlying laws; next, the essential grammar and, finally, the reading of texts. Once mastered, that was that: Latin was Latin and forever after would always be Latin. History, once learned, was history. And biology was precisely biology, a vast array of hard facts to be learned as fundamentals, followed by a reading of the texts.[7]

As you see, Thomas here describes the disease of Gradgrind and his ilk. He goes on to say that the best approach to teaching science is first to realize oneself that the ground of science is constantly shifting, that today's "fact" may be tomorrow's exploded theory (remember "cold fusion"?). He compares the ground of science to poetry, which he says is always "a moving target." A side-note: readers who work in computer science know more than most just what "a moving target" is: not only does the sum of computer knowledge grow each hour, old models shift or fall into the trash, new models demand testing every day, and the old Radio Shack TRS-80 and the Apple toaster both sit forgotten in dusty garages. (Radio Shack, by the way, outsold Apple three times over during the early 1980s; in 2015, they filed for bankruptcy). The state of knowledge changes every hour in science, most obviously in computer science; how do readers of this collection form themselves to reflect that change in their/our approach to our/their various subjects? If we don't—if we repeat our old notes each year without change—then we are not practicing the formation, and the stewardship, that Laine Scales insists upon in her essay as part of what we profess as we build Baylor's community.

7. Thomas, "Art of Teaching Science," SM89.

Insights from the Community

Consider Prof. Scales' essay as a springboard into brief reflections on some of the essays in this collection—reflections meant to stir your thoughts about what you'd like to take away from these essays.

As I just noted, Laine Scales spoke about our task in forming a *community* made up of scholars-teachers-ministers to one another. Others have spoken in the same area, looking at answers to the question "How do I define and follow my calling in a Christian University—that is, in Baylor University? A Christian University, moreover, that pursues and teaches research often highly secular?" Dr. Candi Cann represents a growing number of Baylor faculty who have taken their calling, and the idea of community, to what may be its ultimate point: she has moved in with the students as a faculty member in Baylor's residence halls (North Village). And it isn't just that *she* has moved in: she moved her entire family (her daughter and their dog) in, and they have become part of Dr. Cann's approach to engagement. As she reminds us, you and I, as teachers, are mixtures of family, academic field, church, and much more. Perry Glanzer and Nathan Alleman also reminded us of the complexity of a call to teach. They reported on their major survey that discusses the simple fact that we have many identities: not just teachers but "spouses, parents, Democrats or Republicans, Jews or Muslims, environmentalists, feminists, members of particular ethnic or racial groups, a country, a particular sexual identity and more." We try to excel in each of these categories: how we put them together in search of excellence in our teaching is how we answer the question of following our call. Professors Glanzer and Alleman present in their essay some guidelines for that task of helping ourselves and our students to grow.

Further, and as Professor Byron Newberry points out above, Baylor gives us tools to work within our self-chosen task of helping our students grow in wisdom and in stature, and in favor with God and their fellow humans. Baylor teachers have a great deal of formal authority, he notes: most obviously, we assign students' grades. Byron adds that we also, and in part owing to our formal authority, have a referent authority which allows us, as he puts it, "to excite and motivate a student and to make the learning feel personal." (Prof. Newberry refers to real Socratic engagement and dialogue, not to Gradgrindism.)

Chaplain Burt Burleson's contribution offers stimulating, even exciting suggestions about an authority we share with our students. He discusses how our students, and how *we*, contain and embody the image of God, and thus share a spiritual being with God and with each other. We are *made*, Burt says, for spiritual, intellectual, and moral maturing in community (cf. Thomas's first comment above in this epilogue). That maturing, he adds, does not always take place—but teachers can help prepare the ground for the good seed. He names five *spiritual capacities* that we can help our students develop, five preparing steps we can help ourselves and our students attain through what Chaplain Burleson calls awakening, finding path and purpose, and practicing the habits of humility, presence, and perseverance.

Associate Dean Betsy Vardaman has devoted herself to helping students find their callings through international awards like the Fulbright, the Rotary Global Grant, the incredible Marshall Award, and others both national and international. She has much more than tripled the number of these scholarships won by our students since she took on this task. During the symposium, and typically, she did not discuss her own efforts; instead, she pointed to the footprints other teachers left to lead her to her own calling. She pointed out instances from their teaching, instances of "those carefully planned moments when lights seem almost magically to ignite and students are stunned at the conversation with themselves that a teacher has provoked or inspired." Those teaching moments, Betsy says, "can well be regarded as sacred acts, ways . . . we, as professors, do our best to live out our faith commitment to and in Christ."

Others in the symposium and in this collection—like Professor Trey Cade, with his paper on space weather as an example of how he teaches inquiry-based learning—have taken specific classroom practices as examples of or pointers to our being "called to teach." Like many of us, Trey insists upon *dialogue*; monologue, though useful in small doses, is not his preferred path to his calling or to prompting his students to find their calling. Professor Anne-Marie Schultz likewise insists on inquiry in dialogue as she notes how Plato's dialogues can help graduate students to recognize, develop, and follow the teaching/learning vocation we profess. Dialogue—teacher-student dialogue—was clearly a theme of the symposium, as appeared also in the material from Jon Singletary. He and his colleagues—again including Professor Scales—based an entire essay on dialogue. They simply interviewed students, asking them a series of questions designed to help the students think through what influenced them to move toward their personal calling. And he and his colleagues *listened*. Initiate a dialogue with a student, the "dialogue group" urges, and that will help students begin dialogues with themselves. Some teachers may be a bit shy about initiating such dialogues with their students; those who retreat from interaction with students may want to realize that one of the major reasons students leave one college/university to find another is that they found in the first school no teacher who would engage with them. So they left, seeking one who would.[8]

Professors Mona Choucair and Laurel Zeiss present some carefully thought-out approaches to using the material we teach, and the way we teach, to engage with students and to point out to them not just parts of *our* vocations, but hints or outright suggestions for *their* callings. Professor Choucair points out that we have all hated the skin we were in at some time, if only when agonizing over teen acne or—at the other end of the scale—wrinkles. She wants to use that community of feeling. Professor Zeiss likewise points to the universal in her class material: how many of us, she asks, have listened to music at some point just today? She adds a mention of weddings, funerals, graduations—"Have you been to one without music?" she asks. Music permeates our world, she adds—and she can use the ear-budded approach of our students to help them realize the purpose of all art, the goal appearing in music, or painting, or sculpture, or poetry: a model of order amidst chaos; the struggle against dishonesty and injustice with honesty and truth; and the offering of prayers of lamentation, confession, and praise. Professors Bill Bellinger and Rebecca

8. A useful survey of student responses to the college/university experience is the annual National Survey of Student Engagement. Two more specifically focused studies are Bonet and Walters, "High Impact Practices," 224–35, and Flynn, "Baccalaureate Attainment of College Students," 467–93. Flynn's study is perhaps the most compelling work in this area: he opens by citing a study from 1975 that observed that "it is the individual's integration into the academic and social systems of the college that most directly related to his continuance in that college (quoting Vincent Tinto, *Review of Educational Research* 45.10 (1975) 89); his conclusions, based largely on data collected by the National Center for Education Statistics' (NCES) 2004/09 Beginning Postsecondary Students Longitudinal Study (BPS:04/09), support findings that student engagement with peers and with faculty (out of class as well as in) increase student retention and completion in the 4–6 year normal period of enrollment. Bonet and Walters discuss retention and persistence in two-year colleges especially as affected by "learning communities" in which, as they write, "A key and overarching goal . . . has been the development of cooperative relationships among students, instructors, tutors, and advisors, focused on student learning outcomes. Faculty development and enrichment . . . play a key role in the learning community experience" (225). They report gratifying results of their conjunct peer-faculty "learning communities" with respect to persistence (course completion, specifically: see p. 229). Burnette, "College Academic Engagement," called the latter two sources to my mind. I am indebted.

Poe Hays, in their approach to teaching Psalms, likewise note prayers of lamentation, confession, and praise—and also blistering *anger*—in their approach to that book of Hebrew poetry. They help their students to realize more fully, more *presently*, their relationship to a part of the tradition which the students consider holy without fully understanding that part of their heritage. Their goal, Professors Bellinger and Hays state, is to help their students to look more closely. As Prof. Hays puts it, "I came to Baylor to pursue . . . a vocational call similar to Dr. Bellinger's . . . [:] to help the church be better, more informed, and more faithful." In her travel toward that goal, she accepts hitchhikers: the students she and Prof. Bellinger share come along on the journey (for the most part).

More classroom practices come our way in this collection; for another example, Professor Andrew Arterbury pointed out that wrong answers and bad questions—seemingly *not* fertile fields for the classroom—can, if we use them well, actually lead to light-bringing engagement. He presents examples in his essay. And I must not fail to cite the classroom practices of one of Baylor's master teachers: Professor Roger Kirk. Professor Alex Beaujean writes above that he decided to sit in on Prof. Kirk's class for an entire semester, simply observing and taking notes on habits like coming to class early and talking with students (and later making notes on the conversations, and still later recalling the subjects of those conversations to the students—professor-student engagement in action).

Conclusion

All in all, these essays present suggestions for classroom practice, observations about how we are made in an Image which prompts us to engage and share, notes on how we must realize that we have multiple identities that can interact with our students to their benefit. Most of all, we have heard again Prof. Scales' three rules for successful teaching or even administering: Listen! Listen! Listen!

That three-word mantra is my conclusion. As we did at this point in the symposium, you may want now—if you haven't already—to take a handy sheet of paper and simply list what you see as the two most important elements reported in the essays. And for the daring, I challenge you to narrow your focus to one central insight. Those reflections—once in your own hand—will, perhaps, make up your major takeaways from the collection. In a sense, you will write your own epilogue. I invite you to begin now—even on the flyleaf.

References

Bonet, Giselle, and Barbara R. Walters. "High Impact Practices: Student Engagement and Retention." *College Student Journal* 50.2 (2016) 224–35.

Burnette, Monica. "College Academic Engagement and First-Year Students' Intention to Persist." PhD diss., Seton Hall University, 2017.

Chomsky, Noam. "Creation & Culture." Lecture at Institute of North American Studies, Barcelona, Spain, November 25, 1992. Alternativeradio.org.

Dickens, Charles. *Hard Times*. London: Bradbury & Evans, 1854.

Flynn, Daniel. "Baccalaureate Attainment of College Students at 4-year Institutions as a Function of Student Engagement Behaviors: Social and Academic Student Engagement Behaviors Matter." *Research in Higher Education* 55.5 (2014) 467–93.

Frost, Robert. "Two Tramps in Mud Time." In *The Poetry of Robert Frost: The Collected Poems, Complete and Unabridged*, edited by Edward Connery Lathem, 275–77. New York: Henry Holt, 1979.

National Survey of Student Engagement. *Engagement Insights: Survey Findings on the Quality of Undergraduate Education—Annual Results 2018*. Bloomington: Indiana University Center for Postsecondary Research, 2018. http://nsse.indiana.edu/NSSE_2018_Results/pdf/NSSE_2018_Annual_Results.pdf.

Thomas, Lewis, "The Art of Teaching Science." *New York Times*, March 14, 1982, SM89, 91–93.

———. "On Science and Uncertainty." *Discover*, October 1980, 58–59.

CPSIA information can be obtained
at www.ICGtesting.com
Printed in the USA
FSHW012006100820
72849FS